JUDICIAL
LEGISLATION

A STUDY IN
AMERICAN LEGAL THEORY

By

FRED V. CAHILL, Jr.

ASSISTANT PROFESSOR OF POLITICAL SCIENCE
YALE UNIVERSITY

THE RONALD PRESS COMPANY · NEW YORK

Library of Congress Catalog Card Number: 52-7873

PRINTED IN THE UNITED STATES OF AMERICA

To Nan

PREFACE

Perhaps because of our own development or possibly because it was forced upon us by events beyond our borders, the twentieth century has been for the United States a period of vigorous re-examination of fundamental ideas. The literary aspects of this development are more or less familiar, and agile indeed must be the person who has escaped the energetic and sometimes illuminating controversies in the fields of economics and politics. That the philosophy of law has been undergoing a similar re-evaluation is not so well known. This book discusses certain phases of that reassessment as it pertains to one of the basic problems of our legal system—the legislative function of the judiciary.

The issues can be quite simply stated. The legal philosophy dominant when our government was established did not contemplate judicial legislation in any form. Since that time, however, there has developed a sizable volume of literature that holds as a matter of analysis that judges do legislate, whatever may be the official doctrine. Sometimes the practice is approved, sometimes not, but, in any event, skepticism of the original theory of our legal system has become widespread.

The tendency to question whether the traditional conception of the judicial function is adequate, either as an explanation of our legal history or as a governmental device to serve for the future, has not been an isolated phenomenon. In formulating their criticisms of our standard theory and in laying down their norms for future judicial conduct, American jurists have openly and conscientiously borrowed from the work of contemporary philosophers, economists, sociologists, and political scientists—not to mention psychologists. And a certain urgency has been added to their efforts by the very real constitutional impasse which culminated in the early 1930's and was by-passed, but not settled, by the Roosevelt appointments.

It has been my conviction that despite the legalistic terms of reference within which the controversy has been conducted, the underlying issue has been governmental in a broad sense and that the whole question of popular control of the legislative process has been involved. I have felt that this issue has been inadequately recognized both by the newer critics and by many of the defenders of the traditional faith. It is my hope that this book will contribute to an appreciation of that fact.

When offering a discussion of this sort, an author becomes conscious of his many debts and the fact that his individual contribution probably includes many errors of fact or interpretation resulting from either his inattention or his stubbornness. That there are not more should be attributed to the efforts of kind friends who, without being implicated in the result, have in their various ways aided in seeing this volume through to publication. Among those to whom I am especially indebted are Francis W. Coker, Luella Gettys Key and V. O. Key, Jr., George D. Braden, the Honorable C. E. Clark, and the Honorable Jerome Frank, who read and criticized all or parts of the manuscript. Nan Hardin Cahill has been of great assistance in the preparation of the index. Virginia Cooper, Helen Livingston, W. Ross Yates, and J. J. Inskeep contributed constructive suggestions in matters of composition.

F. V. C.

ACKNOWLEDGMENTS

The author wishes gratefully to acknowledge the permission to quote from the following publications: ·

The Academy of Political Science, *Proceedings* (July, 1923); *American Bar Association Journal*, Vols. 13, 14, 31, 32, and 36 (and to Ben W. Palmer for permission to quote from his articles in the *American Bar Association Journal*); *Atlantic Monthly*, Vol. 55; *California Law Review*, Vol. 6, Callaghan & Company: *The Works of James Wilson*; University of Chicago Press: Arthur F. Bentley, *The Process of Government*, Albion W. Small, *General Sociology, University of Chicago Magazine*, Vol. 3; Claremont College, Claremont, Calif.: Roscoe Pound, *Contemporary Juristic Theory*; Felix Cohen: M. R. Cohen, *Law and the Social Order*; Columbia University: *Law School Announcements*; Columbia University Press: Harlan F. Stone, *Law and Its Administration*, Edwin Garlan, *Legal Realism and Justice*, Benjamin N. Cardozo, *The Paradoxes of Legal Science; Columbia Law Review*, Vols. 8, 31, 34, 46, and 49; *Connecticut Bar Journal*, Vols. 2 and 3; Mrs. Grace Coolidge: Calvin Coolidge, *Have Faith in Massachusetts; Cornell Law Quarterly*, Vol. 10; Coward-McCann, Inc.: Jerome Frank, *Law and the Modern Mind*; Ginn & Company: William G. Sumner, *Folkways*; Harcourt, Brace & Company, Inc.: Felix Frankfurter *Law and Politics,* Oliver W. Holmes, *Collected Legal Papers,* Felix Cohen, *Ethical Systems and Legal Ideals*; Fred Rodell, *Woe Unto You, Lawyers!*; Harper & Brothers: George A. Lundberg, *et al, Trends in American Sociology*; Harvard University Press: John Dickinson, *Administrative Justice and the Supremacy of Law in the United States*, Felix Frankfurter, *Mr. Justice Holmes and the Supreme Court*, Roscoe Pound, *The Interpretation of Legal History*, Julius Stone, *The Province and Function of Law*; The Law School of Harvard University: *The Official Register of Harvard University: The Law School; Harvard Law Review*, Vols. 27, 29, and 44, and Harlan F. Stone, *The Common Law in the United States*; Norman W. Henley Publishing Company: Henry C. Carey, *The Unity of Law*; Henry Holt & Company, Inc.: *The Federalist Papers*, John Dewey, *The Influence of Darwin on Philosophy*, and *Reconstruction in Philosophy*; Houghton Mifflin Company: William F. Ogburn and A. A. Goldenweiser, *The Social Sciences and Their Interrelationships*; Johns Hopkins Press: *Johns Hopkins University Circular*, 1932; *Illinois Law Review*, Vols. 9 and 25; A. A. Knopf: Robert H. Jackson, *The Struggle for Judicial Supremacy*; Association of American Law Schools, edited by the Faculty of Law, Duke University: *Journal of Legal Education*, Vol. 3; Little, Brown & Company:

Oliver W. Holmes, *The Common Law*, Roscoe Pound, *The Formative Era in American Law*; Karl N. Llewellyn: *The Bramble Bush*; Longmans, Green & Company, Inc.: William James, *Pragmatism*; The Macmillan Company: Brooks Adams, *The Theory of Social Revolutions*, Frank J. Goodnow, *Social Reform and The Constitution*, Edward A. Ross, *Social Control*; *Michigan Law Review*, Vol. 11; John Murray, Ltd.: John Austin, *Lectures on Jurisprudence*; University of North Carolina Press: Huntington Cairns, *Theory of Legal Science; New York University Law Quarterly*, Vol. 15; New York University Press: *Law, A Century of Progress*; Clarendon Press, Oxford: Carleton K. Allen, *Law in the Making*; University of Pennsylvania Press: Richard Hofstadfer, *Social Darwinism; University of Pennsylvania Law Review*, Vols. 74 and 78; G. P. Putnam's Sons: John Dewey, *The Quest for Certainty and Liberalism and Social Action*, and Paul L. Ford, *The Writings of Thomas Jefferson*; Random House, Inc.: William James, *The Philosophy of William James*, and *The Federalist Papers*; Viking Press: Thorstein Veblen, *What Veblen Taught*; West Publishing Company: *American Law School Review*, Vols. 6 and 7; *Yale Law Journal*, Vols. 34, 38, and 44; Yale University Press: Thurman Arnold, *The Folklore of Capitalism* and *The Symbols of Government*, Benjamin N. Cardozo, *The Growth of the Law* and *The Nature of the Judicial Process*, Charles E. Clark and Harry N. Shulman, *A Study of Law Administration in Connecticut*, Max Radin, *Law as Logic and Experience*, William G. Sumner, *The Challenge of Facts* and *What Social Classes Owe to Each Other*, William H. Taft, *Popular Government*.

CONTENTS

CHAPTER   PAGE

1 INTRODUCTION 3

2 OLIVER WENDELL HOLMES 32

3 JUDICIAL REVIEW AND JUDICIAL LEGISLATION . . . 46

4 SOCIOLOGICAL JURISPRUDENCE 70

5 LEGAL REALISM: THE BEGINNING 97

6 LEGAL REALISM: THE EXPOSITION 113

7 LEGAL REALISM: THE CRITICISM AND RESTATEMENT . 138

8 CONCLUSION 149

INDEX 161

JUDICIAL LEGISLATION

Chapter 1

INTRODUCTION

I

Adjustment to change has been a continuing problem of the American legal system. The necessity of accommodating our governmental and legal arrangements to a communal life characterized by far-reaching social and economic developments has lent impetus to the search for a method by which to assure the viability of our law and its agencies. As part of that search we have been led to reconsider our traditional legal theory and our conception of the judicial function. Originally, our constitutions were based upon the theory that judges merely apply the law, but do not create it. In the past seventy or eighty years, however, there has grown up an increasingly important body of legal theory that holds that judges not only can legislate, but also ought consciously to do so. Legal writers who hold these views urge in effect that judges should cease to be merely the dispassionate oracles of the law and should assume an active role in the creation of the legal rules themselves. It is with these theories of judicial legislation that we are concerned.

Although jurisprudence is usually considered of primary interest to scholars only, the problem of the judicial function reaches beyond academic confines and has a practical importance. The location of the legislative power presents an important constitutional problem in any government, and especially in the United States, where the peculiar powers exercised by our courts make their activities of great interest. Further, to endow the courts with legislative power means that the function of legislation will be, in part at least, performed in ways that derive from the methods of operation peculiar to courts. In addition, therefore, to the examination of the broader question of the position of government in society, of which the newer jurisprudence is a part, there are involved the narrower questions of the locus of power within the government and the type of governmental action which the citizen can expect. In certain circumstances these are matters of considerable moment. Further, the courts of the United States are surrounded by constitutional protections not enjoyed by other agencies of the government. If our concept of the judicial function is to be changed from that which underlay the original constitutional theory, we may well be forced into a revaluation of these safeguards and protections. Finally, to impute legislative functions to the judiciary and at the same time to seek to hold to the premises of free and representative government is to raise questions as to the necessity of many of the mechanisms we have always considered fundamental to the representative process. It may be that our electoral processes are inadequate, since the product of our elected legislative bodies has proved to be inadequate; the advocate of judicial legislation, however, by suggesting legislative action by nonelected and formally unresponsible agencies, comes close to questioning the necessity of electoral processes as we now understand them.

American legal theorists have, for obvious reasons, been greatly concerned with the issues arising from the powers of our courts to invalidate statutes. Judicial review in this form is indeed an important problem, and it is quite understandable that it should arouse great interest, both in this country and abroad. This interest, however, should not be allowed to obscure the presence of even broader legal problems, of which judicial legislation is one.

The distinctions and relationships between judicial review and judicial legislation are intricate. That the two are not the same is witnessed by the fact that discussions of judicial legislation both antedate judicial review as it is found in the United States and also occur in legal systems in which courts do not exercise constitutional supervision over statutes. At the same time, the actual exercise of judicial review, as it appears from a survey of our legal history, provides perhaps our best example of judicial legislation in action.

This does not mean, of course, that, logically, judicial review is always judicial legislation; what it does mean is that judicial review is sometimes judicial legislation. If a court were to refuse to enforce a statute that clearly violates some explicit constitutional limitation, a statute, for example, to the effect that a person only thirty years of age may be president, that would probably not be judicial legislation, although it would be judicial review. The difficulty is, of course, that such cases do not arise. From this point, however, one moves into areas of increasing vagueness, until he finally arrives at constitutional provisions that have little or no meaning in themselves—"due process of law," for example.[1] In cases involving such clauses, the invalidation of statutes becomes almost pure judicial legislation, although the judges themselves usually refuse to admit it and try to appear not to be legislating by being very "sure" of their reading of the provision in question. Such provisions constitute a thorny problem for those who want to retain judicial review, and yet do not like judicial legislation; and though there are various suggestions for solving the dilemma, none thus far appears to be completely satisfactory.

The problem takes another turn when it is realized that when dealing with constitutionality of legislation the courts are concerned with *limitations* on governmental action. It would seem to follow that whatever legislation the courts are formulating is negative, and it is sometimes suggested that this is scarcely legislation, since it merely preserves the *status quo* against change. Such an argument, in addition to being based upon the rather dubious identification of legislation and innovation, neglects certain important considerations. From the viewpoint of the content of a constitution, such "negative" action is quite positive, since it adds meanings that were not theretofore present. "Due process" means more, and different things, in 1950 than it did in 1850. It is also true that a denial of policy is also the affirmation of policy. To hold, for example, that a municipality may not require a peddler's license of Jehovah's Witnesses [2] means that that group is free to circulate its literature. To say that the town of Irvington was making a legislative judgment and that the Court was not is to draw matters rather fine. And, as a matter of fact, if society is regarded as a congeries of competing groups, each of which seeks to avail itself of governmental power or protection in the furtherance of its own program or desires, the whole question of positive or negative legislation becomes less meaningful. The judicial invalidation of a statute means that certain groups receive judicial protection against other groups that had attained a legislative advantage.

[1] This is quite apart from the fact, of course, that there is broad disagreement among judges how to find the "meaning" of the Constitution. Compare the clash of views in *Home Loan Assn.* v. *Blaisdell,* 290 US 398 (1934), in which Chief Justice Hughes appears to be saying that the Constitution means (or ought to mean) what the Founding Fathers would do in present circumstances (p. 443). Mr. Justice Sutherland, on the other hand, maintains that it "means" now what it meant in 1789.

[2] *Schneider* v. *Irvington,* 308 US 147 (1939).

In either case, there is governmental action and in either case a positive policy determination is involved.

To the degree that these questions arise out of the institution of judicial review, they are relevant to a study of judicial legislation, but to discuss them alone would not exhaust the subject. Much of the legal theory with which we are here concerned does not deal with judicial review and can be said to arise from it only in the sense that judicial review has created a constitutional system in which the problem of the judicial function has become of pressing importance. Moreover, in addition to their policy-determining activities under the guise of judicial review, the courts can also impose their views of policy in the course of statutory interpretation and in the application of the common law. Whether they do or not and whether they ought to do so are major problems for the modern American jurist. And, further, these questions are in themselves constitutional questions, although they do not involve judicial review.

These considerations, however, are complexities within a broader problem that in outline, at least, can be given a fairly simple statement. Basically, the issue is to maintain congruity between a communal life that is assumed to be dynamic and a legal system that is assumed to be static. In political terms, the adaptation of government to the demands of modern society has taken the form of the "positive" or "service" state. In more purely intellectual terms, there has been the growth of relativistic theories in sociology, economics, and philosophy. The emergence of the newer American jurisprudence ought to be seen, then, as the legal reflection of a broader social and intellectual development that has been and is now taking place in the United States.

All these factors must enter into any attempt to explain the peculiar relevance of modern American jurisprudence to the issues of American government, the problems it attacks, the concepts it uses, and why it chooses to set some problems aside as being relatively unimportant. Of the many elements that enter into recent American legal theory, three appear to be of sufficient interest, however, to warrant separate discussion. These are: the traditional theory of the law and the judicial function, from which modern legal theory must take its start; the actual legal system which developed under the auspices of the traditional legal theory and the political and legal problems created by that system; and, finally, the general intellectual ferment in the latter part of the nineteenth century in the United States and later, that provided so much of the vocabulary of the newer jurisprudence and influenced its lines of development.

II

That the American judiciary occupies a paradoxical position has often been pointed out by both American and foreign scholars. More than any country in the world, we have imposed upon our judges delicate and important functions that interject the courts into the very heart of the governmental process. And yet, as the tremendous and emotional opposition to President Roosevelt's ill-starred Court Plan of 1937 indicates, we persistently refuse to accept the idea that the courts are in any way political bodies. The difficult character of the problem can be best illustrated by two sentences, each taken from an opinion of a justice of the Supreme Court of the United States. In 1875, in the course of an opinion dealing with municipal taxation, Mr. Justice Miller remarked: "The theory of our governments, state and national, is opposed to the deposit of unlimited power anywhere." [3] In 1936, Mr. Justice Stone protested in the following terms against what he considered to be an unwarranted use of the judicial veto:

> . . . while unconstitutional exercise of power by the executive and legislative branches of government is subject to judicial restraint, the only check upon our own exercise of power is our own sense of self-restraint.[4]

Despite the seeming contradiction between the two passages, both Justices Stone and Miller are correctly expressing our idea of the judiciary. So also was Mr. Justice Frankfurter when he called the judicial power "oligarchic." [5] But it is necessary to supply a missing element before all of the positions became mutually reconcilable. The oligarchic character of the American judiciary and the final power of the judges can be reconciled with the concept of limited government only by the doctrine that judicial power is of such nature and will be used only in such ways that the apparent conflict between the two positions is prevented. That doctrine is the traditional conception of the judicial function.

[3] *Citizen's Savings and Loan Association* v. *Topeka,* 20 Wall. 655, 663 (1875).
[4] Dissenting in *U.S.* v. *Butler,* 297 US 1, 79 (1936).
[5] *American Federation of Labor* v. *American Sash and Door Co.,* 335 US 538, 555 (1949).

At base, the traditional American theory of the judicial function is negative. This is not to say that the courts are not expected to do positive things. Courts are expected to and do put people in jail, extend protections to property, and can even halt the Congress of the United States. But in theory, at least, it is not the courts that do these things. Rather it is the law operating through the courts that is responsible. In relation to that law, the courts are purely passive. They neither approve nor disapprove its policy. They neither make nor modify its rules. They merely discover and apply it. And, to carry the argument one step further, the extraordinary protections within which the courts operate were devised in order to guarantee that the responsible element in the process would always be, in so far as we could humanly arrange it, the law and not the courts. The courts were not protected in order that they might, in their wisdom, govern us; they were protected so that there would be no interference with the law's governing us. Mr. Justice Frankfurter recognized, as would all Americans, that in the scheme of American government an oligarchic power is anomalous. The problem presented by an oligarchic judiciary can be solved in either of two ways: by removing those protections that render the courts oligarchic, or by endowing the courts with those powers only that can safely be entrusted to an oligarchy. The latter represents the traditional American approach to the problem.

Whether in the light of our legal development such a theory can be accepted as a serious description of what the courts have actually done is not so important as the fact that it has held its place throughout our history as the official doctrine of the judicial function.[6] Although, as will be seen, it has been increasingly under attack by the legal scholars to be considered, there are indications that the traditional, negative theory of the judicial function has been seriously accepted in the United States for the greater part of its legal history. There are two sorts of data that appear to suggest this acceptance. The first is that, although the discussions of the judicial function in American jurisprudence are not as extensive as might be hoped, when

[6] Professor Carleton K. Allen, in his criticism of the legal realists, suggests that they are overstating their case: "So far as the realist theory denounces the Blackstonian doctrine of infallible, immemorial, immutable law, it seems to flog a dead horse, since nobody with the least appreciation of the growth of the Common Law has believed this 'myth' for many a long day past." *Law in the Making* (4th ed.; Toronto, 1946), p. 45. See also Arthur L. Goodhart, "Some American Interpretations of Law," *Modern Theories of Law* (London, 1933).

American writers do discuss it, their consideration of it tends to be along the lines indicated. The second is that it is very difficult to find evidence among American legal writers that any other theory was accepted. Both of these statements are subject to the reservation, of course, that they do not include the sociological jurists and the legal realists whose theories of the judicial function are interesting precisely because they are not orthodox.

As to the first point, it will be well to begin with what was said by the English writers. The American bar was originally trained in the British tradition—either in England, or, if in America, from British books—and can be expected to have absorbed British ideas on the judicial function as well as on other points. And of the British writers available to Americans at the time of the adoption of the Constitution, a time at which our original constitutional theory was being formulated, none was more important than Blackstone.[7]

Blackstone's views on the judicial function emerge clearly in his discussion of the authority of custom and how customs are to be determined. To him this was a responsibility of the judges, whom he described as "the depositories of the law; the living oracles, who must decide in all cases of doubt, and who are bound by an oath to decide according to the law of the land . . ."[8] Even that the judges at times changed their rulings on points of law did not, to him, imply any legislative function on their part:

> But even in such cases the subsequent judges do not pretend to make a new law, but to vindicate the old one from misrepresentation as manifestly absurd or unjust, it is declared, not that such a sentence was *bad law,* but that it was *not law* . . .[9]

American statements of Blackstone's position appear most frequently in connection with discussions of judicial review. Although

---

[7] There can be no doubt of the popularity of Blackstone's *Commentaries* in America. It has been estimated that in the years before the Revolution probably 2,500 copies of his work were sold in this country. The 1,000 copies of the first edition sold in America exceeded the number of sales in England, Francis R. Aumann, *The Changing American Legal System* (Columbus, 1940), p. 31n. There was an American edition of the work published in 1771-72 and another in 1773. The first American edition had a prepublication sale of 1,400 copies, David A. Lockmiller, *Sir William Blackstone* (Chapel Hill, 1938), chap. X. See also *Two Centuries of Growth of American Law, 1791-1901* (New York, 1901); James B. Thayer, *Legal Essays* (Boston, 1908), p. 367; Roscoe Pound, *The Spirit of the Common Law* (Boston, 1921), pp. 96, 100-2, 150-51.

[8] George Sharswood, ed. (Philadelphia, 1872), p. 69.

[9] *Loc. cit.*

the problem of judicial review is, as has been said, narrower than that of the judicial function, that American writers tend to connect the two somewhat different ideas is of considerable importance. As a matter of fact, the Blackstone theory of the judicial function does not of itself explain judicial review. That Americans tended to justify judicial review in Blackstonian terms indicates, however, that although they were concerned with justifying a unique American legal institution, they nevertheless tried to do it by considering judicial review to be no more than a particular application of a generally accepted idea of the judicial function. Their doing so throws light on two questions: what was the underlying legal theory of the Constitution, and, second, why has the negative theory of the judicial function continued to find acceptance well into the twentieth century? And it can be hazarded that at the outset of our history under the Constitution, judicial review was acceptable because of the general adherence to Blackstone's notion of the judicial function. In the course of time, the general adherence to judicial review operated to sustain the Blackstonian theory.

The more general idea and its particular applications in American constitutional terms are combined in Alexander Hamilton's classic statement in *The Federalist,* No. 78. His premise was the notion that the construction of the Constitution falls naturally to the judges because it was merely another aspect of the application of the law in the decision of cases, an activity essentially judicial.

> The interpretation of the laws is the proper and peculiar province of the courts. A constitution is, in fact, and must be regarded by the judges, as a fundamental law. It therefore belongs to them to ascertain its meaning, as well as the meaning of any particular act proceeding from the legislative body . . .[10]

The assumptions that the judge merely applies the Constitution because it is law, and that the relation of the judge to any rule of law is one of application merely, enables Hamilton to say also:

> Nor does this conclusion by any means suppose a superiority of the judicial to the legislative power. It only supposes that the power of the people is superior to both; and that where the will of the legislature, declared in its statutes, stands in opposition to that of the people, declared in the Constitution, the judges ought to be governed by the latter rather than the former.[11]

[10] Paul L. Ford, ed. (New York, 1898), p. 521.
[11] *Ibid.,* pp. 521–22.

That he was conscious that his position depended upon the theory of the judicial function as he understood it is shown also by his setting up the "general nature of the judicial power" as one of his final defenses against the argument that the judicial power for which he contended might be abused.[12]

The *Federalist* papers were political pamphlets written to secure support for the proposed constitution, but Hamilton's argument in support of judicial review was not restricted to the arena of popular debate. It appeared also in the lectures published in 1790–92 by James Wilson, one of the leading lawyers of the day and an associate justice of the Supreme Court:

> The business and design of the judicial power is to administer justice according to the law of the land. According to two contradictory rules, justice, in the nature of things, cannot possibly be administered. One of them must, of necessity give place to the other . . . It is the right and it is the duty of the court to decide upon them: its decision must be made, for justice must be administered according to the law of the land. When the question occurs—What is the law of the land?—it must also decide this question.[13]

For Wilson, as for Hamilton, the same Constitution governed the legislative and judicial powers; there is nothing more than purely comparative action in the judicial function. His argument has no place for any creative activity on the part of the judiciary. There is an element of choice between which of two rules to apply in a given case, but even that choice is predetermined by the Constitution's own declaration of superiority. The judge has no real discretion. To paraphrase Hamilton's phraseology, the function involves the exercise of "judgment, not will." [14]

[12] "It may in the last place be observed that the supposed danger by judiciary encroachments on the legislative authority, which has been upon occasions reiterated, is in reality a phantom. Particular misconstructions and contraventions of the will of the legislature may now and then happen; but they can never be so extensive as to amount to an inconvenience, or in any sensible degree to affect the order of the political system. This may be inferred with certainty, *from the general nature of the judicial power,* from the objects to which it relates, *from the manner in which it is exercised,* from its comparative weakness, and from its total incapacity to support its usurpation by force." *The Federalist,* No. 81, (ed. Paul L. Ford), p. 542. Emphasis supplied.

[13] *Works,* ed. James DeW. Andrews, I (Chicago, 1896), p. 416.

[14] *The Federalist,* No. 78 (Modern Library ed.), p. 508. Much the same argument can be found in Justice Paterson's opinion in *Van Horne's Lessee* v. *Dorrance,* 2 Dallas 304 (1795). To Paterson, the Constitution was "the form of government, delineated by the mighty hand of the people, in which certain first principles of

There is a close resemblance between these statements and the more forceful words of Marshall in *Marbury* v. *Madison*.[15] What Marshall did essentially was to take Hamilton's argument, rephrase it and give it official sanction:

> It is emphatically the province and duty of the judicial department to say what the law is. Those who apply the rule to particular cases, must of necessity expound and interpret the rule. If two laws conflict with each other, the courts must decide on the operation of each.[16]

The Constitution, Marshall argued, by its own words indicates its supremacy. It is therefore as binding upon the courts as upon the legislature. The question, disregarding the semantic difficulties involved in such a statement, is not whether the legislature can pass an unconstitutional law, but whether the courts can enforce one, should it be passed. The basic problem is the judicial function and its limits, however much it may appear to be a matter of the limitation of legislative power:

> From these and many other selections which might be made, it is apparent, that the framers of the constitution contemplated that instrument as a rule for the government of *courts,* as well as of the legislature.[17]

There would be little point in multiplying instances. Substantially unchanged, this conception of the judicial function underlies the discussion of judicial review by Joseph Story,[18] James Kent,[19] and Thomas M. Cooley,[20] and their authority is warrant for its broader

---

fundamental laws are established" (p. 308). He made it abundantly clear that when a law was unconstitutional, the primary responsibility was on the Constitution and not upon the judge construing it: "I take it to be a clear position; that if a legislative act oppugns a constitutional principle, the former must give way, and be rejected on the score of repugnance. I hold it to be a position equally clear and sound, that, in such case, it will be the duty of the Court to adhere to the Constitution, and to declare the act null and void. The Constitution is the basis of all legislative authority; it lies at the foundation of all law, and is a rule and commission by which both legislators and Judges are to proceed." (P. 309.)

[15] 1 Cranch 137 (1803).

[16] *Ibid.,* p. 177.

[17] *Ibid.,* pp. 179–80.

[18] *Commentaries on the Constitution of the United States,* 3 vols. (Boston, 1833). It is of both interest and significance that the work is dedicated to Marshall. Story's direct consideration of the problem and of the judicial function appears in Vol. I, chaps. V and LV; and Vol. III, chap. XXXVIII.

[19] *Commentaries,* I (5th ed.; New York, 1844), p. 295.

[20] *Constitutional Limitations* (Boston, 1868). Cooley goes beyond mere justification, of course, and seeks to formulate rules to guide the exercise of judicial review. His basic assumption remains that of the uncreative judicial function.

acceptance. The ability of the idea to persist into the quite recent past scarcely needs demonstration beyond the citation of Mr. Justice Roberts' classic statement in *United States* v. *Butler* which, despite its length, deserves to be quoted in full:

> There should be no misunderstanding as to the function of this court . . . It is sometimes said that the court assumes a power to over-rule or control the action of the people's representatives. This is a mis-conception. The Constitution is the supreme law of the land ordained and established by the people. All legislation must conform to the prin-ciples it lays down. When an act of Congress is appropriately chal-lenged in the courts as not conforming to the constitutional mandate the judicial branch of the Government has only one duty,—to lay the article of the Constitution which is invoked beside the statute which is chal-lenged and to decide whether the latter squares with the former. All the court does, or can do, is to announce its considered judgment upon the question. The only power it has, if such it may be called, is the power of judgment. This court neither approves nor condemns any legislative policy. Its delicate and difficult office is to ascertain and declare whether the legislation is in accordance with, or in contravention of, the pro-visions of the Constitution; and, having done that, its duty ends.[21]

The remarkable tenacity of these ideas is due, perhaps, only in part to their theoretical soundness. Even granting that some such theory of the judicial function is most helpful in justifying the in-stitution of judicial review, it is nevertheless of interest that in the post-Civil War period this particular theory of judicial review, and, by implication, of the judicial function, became more closely iden-tified with those groups in the community to whom judicial review was an important protection against the rising tide of social reform.[22] A direct connection between social policy and orthodox legal theory is difficult to prove. That the defenders of the traditional theory were perhaps so influenced by nonlegal considerations is suggested,

---

[21] 297 US 1, 62–63 (1936). Students of constitutional law will perhaps agree that this is the clearest part of the opinion. The capability of this theory of the judicial function to convey a total view of life is suggested in the following: "Men do not make laws. They do but discover them. Laws must be justified by something more than the will of the majority. They must rest on the eternal foundation of righteousness. That state is most fortunate in its form of govern-ment which has the aptest instruments for the discovery of laws . . ." Calvin Coolidge, *Have Faith in Massachusetts* (Boston, 1919), pp. 4–5.

[22] "It is always the dynamic party of change which is frustrated by the court's attitude, for the conservative party, resting on the policy of letting well enough alone, presents for review little legislation that is untried or novel." Robert H. Jackson, *The Struggle for Judicial Supremacy* (New York, 1941), pp. 320–21.

however, in Mr. Justice Lurton's article, impressively entitled "A Government of Laws or of Men?" in which it is implied that the growing attack on judicial review and the loss of our Americanism are not unconnected.[23] Moreover, when Theodore Roosevelt, who was not exactly a recent immigrant, led the Bull Moose Party in a campaign that included a demand for the recall of judicial decisions, distinguished defenders of the judiciary rallied in a fashion that suggests the stirring days of President Franklin Roosevelt's Court Plan. Among those who spoke for the traditional theory was Elihu Root, whose statement is typical of the conservative viewpoint:

> It is not the duty of our courts to be leaders in reform, or to espouse or to enforce economic social theories, or, except in very narrow limits to readjust our laws to new social conditions. The judge is always confined within the narrow limits of reasonable interpretation. It is not his function or within his power to enlarge or improve the law. His duty is to maintain it, to enforce it, whether it be good or bad, wise or foolish, accordant with sound or unsound economic policy. By virtue of the special duty imposed upon them, our courts are excluded from playing the part of reformer. Their duty is to interpret the law as it is, in sincerity and truth, under the sanction of their oaths and in the spirit of justice.[24]

Of the various statements tending to show the official conception of the judicial function as it has been held throughout most of our

[23] "But of late, with the great influx of an enormous mass of immigrants unaccustomed to democratic government and wholly unfamiliar with the American constitutional idea, there has been a great increase in the number of those voters who object to any restraint upon the will of the majority . . . and therefore consider this power to annul a law as the usurpation of legislative authority." 93 *North American Review* 17 (1911).

[24] "The Importance of an Independent Judiciary," 72 *The Independent* 704 (1912). See also William Howard Taft's statement of a few years later. "In the United States, however, we have a written Constitution. It declares the fundamental law and it imposes limitations upon the powers of all branches of the Government. Now if any branch of the Government exceeds those powers to which it is thus limited, the act is without authority and must be void. The question is who is to determine whether the act does exceed the authority given. The action of the Supreme Court is confined to the hearing and decision of real litigated cases and the exercise of judicial power between parties. It is essential to the carrying out of this jurisdiction that the Court should determine what the law is governing the issue between the litigants." *Popular Government* (New Haven, 1913), p. 163. The high importance which Taft attached to the judicial function is evidenced by the following passage from a letter written in 1929: "I am older and slower and less acute and more confused. However, as long as things continue as they are, and I am able to answer in my place, I must stay on the court in order to prevent the Bolsheviki from getting control . . ." Quoted in Charles H. Pritchett, *The Roosevelt Court* (New York, 1948), p. 18. As Pritchett points out, this letter was written during the Hoover Administration.

history, several things are noteworthy. The general theory of the judicial function is incidental to the more important political problem of judicial review. It can therefore be suggested that the forces favoring the retention of judicial review were important in maintaining the orthodox theory of the judicial function, despite the fact that, as we approach the present, the standard argument for judicial review scarcely sustains the actual practice of the courts. Then, too, the theory, as stated, is a static one. Even the latest writers add nothing to what Hamilton and Marshall said on the subject. The inference here would seem fairly clear, although it is not that no one accepted the theory, as Professor Allen implies, but rather that there was a general tendency to accept it.[25]

[25] In this connection it is of interest to note that rarely, if ever, does one find a court admitting that it is departing from established law, even when it is engaged in overruling precedents. Taken by itself, this proves nothing, of course, but when it is considered together with the "official theory" it at least suggests that overt lawmaking on the part of the judiciary is not even yet considered good form. Much energetic research has gone into the task of proving that courts do make law, but from the viewpoint of the *theory* of the judicial function this proves little, if anything. See particularly Louis B. Boudin, *Government by Judiciary,* 2 vols. (New York, 1932). Boudin finds a number of cases in which the minority accuse the majority of judicial legislation but even this indicates a belief that it is an improper activity. He does cite (p. 270) Justice Brown, in *Downes* v. *Bidwell,* 182 US 244 (1901), as saying, "The case involves the broader question whether the revenue clauses of the Constitution extend of their own force to our newly acquired territories. *The Constitution itself does not answer the question.*" But even here, Mr. Justice Brown was speaking for himself and not for the Court. The other justices who made up the majority were of the mind that their views were those of the Constitution itself. Mr. Justice Johnson, speaking for the court in *Ogden* v. *Saunders,* 12 Wheaton 213 (1827), did come close to a dangerous admission when he said: "The report of the case of *Sturges* v. *Crowningshield* needs also some explanation. The court was, in that case, greatly divided in their views of the doctrine, and the judgment partakes as much of a compromise, as of a legal adjudication. The minority thought it better to yield something than risk the whole." (Pp. 272–73, discussed in Boudin, *op. cit.,* I, pp. 348–66.) But again Mr. Justice Johnson was here speaking for himself, he was speaking in apology, and he was talking about another case. It is not unusual for a judge who wishes to distinguish or overrule a previous holding to imply that the previous court was legislating. As a matter of fact, that is a good reason for overruling an inconvenient precedent, although it would not be a good reason if the practice of judicial legislation were theoretically acceptable. Mr. Boudin may, then, have shown that judges do legislate, but he has not shown that they think that they should legislate. A reading of Mr. Boudin's work is sufficient for a conviction that the only reason that he does not present more conclusive proof is that he did not find it. For a recent instance of candor on the part of a judge, see Mr. Justice Jackson's concurring opinion in *D'Oench, Duhme & Co.* v. *FDIC,* 315 US 447 (1942): "There arises, therefore, the question whether in deciding the case we are bound to apply the law of some particular state or whether, to put it bluntly, we may make our own law from materials found in common law sources." (P. 468.) This case is,

There was no reason to examine the preconceptions of the theory or to question its conclusions because for the most part men were satisfied with it. When men began to doubt the orthodox theory, their suspicions ultimately produced the "realistic" theories that Professor Allen decries.[26]

---

for our purposes, relatively late. The statement in question might well be taken as a measure of the effect which the discussion of the judicial function has had on the judiciary. Note again, however, that the learned justice is speaking for himself, not for the Court.

[26] The suggestion that consent can be implied from silence is not a matter of conjecture merely. Aside from the issue of judicial review, there was at one time a period in our legal history when men might well have questioned the prevailing theory of the judicial function, had they been disposed to do so. That period was the time when the reception of the common law in America was a debated question. Throughout the colonial period, the question of the legal force in the colonies of the common law of England had been a source of trouble. *Winthrop* v. *Lechmere; Phillips* v. *Savage;* discussed in Homer C. Hockett, *The Constitutional History of the United States* I (New York, 1939), pp. 55 ff. After the Revolution, one aspect of the problem was solved since with the rejection of political allegiance there could be no question of this country's being forced to follow English law. The separation from England did not, however, automatically provide the country with a legal system, and for some time it continued to be an open question whether the basic system should be the common law or a code. Opposition to the common law reached a sufficient intensity to motivate the passage of acts forbidding the citation of English decisions (Aumann, *op. cit.,* p. 79), and a concomitant movement toward codification received the support of anti-Federalist and other anti-British groups. (*Ibid.,* chap. VI; Pound, *Spirit of the Common Law, passim.*) Interestingly enough, however, there seems to have been no extensive discussion of the problem from the viewpoint of the judicial function. The common law was opposed because it was British and because it contained rules that were not liked in this country. Codes were urged because they were more democratic and because it was thought that a written law would be at once less complex and easier to understand. The choice was between two types of law, each of which would provide a tolerably complete legal system. For an example of the general type of argument see Joseph Hopkinson, *The Common Law in the United States* (Philadelphia, 1809). As a matter of fact, men like Story and, particularly, Kent, who perhaps more than any other single person achieved the victory for the common lawyers, are the very persons who follow the Blackstonian conception of the judicial function. In passing, it might be noted that Jerome Frank, in *Law and the Modern Mind* (New York, 1949), p. 104, cites one of Kent's letters that says: "I saw where justice lay, and the moral sense decided the court half the time; I then sat down to search the authorities . . . I might once in a while be embarrassed by a technical rule, but *I almost always found principles suited to my view of the case . . .*" Judge Frank finds here support for his general view that the process of decision is essentially a matter of rationalization. Perhaps so, but there are several things to be said in extenuation of Chancellor Kent. For one thing, Kent's view of the moral law and the moral sense were decidedly not as relativistic as those of more modern writers and, also, his moral views were in all likelihood strongly influenced by the "principles" of the law. One wonders what happened when Kent was "embarrassed by a technical rule."

It is interesting to note that not even the possibility of growth, thought by its proponents to be inherent in the common law, suggested any revision in the theory of the judicial function. (Hopkinson, *op. cit.*) The creative element in the common law was not in judicial activity but rather in the changed customs of the people. (Blackstone's *Commentaries*, I, p. 67.) This idea, which permits a combination of the historical approach to jurisprudence with the orthodox notion of the judicial function, can be seen in the work of James C. Carter, a leading opponent of codification in the latter part of the nineteenth century. By his day the problem of the judicial function as such was receiving attention, and this may possibly account for the directness with which he approached the problem. It does not, however, alter the fact that his theory represents a persistence of the traditional theory.

Carter's prevailing note is his dislike for legislation. He believed that all law arose from custom, which for him was the custom of society, not the custom of the judges. In one of his earlier writings he squarely denied that customary law was judicial legislation: "That judges *declare,* and do not *make,* the law is not a fiction or a pretense, but a profound truth. If courts really made the law, they would have and feel the freedom of legislators. They could and would make it in accordance with their own views of justice and expediency . . . I need not say that the case is precisely contrary. . . . they must decide it consistently with established rules . . . Any judge who assumed to possess that measure of *arbitrary* power which a legislator really enjoys would clearly subject himself to impeachment." "The Province of the Written and Unwritten Law," 24 *American Law Review* 1 (1890), p. 21. Carter did not find this belief inconsistent with his opposition to codification, which he disliked because it was, oddly enough, unadaptable. For him the judge was an expert in custom; he could see which customs were for the good of society, and by adopting them the judge gave to the custom the "authenticating stamp of public approval." Still, this did not involve judicial lawmaking. "The conduct drawn in question *is* either right or wrong according to its own qualities; that is to say that its true legal character is already fixed, and the task of the expert—that is, the judge—is to find these true determining qualities, and when he finds these he finds the class to which the transaction belongs and therefore finds the law. He would misconceive his task if he should say that it was a new case and, without a correct ascertainment of its determining features, should arbitrarily declare it to belong to a class under which its real qualities did *not* bring it. Should he do this he would be *making* the law, and, indeed, the judge can only *make* the law by making a wrong declaration—that is, he can only make erroneous law." *Law: Its Origin, Growth and Function* (New York, 1907), pp. 192–93. ". . . human conduct follows its own inherent laws uncontrolled, except in minor matters, even by the deliberate judgments of courts, and . . . if some piece of conduct really in accordance with custom is declared by the courts to be otherwise, society will, if the matter be one of grave importance, pursue its own course, regardless of the decision." *Ibid.,* pp. 82–83. If some of his statements are to be taken literally, although he was not entirely consistent on the point, he carried his reliance on custom to the point of denying any innovating function even to legislation. Contrary to the modern tendency, he tended to assimilate the legislative function to the judicial. See "The Ideal and the Actual in the Law," 24 *American Law Review* 752 (1890), pp. 761, 766.

The premises of Carter's legal thinking are not those of the eighteenth-century natural law theorists or of their nineteenth-century followers. If it were necessary to categorize, he would be more easily placed in the historical school rather than in the earlier group. The wide separation in premises did not, however, prevent a substantial identity of conclusions.

Since, therefore, proponents of the common law method held to the mechanical conception of the judicial function, and certainly those in favor of codification were not seeking to expand the area of judicial discretion, there would seem to have been fairly widespread agreement as to what the judge should do.

Granting, then, that the evidence of detailed and sophisticated thought on the general subject of the judicial function is not as strong as might be desired, it still seems possible to assert that the Blackstonian concept has shown considerable endurance in American legal theory. Translated into constitutional terms, it reveals itself in the arguments sustaining judicial review and we have little or no evidence that it has ever been abandoned as the official theory of the relation between the courts and the law. The deductive thought patterns of the eighteenth century, the general distrust of government of any kind, the theory of the separation of powers, all combine to suggest the incongruity of a theory which would permit the judge to create the law even as he applied it. And in so far as these notions retain their vitality in American thinking, so also does the mechanistic theory of the judicial function. By the same token, when they begin to give way, so also will the mechanical theory of the judicial function be weakened.

III

During the past seventy or eighty years, American legal theorists have shown an increasing tendency to re-examine the traditional theory of the judicial function as it has just been outlined. One of the principal critical themes has been the assertion that the orthodox conception is inadequate as a description of what actually takes place in the decision of cases. The conclusions have been that the courts in the past have actually engaged in legislation and that the results of this legislation have been undesirable. Upon this basis, the modern legal theorists suggest a variety of proposals which range from a return to real adherence to the older theory to arguments that, since many of our legal difficulties result from judicial legislation, the courts should continue to use the power of judicial legislation to solve the problems which they have created.

In attacking the orthodox theory, the Americans had many precursors and undoubtedly evolved their theories in response to several motivations. Open criticism of either the possibility or the desirability of a rigid and mechanical application of general laws is at least as old as Aristotle, who clearly adumbrated some of the most "modern" notions of the judicial function.[27] Bentham also recog-

[27] See particularly *Ethics*, V, 1137b; pp. 126–27 in Everyman's ed.

nized the fact of judicial legislation, although, of course, he did not approve of it.[28] John Austin discusses "judiciary legislation" appreciatively in several passages of his *Jurisprudence,* where he says, for example, "I cannot understand how any person who has considered the subject can suppose that society could possibly have gone on if judges had not legislated, or that there is any danger whatever in allowing them that power which they have in fact exercised, to make up for the negligence or the incapacity of the avowed legislator." [29] On the Continent, also, the necessity and desirability of judicial legislation was discussed by many writers in connection with theories of "sociological jurisprudence" and the "free decision" movement.[30]

The age of the critical tradition and the fact that it flourished in other than American environment render it unlikely that the juristic development of the past seventy-five years arises from causes that are peculiarly American, except perhaps in a very narrow and special sense. In so far as American theories parallel those developed in Europe, the probability is strong that the Americans and the Europeans were responding to similar problems, although our system is basically that of common law as opposed to the Continental European tendency toward codes. Holmes, Frank, Cardozo, and Pound might be mentioned as among those whose writings seem to be based on a general interest in legal problems and not directed exclusively at American problems.

There are, however, some elements of our legal system that render the problem of judicial legislation in the United States peculiarly important. The basic facts are the judicial power to control legislation and the constitutional system that has grown up around that power. On the simplest level, it is possible to say that a part

[28] See *Works,* ed. John Bowring, V (London, 1843), p. 369, for scornful references to *Judge and Company.*

[29] I, p. 224. See also II, Lectures XXXVII–XXXIX. References are to the Robert Campbell ed. (London, 1873).

[30] Of the European jurists who participated in some degree in these movements, mention can be made of Eugen Ehrlich, François Gény, Hans Gmelin, G. Kiss. A very convenient collection is made in *The Science of Legal Method,* Modern Legal Philosophy Series IX (Boston, 1917). The assessment of the direct influence of the Continental writers on American jurists is, of course, exceedingly difficult since the language barrier would have operated to reduce it and the works in question were not available in translation until comparatively late. There is no doubt, however, that Roscoe Pound was very alert to European theories, and Cardozo's work is rich in references to non-English literature. Karl N. Llewellyn might also be mentioned as one who was familiar with German and French theoretical literature. Undoubtedly there were others.

of the interest in judicial legislation arose out of the increasingly un-
satisfactory results of judicial review—a dissatisfaction that came to
an explosive climax in the Roosevelt Court Plan. This problem will
be discussed in some detail at a later point. For the present it is
enough to note that the gap constantly widened between the Constitution as read by the people and their representatives and the Constitution as read by the courts. Such a development can be either
good or bad, depending upon the function a constitution, or a court
system, is expected to perform. That the difference in view existed
and ultimately came to a crisis can scarcely be questioned.

Beyond the problems produced by the thwarting of the popular
will, however, there took place in the latter nineteenth century and
later an institutional development of the greatest importance. For
want of a better term this can be called the merging of the judicial
function with the role of constitutional guardianship. The methods
by which this was accomplished will also be reserved for later discussion. It is sufficient to say here that, from the comparatively
narrow base of accepting the responsibility of deciding clear constitutional conflicts that came to them in the form of legal cases, the
courts constantly expanded their control over the whole governmental process, including new agencies that were being developed. The
courts were therefore in a position to control all legal change. It
followed that any legal theorist interested in making the legal system sufficiently flexible to withstand the strains imposed by modern
society was forced to consider the judicial function. Not, be it understood, because he was necessarily interested in constitutional law,
but rather because the law of the Constitution made the judicial function the key-log in achieving legal change of any sort.

This development is a complex matter and, it must be admitted,
not all of its complications were clearly stated by many of the theorists who were most concerned with combatting it. In the discussion
that follows, however, it will be helpful to remember that underlying the greater part of modern jurisprudence is a realization of a
need for greater governmental participation in social and economic
affairs [31] and a recognition that legal relationships established in a

[31] This statement accepts the common terminology, and, of course, falls into the
familiar fallacy that dogs so much modern American theoretical literature. Briefly
put, the common error is to assume that the "era of negation," as Jackson puts it,
involved any less governmental action than does the era of the "positive" or "service"
state. Unfortunately, the idea is so well-imbedded in the literature, legal as well as

less mechanized age lose their appropriateness when carried over into an urban, industrialized society. In so far as these can be made matters of legislative competence, the modern American jurist seeks to formulate a theory of legislative freedom. Where the courts seem the more appropriate agencies of legal modification, he seeks a theory of judicial legislation.

IV

In addition to its failure to explain the actual operation of the court systems in the United States and its inability to produce socially satisfactory results, the traditional theory of the judicial function was also open to attack on the ground that its basic assumptions had been proved invalid. The fact was that the orthodox conception of the judicial function presupposed a certain method and reflected a general social philosophy. In the course of the nineteenth century, both the method and the underlying philosophy underwent important modifications. In his attempt to justify a theory of judicial legislation, the modern legal theorist seeks to take account of these developments and to make his theory of law congruous with them.

At the outset it should be noted that the attempt to achieve such a relationship is no new development in jurisprudence. Theories of law and of the methods of formulating it usually take on the coloration of the broader thought patterns which seem at the time to express some important truth about reality. The Roman jurist fusing the concepts of Stoicism into the law, and Blackstone, identifying the common law with the law of God and nature, were attempting the

---

otherwise, that there would be little point in trying to disturb it. Whatever may be the case in other jurisdictions, certainly in the United States the choice has not recently been governmental power against a lack of governmental power but rather legislative or administrative authority against judicial power. Even at the height of the "laissez-faire" period, governmental (judicial) power was being appealed to, to protect certain types of economic relationships, but its coming through the court system, cloaked under the traditional theory of the judicial function, made it appear as if the issue lay between governmental action or the absence of it. Certainly, from the viewpoint of a labor-union leader, there was no lack of governmental interference with the economic system in the Debs case, *In re Debs,* 158 US 564 (1895), the Danbury Hatters' Case, *Loewe* v. *Lawlor,* 208 US 274 (1908), or the second Coronado Case, *Coronado Coal Co.* v. *UMW,* 268 US 295 (1925), and see *Truax* v. *Corrigan,* 257 US 312 (1921). In truth, everyone short of the anarchist wants governmental action of some sort. The choice, therefore, really comes down to a question of policy: at what points, and in the protection of what interests is governmental power to be brought to bear?

same thing that Jerome Frank is trying to do when he seeks to bring
the truths of psychology to bear upon the judicial process. Nine-
teenth- and twentieth-century American legal theories, therefore, are
not exceptional in this effort.

The appearance in the mid-nineteenth century of the concept of
evolution was an event of transcending importance to the development of American jurisprudence. The evolutionary hypothesis had
an influence that went beyond the conclusions of Herbert Spencer,
which operated merely to reinforce antigovernmental notions already
current in American thought,[32] or in the somewhat later interpretations in which the evolutionary hypothesis was turned to the support
of social activism, as in the work of Charles Horton Cooley.[33]
Rather, our concern here is with a change which evolutionism
brought about in the presuppositions of social thinking. The alteration in outlook as applied to the law ultimately contributed heavily to the attacks on the accepted theory of the judicial function
which are our major concern.

What this involved might be summarized as a shift in the methods of social analysis from the rationalistic, deductive pattern, characteristic of the pre-Darwinian period, to the empirical, evolutionary
approach that is followed in many areas of social studies today. The
substitution of the method of biology for what was essentially that
of eighteenth-century physics reflected a change in the attitude of the
social observer. It is this change in attitude that has proved almost

---

[32] Professor Corwin points out that even before the Civil War the courts were
using the due process concept in a way which adumbrated later developments.
Wynehamer v. *People,* 13 NY 378 (1856) ; and *Dred Scott* v. *Sanford, supra.*
See Edward S. Corwin, *Liberty against Government,* chap. II. These cases are,
of course, too early to represent the impact of evolutionism. It is more likely that
such cases indicate the emergence into constitutional law of classical economic doctrines, and it is possible to suggest that perhaps the constitutional developments
later attributed to Spencerianism might have come about in any event. No one
would wish to deny that Spencerianism may have contributed to the result. That
classical economics and Spencerian economics came to the same conclusions is, of
course, of great importance and may have had the result of delaying the impact of
the evolutionary hypothesis on economic science. See Richard Hofstadter, *Social
Darwinism* (New York, 1943). The coincidence in conclusions between Spencerianism and the older individualism, in fields other than economics, certainly made
easier the adoption of evolutionary concepts. Ralph H. Gabriel, *The Course of
American Democratic Thought* (New York, 1940), chaps. XIII–XVIII.

[33] *Social Organization* (New York, 1909). For an illuminating discussion see
E. S. Corwin, "The Impact of the Idea of Evolution on the American Political and
Constitutional Tradition," in *Evolutionary Thought in America,* Stowe Persons, ed.
(New Haven, 1950).

more disruptive for the older philosophy than any of the scientific data which may have been assembled and analyzed. It is essential to note, however, that this process was at first concealed by the similarity in conclusions between the older philosophy and the new.

A striking, although by no means the only, figure in this transition was William Graham Sumner, of Yale, who illustrates in vivid fashion both the immediate application of the evolutionary hypothesis to reinforce the antigovernmental tone of classical economics and the secondary effects which resulted in the development of an empirical, relativistic approach to social problems. In general, his social philosophy was almost deceptively clear. His conclusions were reached by logical deduction from the basic principle of governmental nonintervention, and he calmly accepted the inevitability of both disparity of wealth as a result of the competitive process and the suffering endured by the unfit in the process of being eliminated. Like Spencer, he felt that freedom was the natural method by which societies developed. To seek to interfere with the process was merely to interfere with nature: ". . . we have inherited a vast number of social ills which never came from Nature. They are the complicated products of all the tinkering, muddling, and blundering of social doctors in the past." [34]

This statement undoubtedly was extremely congenial to those who had arrived at the same conclusion on the basis of the natural-law doctrine that "that government is best which governs least." At the same time, one should not overlook the significance of another sentence in the same passage, "Human society tries hard to adapt itself to any conditions in which it finds itself. . . ." Or that of the clause, "If we can acquire a science of society, based on observation of phenomena and study of forces . . ." Similarly interesting is the sentence, "We have a body of laws and institutions which have grown up as occasion has occurred for adjusting rights." Here Sumner appears to suggest that the Darwinian hypothesis can be used to explain the development of social forms. In so doing, he departed from the usual tendency to picture evolution as applying only to individuals functioning in an environment that was really an abstraction of the industrial culture of the late nineteenth century.

[34] *What Social Classes Owe to Each Other* (New Haven, 1925), p. 118.

The subversive factor is to be found in his concept that societal forms are themselves the product of development. In Sumner's theory, these were the *folkways* and *mores*. Basically, the definition of the two terms is utilitarian—they are ways of social action best adapted to societal welfare as measured by pleasure and pain, the ability to distinguish between the two being assumed.[35] These factors taken together account for the development of philosophy, morals, and ethics. "The morality of a group at a time is the sum of the taboos and prescriptions in the folkways by which right conduct is defined. Therefore morals can never be intuitive. They are historical, institutional, and empirical."[36] Or again, "At every turn we find new evidence that the mores can make anything right."[37] Although Sumner never admitted it, the principles to be used in government, it would follow, ought to be based upon the analysis of a particular society. But this means that such principles become functions of time and place. The growth of this type of social analysis, of which Sumner is but a convenient example, represents a development completely contrary to the older presuppositions. That the recognition of this conflict was delayed can be attributed, as has been suggested, to the fact that individualistic conclusions were drawn from both the older and newer philosophies.

The impact of this type of analysis on the social sciences can perhaps be best shown by illustration. Compare the economic analysis followed by an early American economist, Francis Wayland, with the credo of the American Economic Association, organized in 1885. In the Introduction to his *Elements of Political Economy,* first published in 1833, the Reverend Mr. Wayland defined his subject as the "science of wealth." To him a science was "a systematic knowledge of the laws which God has established of any department of human knowledge," and he thought it ". . . obvious, upon the slightest reflection, that the Creator has subjected the accumulation of the blessings of this life to some determinate laws."[38] Contrast with this

[35] W. G. Sumner, *Folkways* (Boston, 1906), p. 3.

[36] *Ibid.,* p. 29.

[37] *Ibid.,* p. 521.

[38] The passages quoted are from the 4th edition (Boston, 1853). Henry C. Carey, although very unorthodox in some of his economic conclusions, illustrates the same approach. The following is from the Preface to the *Unity of Law* (Philadelphia, 1872) : "In the whole range of law there is nothing more beautiful than this; nothing furnishing more thorough proof that the High Intelligence to which man stands indebted for the wonderful mechanism of each and every part of his

the statement of principles adopted by the American Economic Association:

> We believe that political economy is still in an early stage of development . . . and we look not so much to speculation as to historical and statistical study of actual conditions of economic life for the satisfactory accomplishment of that study.[39]

The break with the older thought pattern becomes even more explicit when one turns to a figure like Thorstein Veblen, whose theoretical approach has been of great influence in later social thought and not least in the field of jurisprudence. A tolerably clear statement of his position can be found in his essay, "The Limitations of Marginal Utility":

> In so far as it is a science in the current sense of the term, any science, such as economics, which has to do with human conduct, becomes a genetic inquiry into the human scheme of life; and where, as in economics, the subject of inquiry is the conduct of man in his dealings with the material means of life, the science is necessarily an inquiry into the life-history of material civilization, on a more or less extended or restricted plan.[40]

The fundamental difficulty, as he understood it, was the tendency of economists, unaware of their own assumptions, to posit stability in the institutions which they were analyzing. In contrast, he was more concerned with the assumptions themselves. There resulted an application of the destructive Sumnerian analysis to the principles and values of economic life:

> . . . it would be mere absent-mindedness in any student of civilization therefore to admit that these or any other human institutions have this stability which is currently imputed to them or that they are in this way intrinsic to the nature of things. The acceptance by the economists of

---

physical form, had not failed to provide the societary body laws fully fitted to prepare him for becoming master of nature, master of himself, and prompt to unite with his fellowmen in all measures tending to thorough development of the highest faculties with which he and they had been endowed." (P. xvii.)

[39] Quoted in Gabriel, *op. cit.,* p. 298. It is interesting to note that Sumner himself refused to become a member of the Association. What he thought of the whole venture may be found in his "The Absurd Effort to Make the World Over," *Selected Essays of W. G. Sumner,* ed. Albert G. Keller and Maurice C. Davie (New Haven, 1924), p. 234.

[40] Thorstein Veblen, *What Veblen Taught,* ed. Wesley C. Mitchell (New York, 1936), pp. 162–63, reprinted from *The Place of Science in Modern Civilization* (1919), and first appearing in 17 *The Journal of Political Economy* (1909).

these or other institutional elements as given and immutable limits their
inquiry in a particular and decisive way. It shuts off the inquiry at the
point where the modern scientific interest sets in. The institutions in
question are no doubt good for their purposes as institutions, but they
are not good as premises for a scientific inquiry into the nature, origin,
growth, and effects of these institutions and of the mutations which they
undergo and which they bring to pass in the community's scheme of
life.[41]

That the application of concepts such as those of Sumner and
Veblen would have important consequences in the field of legal study
is immediately apparent. There was, however, still another offshoot
of the evolutionary concept, which was of possibly even greater importance for the development of legal theory. This was the philosophical movement known as Pragmatism.

To understand the place which Pragmatism occupies in the scheme
of American intellectual history, it must be borne in mind that the
immediate result of the introduction of the evolutionary hypothesis
was merely to replace one type of natural law with another. The
eighteenth-century social philosopher was an observer of a finely
articulated natural order, mechanical in operation. Although many
nineteenth-century social philosophers accepted the concept of development, they were equally observers of a natural order. As Sumner said, "The truth is that the social order is fixed by laws of nature
precisely analogous to those of the physical order." [42] Pragmatism
should be seen as a reaction against this aspect of nineteenth-century
social philosophy. It refused to accept the grim determinism involved
in the "survival of the fittest" and the "elimination of the unfit," the
method of progress as seen by Spencer and Sumner. It represents,
therefore, a reassertion of the principle of the free individual.

The formulation of this new philosophic attitude came about at
the same time as Sumner's statements of deterministic laissez faire.
It was quickly absorbed into the general stream of contemporary liberal thought. Just as Sumner's contribution freed men from the
concept of inherent moral laws which should govern human association, so did that of the Pragmatists release thought from the burden of an eternal and abiding "truth" to which men had but to conform. Pragmatism was not an attempt to escape unpleasant con-

[41] Veblen, *op. cit.*, pp. 161–62.
[42] "The Challenge of Facts," *The Challenge of Facts and Other Essays* (New
Haven, 1914), p. 37.

clusions by substituting one set of philosophical assumptions for another. It rather involved a fundamental redefinition of truth and man's relation to it. It is difficult to underestimate the importance of a departure so basic that it not only disputed the corpus of philosophic truth upon which men had depended but asserted that no comparable body of doctrine was even possible.

In view of the highly practical uses to which the Pragmatic philosophy has been put by the modern jurist, no exploration into its metaphysic and more esoteric sources will be attempted.[43] In its development and application, however, it illustrates the dual influence of the evolutionary hypothesis upon social thought. In the hands of Spencer and Sumner, evolutionism led to a passive attitude in the face of social development. In the writings of James and Dewey, it supported activism in social theory and became a doctrine of the conscious direction of social change.[44] It is not the least of the many paradoxes which are encountered in this area, of course, that James's effort to reassert the values and importance of the free individual has been turned so readily to the purposes of social control. In this sense, Pragmatism is symbolic of the whole liberal movement.

Whatever James's intention may have been, however, we can say that his primary influence was in making popular an attitude which was exceedingly appropriate to the scientific character of the age. For the purpose of modern jurisprudence, the conception of truth at which he arrived is extremely significant. And though James turned

[43] For discussions of the influence of Peirce and others see Hofstadter, *op. cit.,* p. 106; Herbert W. Schneider, *A History of American Philosophy* (New York, 1946), pp. 511 ff.; Harvey G. Townsend, *Philosophical Ideas in the United States* (New York, 1934), chaps. IX–XII.

[44] Dewey specifies the influence of Darwinism as follows: "That the combination of the very words origin and species embodied an intellectual revolt and introduced a new intellectual temper is easily overlooked by the expert. The conceptions that had reigned in the philosophy of nature and knowledge for two thousand years, the conceptions that had become familiar furniture of the mind, rested on the assumption of the superiority of the fixed and final; they rested upon treating change and origin as signs of defect and unreality. In laying hands upon the sacred ark of absolute permanency, in treating the forms that had been regarded as types of fixity and perfection as originating and passing away, the 'Origin of Species' introduced a mode of thinking that in the end was bound to transform the logic of knowledge, and hence the treatment of morals, politics, and religion." *The Influence of Darwinism on Philosophy* (New York, 1910), pp. 1–2. Professor Corwin suggests that a distinction should be made between the influence of Spencerianism, which pointed toward restricting governmental activity, and that of Darwinism, which, he believes, always supported social activism. "The Impact of the Idea of Evolutionism on the American Political and Constitutional Tradition," in S. Persons, ed., *op. cit.*

it to a different purpose, it is really a statement in broader terms of the attitude which underlay Sumner's science of society.

Primarily, it took the form of a frontal attack upon the concept of truth as something inherent in things, independently existing, and but waiting to be discovered by man. As James himself puts it:

> He (the pragmatist) turns away from abstraction and insufficiency, from verbal solutions, from bad *a priori* reasons, from fixed principles, closed systems, and pretended absolutes and origins. He turns toward concreteness and adequacy, towards facts, towards action and towards power. That means the empiricist temper regnant and the rationalist temper sincerely given up. It means the open air and possibilities of nature, as against dogma, artificiality, and the pretense of finality in truth.

> At the same time it does not stand for any special results. It is a method only.[45]

For James truth was not so much in ideas themselves as in the fact that they were believed and that efforts were made to achieve them:

> The truth of an idea is not a stagnant property inherent in it. Truth *happens* to an idea. It *becomes* true, it is *made* true by events. Its verity *is* in fact an event, a process: the process namely of its verifying itself, its *verification*. Its validity is the process of its *validation*.[46]

The test of the verity of an idea, then, was the results to be achieved by adopting it. The general attitude was indeed one of empiricism:

> The pragmatic rule is that the meaning of a concept may always be found, if not in some sensible particular which it directly designates, then in some particular difference in the course of human experience which its being will make.[47]

James may have had the immediate effect of glorifying the active, energetic individual and of furnishing him with a new battery of arguments. The acceptance of Pragmatism, however, involved a relativism which served to mark how far the old order had shifted on its foundations. The open break is best illustrated by a selection from the writings of John Dewey:

> The doctrine that nature is inherently rational was a costly one. It entailed the idea that reason in man is an outside spectator of a rationality already complete in itself. It deprived reason in man of an active and

---

[45] *Pragmatism* (New York, 1919), p. 51.   [46] *Ibid.,* p. 201.
[47] *The Philosophy of William James,* ed. H. M. Kallen (Modern Library ed.), p. 82.

creative office; its business was simply to copy, to represent symbolically, to view a given rational structure . . .

Its paralyzing effect on human action is seen in the part it played in the eighteenth and nineteenth century in the theory of "natural laws" in human affairs, in social matters.[48]

Laissez faire typifies the results when such an untrue concept is applied to the fields of economics and government, Dewey thought. In opposition to it he placed a theory of knowledge by participation, which admits of active effort toward change. In so far as natural law did lead to the paralysis of men's minds, there was substituted for it a concept expressly designed to release them from that bondage and to redirect their thinking into more profitable channels.[49]

This type of thought indeed implied a revolution, but it implied even more than that. It meant, in so far as it was accepted, not only a revolution, but a permanent revolution of a type fundamentally different from the eighteenth-century doctrine of progress from one stability to another. For these new thinkers stability was an impossible—even an undesirable—condition. The concept of change had been elevated into a principle of social theory. The belief in progress remained, but it was no longer based upon the mutual interactions of a Newtonian universe, and in place of the somehow beneficent operation of the principle of natural selection there was substituted the capacity of man to adapt himself, and through purposive action to solve his problems as they arise.[50] True, not all develop-

[48] *The Quest for Certainty* (New York, 1929), p. 211.

[49] "Philosophy forswears inquiry after absolute origins and absolute finalities in order to explore specific values and the specific conditions that generate them. . . . Finally, the new logic introduces responsibility into the intellectual life. To idealize and rationalize the universe at large is after all a confession of inability to master the courses of things that specifically concern us. As long as mankind suffered from this impotency, it naturally shifted a burden of responsibility that it could not carry over to the more competent shoulders of the transcendent cause. But if insight into specific conditions of value and into specific consequences of ideas is possible, philosophy must in time become a method of locating and interpreting the more serious of the conflicts that occur in life, and a method of projecting ways for dealing with them: a method of moral and political diagnosis and prognosis. . . . In having modesty forced upon it, philosophy also acquires responsibility." Dewey, *The Influence of Darwinism on Philosophy,* pp. 13–18.

[50] "Man lives in such a changing and progressive environment that in his case it is flexibility, readiness to adjust to the conditions of the morrow as well as the present, that constitutes fitness. As the meaning of environment changes, the meaning of the struggle for existence changes also. The biological promptings of self-assertion have potentialities for good as well as evil. The essence of the human problem is controlled foresight—ability to maintain the institutions of the past while remaking them to suit new conditions. . . ." Hofstadter, *op. cit.,* p. 118.

mentalists or even all pragmatists drew the same conclusions as to
what to do in the face of change, but taken together their common
reliance upon relativism and instability marks their complete divorce-
ment from their predecessors.

V

The turn of the century, then, found the older order under attack
from all directions. The strength of the criticism was too strong for
mere denial. The only answer would seem to be accommodation to
the forces demanding change. It remains for us to consider what
was the result of the new way of thinking upon notions of the judicial
function. The original conception had been consistent with a long
intellectual tradition and consonant with the broader philosophical
tenets of the time. Its inconsistency with the newer thought patterns and its inconvenience in the newer conditions were manifest.
This inconsistency was rendered more pressing by the fact of judicial
power. It is this incongruity with which the modern jurists have
concerned themselves.

The three factors that we have discussed set the dimensions of the
problem which the modern jurist attempts to solve and in measure
they dictate the solution he offers. It is well, however, to be as clear
as possible how they enter into combination. Basically, there are two
issues: first, the political necessity to formulate a legal theory that
would permit the type of governmental action demanded by the social
and economic circumstances; second, the constitutional power and
evident willingness of the courts to prevent that action. In dealing
with these issues, modern legal theory turns to its purpose concepts
developed in other fields of social study and in philosophy, both as
weapons of criticism and as materials from which to construct new
theories.

The theories discussed below must, therefore, be seen as an aspect
of the legal situation that called them forth. The very fact that
they emerged is strong evidence of the nature of the legal difficulties
which the country was experiencing in its attempt to construct a
modern government and a viable administration of justice. The
subsiding of interest in questions that so profoundly agitated the
members of the "sociological" and "realistic" groups is equally good
evidence that in part, at least, the immediate crisis has passed.

In longer terms, however, the problems which these writers attempted to solve, not to speak of the questions raised by the solutions themselves, are by no means settled. The actual result of the juristic theories of the past seventy or eighty years has been to elevate the courts to an even higher position than that which they held before. Comparative satisfaction with the constitutional changes of the past fifteen years should not conceal the fact that those changes came about by the exercise of the judicial power. Taken together, the constitutional decisions of the period since 1937 give us a new Constitution, but it is a judicially formulated Constitution quite to the same degree as was the one that preceded it. The difference is that such judicial activity now has a theoretical sanction that it did not previously have.

Any theory that seeks to alter the functioning of an agency of government leads to constitutional problems because it affects the basic relationship between the government and the people. Traditionally, we have clung to the proposition that such relationships are matters to be decided by the people themselves. It has been remarked that one solution to the problem of an oligarchic power in a free society would be to limit the power of the oligarchy to that which an oligarchy may safely be permitted to exercise. In essence, this is the solution offered by the traditional theory of the judicial function. It may be, of course, that this choice is not open to us. If such is the case, however, and the powers of our judicial oligarchy must in the nature of things be extensive, it may perhaps be worth considering whether the judiciary ought to remain an oligarchy. In any event, the implications of whatever position we adopt, or are forced into—if "adopt" implies too much freedom of choice—ought to be made plain.

To know what you want and why you think that such a measure will help it is the first but by no means the last step towards intelligent legal reform. The other, and more difficult one is to realize what you must give up to get it, and to consider whether you are ready to pay the price.[51]

[51] O. W. Holmes, "Ideals and Doubts," *Collected Legal Papers* (New York, 1920), p. 307.

Chapter 2

OLIVER WENDELL HOLMES

Oliver Wendell Holmes, Jr., stands among the great figures of American jurisprudence and American intellectual history. His long life spans one of the decisive periods in the development of American culture, just as his long judicial career spans a crucial period in the growth of American law. His philosophy is now almost a premise for those writers responsible for the major portion of contemporary juristic literature. Less than twenty years after his death, most of his constitutional views as he stated them in dissent have become the law of the Constitution. Claimed by modern jurists of all schools, he is famous as an historian of the law, a great judge, and an original thinker.[1] He occupies in great measure the position of official judicial philosopher for the modern age.[2]

The breadth of his influence makes it extremely difficult to treat him in isolation. He could be considered with some show of consistency in connection with almost any of the more recent groups of legal writers, and yet one cannot be certain that he belongs to any of them. The claims and counterclaims of various of his disciples to the inheritance of the true Holmes tradition are enough to discourage the temptation to associate him too closely with any of them. Rather, in Holmes is found the starting point for almost all recent American legal writers, the foundations upon which many men have built. Whether the additions have really been so important as the

[1] The literature concerning Holmes has already reached sizable proportions. The reader is referred to Silas Bent, *Justice Oliver Wendell Holmes* (New York, 1932) ; Felix Frankfurter, *Mr. Justice Holmes and the Supreme Court* (Cambridge, Mass., 1938) ; *Mr. Justice Holmes,* ed. Felix Frankfurter (New York, 1931) ; Richardson Dorsey, *The Constitutional Doctrines of Mr. Justice Holmes* (Baltimore, 1924) ; Katherine Drinker Bowen, *Yankee from Olympus* (Boston, 1945) ; Francis Biddle, *Mr. Justice Holmes* (New York, 1942) ; Max Lerner, *The Mind and Faith of Mr. Justice Holmes* (New York, 1942). See also the *Holmes-Pollock Correspondence,* ed. Mark DeW. Howe, 2 vols. (Cambridge, Mass., 1941). Lerner, *op. cit.,* includes a large bibliography of periodical material.

[2] Even Holmes's critics acknowledge his pre-eminence. See, for example, Harold R. McKinnon, "The Secret of Mr. Justice Holmes," 36 *American Bar Association Journal* 261 (1950).

groundwork remains to be seen. Holmes himself always insisted that the architect was the most important man in the building of a house, and this in many ways represents his own position in modern American legal theory. That his ideas, expressed early as they were in a movement that emphasizes development, should continue to exert such influence indicates how well he understood the necessities of his time.

Holmes's legal philosophy was a reflection of his general philosophical outlook.[3] Although he spent his life in the law, even a superficial glance at his correspondence with Sir Frederick Pollock indicates the breadth of his interests. It was one aspect of his greatness that he refused to set his legal philosophy apart in a realm of its own and insisted on relating it to what he thought to be true in broader areas.

In his general outlook, Holmes was a striking example of the "rationalist temper sincerely given up."[4] He distrusted systems and systematizers and defined truth as what he could not "help believing."[5] In his governmental and legal thinking, therefore, he rejected the notion of natural and universal principles characteristic of eighteenth-century social philosophy.[6] The criterion that he sought to

[3] The principal sources are: *The Common Law* (first published in Boston, 1881; 40th printing, 1946); the *Collected Legal Papers* (New York, 1920); *Book Notices and Uncollected Letters and Papers* (New York, 1936); and the *Holmes-Pollock Correspondence*. There are in addition several collections of Holmes's opinions, both state and federal.

[4] William James, *Pragmatism*, p. 51.

[5] This is one of the points upon which contemporary critics of Holmes are prone to seize. For example: "In harmony with the fashion of the day, Holmes said that traditional thought is childish in looking for superlatives. Actually, that was the fault of Holmes himself, who made such extravagant demands of proof that he was left with impoverished convictions. If he had only ceased asking for thunderclaps and been a little quieter and a little humbler he might have found that his famous can't-helps were not merely the indefeasible offspring of his own mind but the cosmic first principles of human reason." H. R. McKinnon, *op. cit.*, p. 346.

[6] Since the revival of some sort of natural law appears to be the goal of many of the participants in the current tendency to attribute the majority of our social ills to Holmes, it may be appropriate at this point to indicate the breadth of contemporary explanations for the decline of 18th-century natural law concepts. Mr. Ben W. Palmer, in his "Defense against Leviathan," 32 *American Bar Association Journal* 328 (1946), in which he says, "The implications of the philosophy of Mr. Justice Holmes . . . lead straight to Hitler" (p. 328), cites thirteen contributing factors. These are: "1. Rise of nationalism; 2. Rise of Capitalism; 3. Relativism; 4. Anti-Intellectualism of Rousseau and the Romanticists; 5. Certain adverse tendencies of modern science; 6. Cooperation of laissez-faire with evolutionary theories; 7. Utilitarianism; 8. Austinian jurisprudence [which, by some mysterious alchemy, has become a doctrine of "no challenge to commands of the sovereign state"]; 9. Denial

substitute is far more modest and utilitarian. Holmes's conception of government should be contrasted with the definiteness and assurance of the eighteenth-century political philosophers. In a sense, it sets the key for his entire discussion of law and the judicial function.

> What proximate test of excellence can be found except correspondence to the actual equilibrium of force in the community—that is, conformity to the wishes of the dominant power? Of course, such conformity may lead to destruction, and it is desirable that the dominant power should be wise. But wise or not, the proximate test of a good government is that the dominant power has its way.[7]

His approach to law and legal theory is of much the same character. Holmes was a legal historian, but he was not interested in history for its own sake. To him law was a practical thing. It was less an end than an instrument to be employed by society for the satisfaction of its wants. The standard by which it must be measured is always its contemporary usefulness. Like Jefferson, he be-

---

of rationality of human conduct and of man's free will; 10. Pragmatism; 11. The case system of teaching law [which is credited with "isolating law from the social sciences and from morals"]; 12. The spate of legislative law ["In an earlier day there was a greater tendency to regard law as the embodiment of reason because [!] law was primarily the law of decided cases"]; 13. The discrediting of true natural law by a pseudo-natural law of the late nineteenth century." To some observers it may appear that the list is at least as inclusive as it is discriminating. The conclusion would seem to be that the nineteenth century contributed to the decline of natural law theory.

[7] "Introduction to Montesquieu, *Spirit of the Laws*," *Collected Legal Papers*, p. 258. Holmes's legal positivism as here expressed has been credited with the most dire potentialities, although the discussion, involving as it does the canons of evidence themselves, has its own difficulties. For example: ". . . we must be alert against an insidious absolutist approach. If totalitarianism comes to America . . . it will come through dominance in the judiciary of men who have accepted a philosophy of law that has its roots in Hobbes and its fruition in implications from the philosophy of Holmes." Ben W. Palmer, "Hobbes, Holmes and Hitler," 31 *American Bar Association Journal* 569 (1945), p. 573. For a similar sentiment see also McKinnon, *op. cit.*, p. 261. Professor Mortimer J. Adler, in a Foreword to a reprint of McKinnon's article, quotes Mark DeWolfe Howe's defense of Holmes: "Professor Howe cannot see that the 'rejection of the absolute necessarily entails such destructive consequences.'" Professor Adler then, by what appears to be in the nature of a counteraffirmation, says, "Mr. McKinnon cannot, nor does he try to, open the eyes of those who 'doubt the cosmic significance of human values,' who deny that 'our moral standards have objective . . . significance,' and yet cannot *see* the destructive consequences entailed by such views. He has no cure for such blindness, but his diagnosis is deadly accurate, for he explains the mystery of Holmes' popularity by simply pointing out that such blindness—to be found in our law schools, our universities, and everywhere in our society—is the disease of our age." As indicated above, in the absence of at least commonly accepted visual referents, the dispute would appear inherently destined to be inconclusive.

lieved that the "earth belongs in usufruct to the living." [8] As Holmes put it:

> Everyone instinctively recognizes that in these days the justification of a law for us cannot be found in the fact that our fathers always have followed it. It must be found in some help which the law brings toward reaching a social end which the governing power of the community has made up its mind that it wants.[9]

In this there is the tone of the new legal theory, an emphasis on the fact of change in social relations. It is the reflection in the thought of a discerning man of the idea that the world does not move merely from one stability to another, but is continually in transit. It is also one of the clearest statements in Holmes's theory of his separation of law and ethics and one of the strongest in American legal theory of law as the will of the most powerful group. To Holmes a legal system had no ends of its own. It was a procedure by which groups accomplished their desires.

It is not surprising, then, that Holmes saw little in the prevailing theories of law to express his own views. He could not accept the orthodox idea that the law had an existence apart from the decisions of courts. Law was an instrument, a means. It was real because it was a thing that affected the lives of men. Through the law men got or were denied the things they wanted. They were punished in its name for their transgressions. It was the gratifications, denials, and punishments that made the law a real force. Apart from them Holmes did not believe it to have an existence.

In seeking to determine what the law means, he thought, one should take the view of the person affected by it. The person in need of the law is not interested in the theory, nor is he concerned with legal mechanisms except as they give him what he desires or are a factor to be included in his calculation of costs. Holmes employed the figure of a potential law-breaker—a "bad man." The primary interest of the "bad man" is in what the courts will do to him for breaking the law. He gambles on the chance that he will escape

---

[8] Letter to James Madison, September 6, 1789. *Writings of Thomas Jefferson*, ed. Ford, V, p. 115.

[9] "The Law in Science—Science in Law," *Collected Legal Papers*, p. 225. See also his statement: "It is revolting to have no better reason for a rule of law than that so it was laid down in the time of Henry IV. It is still more revolting if the grounds upon which it was laid down have vanished long since, and the rule simply persists from blind imitation of the past." "The Path of the Law," *ibid.*, p. 187.

punishment. His guess may be good or bad, but there is nothing else upon which to rely. In treating the law in this fashion, Holmes formulated a definition of law that has had a profound effect on modern jurisprudence. "The prophecies of what the courts will do in fact," he said, "and nothing more pretentious, are what I mean by the law." [10] It follows that if the law is a prophecy of what the courts will do, and if different courts do different things when faced with the same problems, then the law differs. The attempt to picture the law as a seamless web is misleading. This conception is reflected in Holmes's reaction to the various decisions of the federal courts under the doctrine of *Swift* v. *Tyson*.[11] In his famous dissent in the "taxicab" case,[12] he said:

> Books written about any branch of the common law treat it as a unit, cite cases from this court, from the circuit courts of appeal, from the state courts, from England and the Colonies of England indiscriminately, and criticize them as right or wrong according to the writer's notion of a single theory. It is very hard to resist the impression that there is one august corpus, to understand which clearly is the only task of any court concerned. . . . But there is no such body of law. The fallacy and illusion that I think exist consist in supposing that there is this outside thing to be found. Law is a word used with different meanings, but law in the sense in which courts speak of it today does not exist without some definite authority behind it.[13]

The important thing to be noted is that Holmes treated a theory as an explanation of facts. It has value precisely to the degree that it is an adequate explanation of phenomena. In this case the facts to be explained are the actions of men motivated, not by theory or explanations, but by the urge to satisfy their wants. In doing the things they want to do, they will not wait for the theorists. When

[10] "The Path of the Law," p. 173.

[11] 16 Peters 1 (1842). In this case, the federal courts began the development of a "general law" covering certain subjects in cases coming into the federal courts purely by reason of diversity of citizenship.

[12] *Black and White Taxicab and Transfer Co.* v. *Brown and Yellow Taxicab and Transfer Co.*, 276 US 518 (1928).

[13] *Ibid.,* p. 533. *Swift* v. *Tyson* has now been overruled and with it the cases based upon it. Mr. Justice Brandeis, speaking for the Court, specifically adopted this doctrine of Mr. Justice Holmes. He further gave approval to the idea that the courts in following the *Swift* case "have invaded rights which in our opinion are reserved by the Constitution to the several states." *Erie Railroad Co.* v. *Tompkins,* 304 US 64 (1938). It is not often that a settled doctrine of the Supreme Court is recognized in one of its own decisions to have been unconstitutional.

theory and practice conflict, it is the theory that suffers. Men will continue to act and will force the law into moulds convenient to that action in spite of the philosophers' best efforts. "A principle which defies convenience is likely to wait some time before it finds itself permanently realized." [14]

Like government, law must reflect the social conditions as they actually exist. Absolute criteria of right and wrong have little relevance. "It is pretty certain that men will make laws which seem to them convenient without troubling themselves very much what principles are encountered by their legislation." [15] The law cannot enforce a perfect standard against the will of those subject to it. There is only one requirement: it is better that things be done within the law than without it.

> The first requirement of a sound body of law is, that it should correspond with the actual feelings and demands of the community, whether right or wrong. If people would gratify the passion of revenge outside of the law, if the law did not help them, the law has no choice but to satisfy the craving itself, and thus avoid the greater evil of private retribution. At the same time, this passion is not one which we encourage, either as private individuals or as lawmakers.[16]

The idea that law is to be judged from the outside and from the standpoint of its capability to satisfy certain needs is now as well-known, perhaps, as Holmes's famous definition of the law. It is doubtful, however, whether any one has more completely raised and disposed of the question of the proper role of law in modern life than did Holmes in this brief discussion.

Correspondence with the desires of the community implies that there must be agreement among the community before the law can give effect to it. There is a measure of interaction between the actual accepted practice of society and the notions of the law as to what those agreements ought to be, but in the end it is the former which will prevail, and it is right that it should do so. It is not the purpose of the law to protect men against the consequences of their own foolishness. "It is quite enough, therefore, for the law, that man, by an instinct which he shares with the domestic dog, and of which the seal gives a most striking example, will not allow himself to be dispossessed . . ." [17] The law does not require further justification.

[14] *The Common Law* (Boston, 1881), p. 211.
[15] *Loc. cit.*
[16] *Ibid.*, pp. 41–42.
[17] *Ibid.*, p. 213.

As long as the instinct remains, it will be more comfortable for the law
to satisfy it in an orderly manner, than to leave people to themselves. If
it should be otherwise, it would become a matter for pedagogues, wholly
devoid of reality.[18]

Holmes was, however, more than a legal commentator. In the
words of a later school, he was a "law-man." Even more, he was a
judge—an official source of the law. Granted his conception of law
as a social institution and the "external standard" by which it is to
be gauged, what was the function of Holmes as a state official peculiarly concerned with the administration of the law? What did
Holmes conceive to be his part in the developing legal process? On
this also, he was explicit—and never more so than when he felt that
what he conceived to be the right principle was being departed from
by his judicial brethren.

He found it necessary first to go behind the assumptions of the
society that he was helping to regulate. Doing this helped him in
weighing the assumptions of the law.

Our system of morality [said Holmes] is a body of imperfect social generalizations expressed in terms of emotion. To get at its truth, it is useful to omit the emotion and ask ourselves what those generalizations are
and how far they are confirmed by fact accurately ascertained. So in
regard to the formulas of the law, I have found it very instructive to
consider what may be the postulates implied. They are generically two:
that such and such a condition or result is desirable and that such and
such means are appropriate to bring it about. In all debatable matters
there are conflicting desires to be accomplished by inconsistent means,
and the further question arises, which is entitled to prevail in the specific
case? Upon such issues logic does not carry us far, and the practical
solution sometimes may assume a cynical shape. But I have found it a
help to clear thinking to try to get behind my conventional assumptions
as a judge whose first business is to see that the game is played according to the rules whether I like them or not. To have doubted one's own
first principles is the mark of a civilized man.[19]

We are led, then, to a consideration of the results of the application
of this skeptical method to legal principles and, incidentally, to an
examination of whether Holmes consistently held to the ideal of a
judge seeing "that the game is played according to the rules."

At the outset Holmes denied the first premise of the older school—
that the instrument of the law is logic. As has been indicated, tra-

[18] *Loc. cit.*
[19] "Ideals and Doubts," *Collected Legal Papers,* pp. 306–7. The resemblance
between Holmes and Veblen is plain. See pp. 25–26, *supra.*

ditional theory demands that logic be the instrument for the application of legal principles in the decision of cases. The principles of law being given in the nature of things, logic is a device both for the extension of these principles and at the same time for limiting the discretion of the judge. As against this view, Holmes held that the law is a growing thing and that its growth is determined, not by logic, but by the "felt necessities of the time." In this growth, the judge is bound to play an active part. The law moves, according to Holmes, in a climate of opinion made up of moral and political beliefs, judgments of policy and even prejudices—all of which affect the judge. To treat the living organism of the law as if it "contain[s] only the axioms and corollaries of a book of mathematics" is an impossible oversimplification.

It must be remembered that Holmes was speaking of all law in the same terms—common law as well as statute. It meant, then, that he minimized the distinction between statute and judge-made law. All legal growth is governed by the same principles. These principles, which we usually conceive applicable only to the product of legislatures, also apply to courts for two reasons. In the first place, judges often give out new law under old labels. That is to say, the content of a given legal rule or term can be seen to change in the course of its development.[20] The second reason was even more unorthodox. Judges really make law, Holmes asserted, because they are motivated by the same considerations as is the legislator.

> The very considerations which the courts most rarely mention, and always with an apology, are the secret root from which the law draws all the juices of life. We mean, of course, considerations of what is expedient for the community concerned. Every important principle which is developed by litigation is in fact and at bottom the result of more or less definitely understood views of public policy; most generally, to be sure, under our practice and traditions, the unconscious result of instinctive preferences and inarticulate convictions, but none the less traceable to public policy in the last analysis.[21]

[20] This was not peculiar to Holmes, of course, but can also be found in comparatively conservative legal writers. Cf. Thomas E. Holland, *Jurisprudence* (Oxford, 1880), pp. 50–51. Holmes's description of the process had it that a certain rule, in the first place, might be adopted for certain reasons. In the course of time the reasons would cease to exist but the rule would remain. Then new reasons, essentially rationalizations—although I do not recall Holmes's using that term—would be supplied to explain the rule. Finally, the new reasons result in a reformulation of the rule. Cf. *The Common Law*, p. 36.

[21] "Common Carriers and the Common Law," 13 *American Law Review* 609 (1879), pp. 630–31.

It is in this fashion that the new content has been added to old rules and new rules formulated, but—and upon this Holmes laid stress— the process is, even on the part of the greater number of judges, unconscious.

At this point, the argument, of course, faces several alternatives. If the "felt necessities of the time" make themselves felt in the law by a species of unconscious judicial legislation, the reader is entitled to ask, "Why talk about it?" Should he conclude that judicial legislation exists and should be prevented? Or should he say, rather, that it should be encouraged? Or should he take yet another view and say that legislation is of the essence of the judicial process, but that it can be guided and thereby improved? Of these, Holmes chose the last. He accepted the fact of judicial legislation and sought to make the process more acceptable. And he did this by making the paradoxical assertion that recognition and acceptance of judicial legislation will improve it by reducing it. In so doing, he exhibited his deep concern with the constitutional development of his time, against which he fought so brilliantly while he was on the Supreme Court.

Having accepted legislative judgments as a legitimate part of the judicial function, Holmes took the attitude that much was to be gained from a frank recognition of the process. The judges were failing to recognize adequately this phase of their duties. By persisting in denying it altogether, they were placing themselves in a very dangerous position and, indeed, were falling into the very error they sought to avoid. A decision for one of the parties to a cause necessarily meant a decision against the other—a matter of no particular importance, perhaps, when the contestants represented only themselves. In many cases, however, the implications reached beyond the individuals involved. Such cases were actually foci for contending social forces. The traditional theory obscured this fact and left the actual legislative choice buried in the judicial mind, where it was not easily separated from prejudice and other unreasoned elements of thought, including the tendency to react unfavorably to anything new.[22] The result was that judges were actually legislating more under the traditional theory than they would have done if they had

[22] "Judges commonly are elderly men, and are more likely to hate at sight any analysis to which they are not accustomed, and which disturbs repose of mind, than to fall in love with novelties." "Law in Science—Science in Law," p. 230.

brought the function into the open and recognized it for what it was.[23] Holmes was of the opinion that the time had come when this aspect of the judicial function could with propriety be publicly discussed. In any event, there was adequate remedy should the judge go wrong in his choice of courses.[24] That this involved a changed judicial tradition, he admitted, but he thought that the necessities of the time both permitted and demanded it.[25] Care must be taken with the application of this idea, however, because, as Holmes presented it, the argument for judicial legislation in reality resolves itself into a plea for judicial moderation and self-restraint.

[23] "I think that the judges themselves have failed adequately to recognize their duty of weighing considerations of social advantage. The duty is inevitable, and the result of the often proclaimed judicial aversion to deal with such considerations is simply to leave the very ground and foundations of judgment inarticulate, and often unconscious, as I have said . . . I cannot but believe that if the training of lawyers led them habitually to consider more definitely and explicitly the social advantage on which the rule they lay down must be justified, they sometimes would hesitate where now they are confident, and see that really they were taking sides upon debatable and often burning questions." "The Path of the Law," p. 184.

[24] "The philosophical habit of the day, the frequency of legislation, and the ease with which the law may be changed to meet the opinions and wishes of the public, all make it natural and unavoidable that judges as well as others should openly discuss the legislative principles upon which their decisions must always rest in the end, and should base their judgments upon broad considerations of policy to which the traditions of the bench would hardly have tolerated a reference fifty years ago." *The Common Law,* p. 78.

[25] At this point it may be appropriate to enter a warning that while Holmes suggested judicial legislation, the suggestion must not be taken out of context. Whatever he may have thought the proper function of the judge in the common law field, he most emphatically did not accept judicial legislation on the constitutional level. One of the complications of the whole problem of judicial legislation was the tendency on the part of the courts to elevate the common law to constitutional status. *Ives* v. *South Buffalo Ry. Co.*, 201 NY 271 (1911). Holmes himself recognized this when he said, "When socialism first began to be talked about, the comfortable classes of the community were a good deal frightened. I suspect that this fear has influenced judicial action both here and in England, yet it is certain that it is not a conscious factor in the decisions to which I refer. I think that something similar has led people who no longer hope to control the legislatures to look to the courts as expounders of the Constitutions, and that in some courts new principles have been discovered outside of the bodies of instruments, which may be generalized into acceptance of the economic doctrines which prevailed about fifty years ago, and a wholesale prohibition of what a tribunal of lawyers does not think about right." "The Path of the Law," p. 184. In so far as this was true, Holmes's assumption of the ease of legislation became progressively less tenable during the first decades of the twentieth century.

Assuming the "ease of legislation," Holmes's argument is not the only possible deduction. Whereas he argues that the ease of legislation should encourage the judiciary to legislate, it can be argued that the "ease of legislation" should put the judiciary out of the field altogether since the law can be changed by legislation. Cf. Learned Hand, "The Contribution of an Independent Judiciary to Civilization," *The Supreme Judicial Court of Massachusetts, 1692–1942* (Boston, 1942), p. 59.

This argument has already been stated by inference, but it can be restated in the following fashion. The ultimate justification for any rule of law must be that "it helps to bring about a social end which we desire." This requires that those charged with giving official sanction to a rule have clearly in their own minds the ends they desire to achieve. This requirement applies to courts as well as to legislatures. However, there is a limit. Holmes did not "expect or think it desirable that the judges should undertake to renovate the law. That is not their province . . ." Their function is rather to decide cases. It is when the cases present them with the task of deciding which complex of forces is to be recognized that the judges must "exercise the sovereign prerogative of choice." [26] In such a situation, of course, logic is a poor instrument. It is the form in which an opinion is cast rather than the factor which impels it. The choice ultimately rests upon other grounds.[27]

The judge must be careful, therefore, to avoid being precipitate in exercising his choice. It is not for him to seek to force a solution, even a solution that appears to him to be wise, or the one that seems to him the final result of a course of development.

> As law embodies beliefs that have triumphed in the battle of ideas and then have translated themselves into action, while there still is doubt, while opposite convictions still keep a battle front against each other, the time for law has not come; the notion destined to prevail is not yet entitled to the field. It is a misfortune if a judge reads his conscious or unconscious sympathy with one side or the other prematurely into the law, and forgets that what seems to him to be first principles are believed by half his fellow men to be wrong.[28]

[26] "Law in Science—Science in Law," p. 239.

[27] "Behind the logical form lies a judgment as to the relative worth and importance of competing legislative grounds, often an inarticulate and unconscious judgment, it is true, and yet the very root and nerve of the whole proceeding. You can always imply a condition in a contract. But why do you imply it? It is because of some belief as to the practice of the community or of a class, or because of some opinion as to policy or, in short, because of some attitude of yours upon a matter not capable of exact quantitative measurement, and therefore not capable of founding exact logical conclusions. Such matters really are battle grounds where the means do not exist for determinations that shall be good for all time, and where the decision can do no more than embody the preference of a given body in a given time and place. We do not realize how large a part of our law is open to reconsideration upon a slight change in the habit of the public mind." "The Path of the Law," p. 181.

[28] "Law and the Court," *Collected Legal Papers*, pp. 294–95. This theme reappears constantly in Holmes's famous constitutional dissents, both in this form and as a ground of protest against the retention of antiquated notions (the reverse of the proposition) as bases for decisions.

The principle applies as well to the constitutional function of the courts as to their activities in other branches of the law, but the fact that a statute is the product of a legislative majority indicates a degree of popular acceptance that should be binding upon the courts.[29] In a sense it is judicial legislation of the most undesirable kind when a court exercises its power in such fashion as to prevent necessary constitutional growth and adaptation.

> . . . the provisions of the Constitution are not mathematical formulas having their essence in their form; they are organic living institutions transplanted from English soil. Their significance is vital, not formal; it is to be gathered not simply by taking the words and a dictionary, but by considering their origin and the line of their growth.[30]

In one class of cases only does Holmes apparently depart from the view that the majority will must prevail. In the area of civil rights, particularly in those cases touching upon freedom of speech and expression, he seems particularly alert to the dangers of governmental power.[31] And yet one cannot be certain that the deviation is not more apparent than real. In general, law was to him a method

[29] See the famous dissent in *Lochner* v. *New York:* "This case is decided upon an economic policy which a large part of the country does not entertain. If it were a question whether I agreed with that theory, I should desire to study it further and long before making up my mind. But I do not conceive that to be my duty, because I strongly believe that my agreement or disagreement has nothing to do with the right of a majority to embody their opinions in law." 198 US 45, 75 (1905).

[30] *Gompers* v. *U.S.*, 233 US 604, 610 (1914). With this view compare the theory of Mr. Justice Sutherland in *Home Building and Loan Association* v. *Blaisdell*, 290 US 398 (1934) : "It [a constitutional provision] does not mean one thing at one time and an entirely different thing at another time." (P. 449.) "The whole aim of construction, as applied to a provision of the Constitution, is to discover the meaning, to ascertain and give effect to the intent, of its framers and the people who adopted it." *Ibid.*, p. 453.

[31] This is an extremely troublesome point in the interpretation of Holmes, and it involves some interesting questions. He did not, of course, believe in absolute freedom of speech. *Schenk* v. *U.S.*, 249 US 47 (1919) ; *Debs* v. *U.S.*, 249 US 211 (1919) ; *Frohwerk* v. *U.S.*, 249 US 204 (1919). At the same time he believed in extending the permissible area of speech as far as possible. *Gitlow* v. *New York*, 268 US 652, 672 (1925) ; *Abrams* v. *U.S.*, 250 US 616, 624 (1919). He also did his best to formulate a plain standard by which to guide judgment in this area. He also apparently was willing to use "due process" as the peg inasmuch as he accepted it in the Gitlow case, although in general he was extremely suspicious of any extension of the Fourteenth Amendment. *Baldwin* v. *Missouri, supra*. See also *Meyer* v. *Nebraska*, 262 US 390 (1923). One surmises that part, at least, of the recent difficulty exhibited by the Supreme Court in dealing with this question arises from this unclarified point since both wings of the Court seem to claim to derive from Holmes. See *Minersville School District* v. *Gobitis*, 310 US 586 (1940) ; *West Virginia* v. *Barnette*, 319 US 624 (1943). On this aspect of Holmes's thought see **Max Lerner**, *op. cit.*, pp. 289 *et seq.*

by which the dominant power achieved its desires, and he was willing to resolve every doubt in favor of the majority's action. It is entirely possible that in these cases again he was concerned principally with method, in these cases with the method by which majorities could come into being, and only secondarily with results.[32]

In the final analysis, Holmes admitted that there would be no rules of eternal validity discovered by his method.

> . . . in the law we only occasionally can reach an absolutely final and quantitative determination, because the worth of the competing social ends which respectively solicit a judgment for the plaintiff or the defendant cannot be reduced to number and accurately fixed. The worth, that is, the intensity of the competing desires, varies with the varying ideals of the time, and, if the desires were constant, we could not get beyond a relative decision that one was greater and one less.[33]

And in his desire that the law of the present should be the law made for the present, Holmes turned from history to science as the final measure. The study of the past has only one legitimate purpose— to throw light on the present, and he looked forward to a time when historical research should give way to "the study of the ends sought to be attained and the reasons for desiring them." [34] He reflected not only the problem, but the faith of his age when he said:

> . . . I have had in mind an ultimate dependence upon science because it is finally for science to determine, so far as it can, the relative worth of our different social ends, and, as I have tried to hint, it is our estimate of the proportions between these, now often blind and unconscious, that leads us to insist upon and to enlarge the sphere of one principle and allow the other to dwindle into atrophy. Very likely it may be that with all the help that statistics and every modern appliance can bring us there never will be a commonwealth in which science is everywhere supreme. But it is an ideal, and without ideals what is life worth? [35]

In some senses, modern American jurisprudence is an effort to fulfill the requirement here laid down by Holmes. Many legal mod-

---

[32] See especially *Gitlow* v. *New York, op. cit.,* p. 673: "If, in the long run, the beliefs expressed in proletarian dictatorship are destined to be accepted by the dominant forces of the community, the only meaning of free speech is that they should be given their chance and have their way." It may be appropriate to indicate here that Holmes was talking about peaceful persuasion. It was he who formulated the "clear and present danger" rule that permits the community to protect itself against other than peaceful methods of social change.

[33] "Law in Science—Science in Law," p. 231.
[34] "The Path of the Law," p. 195.
[35] *Ibid.,* p. 242.

ernists have accepted his dictum that "the man of the future is the man of statistics and the master of economics." [36] The ideas of Holmes will reappear many times in the discussion that follows. So great is his influence that the great bulk of modern American writing on the theory of the judicial function is in a sense an extended commentary, a commentary that perhaps lacks Holmes's characteristic moderation.

Holmes was a relativist and a skeptic. As such, he shone brilliantly in an age not conspicuous for either quality. But the skeptic, however much he criticizes the tendency of his time, nevertheless depends upon the prevailing tendency of affirmation. A major problem in the later theories that so proudly trace their lineage to Holmes is whether the skepticism that serves as a device for criticizing accepted values is equally useful in deriving new values to serve as substitutes.

That Holmes himself may have realized this is indicated by a remark in his Introduction to Wigmore's *Rational Basis of Legal Institutions.*[37] Perhaps he felt that the time had come to call a halt, or perhaps he was merely being skeptical about skepticism. At any rate, he said:

> Law is a plant that lives long before it throws out bulbs. It is rooted for millenniums before it gathers the food and develops the nucleus for a new life that inquires into the reason for its being and for the directions and character of its growth . . .
>
> The present time is experimenting in negations—an amusing sport if it is remembered that while it takes but a few minutes to cut down a tree it takes a century for a tree to grow.

One wonders whether the final judgment of Holmes will be made upon his thought considered by itself or upon the development of his ideas in the work of the men for whom he was the inspiration.

[36] *Ibid.,* p. 187.
[37] (New York, 1923). This book, incidentally, did not receive very high praise from the modern realistic school. See the review by William U. Moore, 23 *Columbia Law Review* 609 (1923).

Chapter 3

JUDICIAL REVIEW AND JUDICIAL LEGISLATION

Although not wholly restricted to the area of constitutional law, the first widespread discussion of the legislative aspects of the judicial function grew out of the problem of judicial review. The reasons for this are not far to seek. The invalidation of legislation not only increased in frequency following the Reconstruction but also involved legislation that affected rising political forces of importance. The issue of judicial power was therefore kept before the people more continuously than theretofore, and the widening social implications of judicial decisions were more readily apparent.[1] There resulted a thorough reconsideration of the whole subject of judicial review from the viewpoint of its historical justification,[2] the his-

[1] Considerable popular agitation over the position of the courts was not, of course, a new phenomenon in American politics. For a branch of the government supposedly above the "petty strife of politics," the courts in general, and the Supreme Court, in particular, have been political storm centers on a distressingly large number of occasions. Examples that come immediately to mind include the enforcement of the Alien and Sedition Acts, the struggles over the constitutionality of the United States Bank, the liability of the states to suit, the Dred Scott decision, the legal tender decisions, the income tax decisions, and most of the first phase of the New Deal and the Court Plan of 1937. The most convenient account is Charles Warren, *The Supreme Court in United States History,* 2 vols. (Boston, 1947). For the New Deal controversy see Robert H. Jackson, *The Struggle for Judicial Supremacy.*

[2] The literature on this point is voluminous. As examples see: William Trickett, "Judicial Nullification of Acts of Congress," 185 *North American Review* 848 (1907), "The Great Usurpation," 40 *American Law Review* 356 (1906), "Judicial Dispensation from Congressional Statutes," 41 *American Law Review* 65 (1907); William R. Meigs, "Some Recent Attacks on the American Doctrine of Judicial Power," 40 *American Law Review* 641 (1906), "The Relation of the Judiciary to the Constitution," 19 *American Law Review* 175 (1885); Edward S. Corwin, *The Doctrine of Judicial Review* (Princeton, 1914); "Judicial Review," *Encyclopedia of the Social Sciences,* VIII, 457; Charles G. Haines, *The American Doctrine of Judicial Supremacy* (University of California Press, 1932); Charles A. Beard, *The Supreme Court and the Constitution* (New York, 1912); Louis B. Boudin, "Government by Judiciary," 26 *Political Science Quarterly* 238 (1911), *Government by Judiciary,* 2 vols. (New York, 1932); Brinton Coxe, *Essay on Judicial Power and Unconstitutional Legislation* (Philadelphia, 1893); Charles P. Curtis, *Lions Under the Throne* (Boston, 1947). Robert H. Jackson, while admitting that there is no direct constitutional grant of power to nullify legislation, concludes that "political evolution has supplied the omission, and the course of history has established that power

torical development of the institution, and the redirection of judicial review to provide a more workable governmental structure. It is in connection with the last of these that there developed searching discussions of judicial legislation as a source of constitutional law,[3] which served not only to dramatize the position of the courts but also to raise broader issues concerning the nature of the judicial function.

The empirical basis from which the modern criticism starts will best be understood after a brief reference to the constitutional and legal problems faced by the United States in its transition toward the positive or service state. It is a commonplace that as compared with other nations in the Western tradition, the United States lagged in this development. The United States is also unique in that the development of the positive state in this country was accompanied

---

in the Supreme Court," *op. cit.,* p. 5. See also Mr. Justice Frankfurter, concurring in *American Federation of Labor* v. *American Sash and Door Co.,* 335 US 538, 556–57 (1949) : "Our right to pass on the validity of legislation is now too much part of our constitutional system to be brought into question."

[3] This aspect of the discussion should be clearly separated from the historical problem of the origin of judicial review, although Charles H. McIlwain in *The High Court of Parliament* (New Haven, 1910) sought to show that the early combination of legislative and judicial functions in Parliament had persisted in the present-day courts. The orthodox treatment of judicial review under the United States Constitution has it that judicial review is a granted power, but that it does not, and presumably should not, involve any legislative function. "The Court lives today, strong, virile, patriotic and able and willing to recognize progress, to treat the Constitution as elastic enough to permit a construction which will conform to the growth and necessities of the country, to view constitutional restriction with reasonable regard to the changes which have taken place in our business and society, and yet determined to enforce the principles of individual rights and the essential limitations upon the branches of the Government which are provided for in our fundamental law. The greatest advantage of our plan of government is the character of the judicial power vested in the Supreme Court." William H. Taft, *Popular Government* (New Haven, 1913), p. 184. "The general run of cases presenting the issue of validity or non-validity, under a fundamental law, does not involve politics at all or anything like legislative discretion. It involves only a lawyer-like construction of the Constitution and the law in question to decide whether they are in conflict." *Ibid.,* pp. 166–67. On the other hand, it is possible to argue, as does J. Allen Smith, that judicial review is consistent with the intention of the Constitution, but that it does eventuate in judicial legislation : "It has been claimed that in this respect our general government is even less democratic than the framers of the Constitution intended. This view, however, is not borne out by facts. The assertion of this far-reaching power by our national judiciary, though not expressly authorized by the Constitution, was nevertheless in harmony with the general spirit and intention of its framers. That the members of the Constitutional Convention declined to confer this power in unequivocal language does not justify the inference that they did not wish and intend that it should be exercised by the Courts." *Spirit of American Government* (New York, 1907), pp. 90–91. Smith's argument that judicial review involved a legislative function is given below.

by a constitutional crisis that was not the less serious because it was long in duration. This constitutional crisis was in the main a conflict between the legislative response to the development of our industrial society and the judicial vetoing of important aspects of that response. The result was a judicially created constitution that took the form of an amazing and fantastically complete set of limitations of governmental activity in some areas and an expansion of governmental power in other directions. Altogether it was a constitution fit for a "laissez-faire" economy, and of it we can note two things: first, it was in important aspects a post-Civil War product; and, second, it was largely a judicial achievement.[4]

The account that follows is a discussion of certain post-Civil War constitutional and legal developments which are important for our purposes. For the sake of convenience, the outline is logical rather than chronological. This does not imply that the development was purposive in the sense that it represents the achievement of a master plan of some sort, and it is undoubtedly true that the broad pattern is clearer now than it was at the time. Nevertheless, a survey of the cases indicates that a new set of legal and constitutional relationships was coming into being—a set of relationships more easily explained in terms of social and economic policy than in the traditional terms of *stare decisis* and the nonlegislative theory of the judicial function. The result was a changed Constitution, both in terms of the locus of power within the total governmental structure and in terms of the relationship between the government and the individual. Although the whole development took place without any change in the formal theory of the judicial function, it actually involved both an elevation of the judicial power into a predominating position and the use of that power to establish protections for certain parts of the emerging industrial system.

The movement of the courts from a peripheral to a central position was a subtle development. It did not require the assertion of any new powers so much as it involved a more frequent use of estab-

---

[4] There is no implication intended here that the courts did not reflect important segments of opinion. At the same time, since the constitution of the post-Civil War era can be sketched largely in terms of holdings that state or federal legislation was unconstitutional, there is indication that the judicial constitution was not the constitution of the majority of the people. One may wish to argue that courts are more representative than legislatures, but this raises questions as to why we have legislatures at all.

lished powers. That this movement was in reality a change of considerable magnitude was concealed by the fact that the institution of judicial review had been "established" since 1803. Following the Civil War, however, two things can be noted about the actual use of judicial review: first, this use appeared more frequently, especially as regards federal legislation; and, second, there was a gradual tendency to base judicial invalidation of statutes upon broad constitutional phrases rather than the comparatively definite provisions that had been used in the Marshall and Taney periods. Taken together, these two developments account for the fact that in the later nineteenth century and the early decades of the twentieth century, our constitution became a judicial constitution in a sense that had not theretofore been true.

Although a number of factors combined to keep the tradition of judicial review alive,[5] the exaggerated deference we now pay to *Marbury* v. *Madison*[6] sometimes conceals the fact that the power to invalidate congressional acts lay practically unused prior to its unfortunate reappearance in *Dred Scott* v. *Sanford*,[7] and the comparatively minor role played by the courts during the Civil War period scarcely contributed to a strengthening of their position.[8]

[5] One could list here the work of the commentators, especially Kent and Story, and the more or less continuous invalidation of state statutes. Although the federal invalidation of state legislation is essentially a different problem from the judicial invalidation of congressional legislation, the two have usually been considered together. There is also evidence of a general acceptance of judicial review in the controversy over the admission of territories. In the Compromise of 1850, special arrangements were made to expedite a ruling by the Supreme Court on the question of slavery in the territories of Utah and New Mexico. Andrew C. McLaughlin, *A Constitutional History of the United States* (New York, 1935), p. 534. See also Warren's story of the maneuvers to force a Supreme Court ruling on the broad issues in the Dred Scott case, *op. cit.*, II, pp. 279–319.

[6] 1 Cranch 137 (1803).

[7] 19 Howard 393 (1857). The only other instances in which federal statutes were declared unconstitutional prior to the Civil War were *U.S.* v. *Benjamin More*, discussed in Warren, *op. cit.*, I, p. 255, a case so minor as scarcely to constitute an exception; and *U.S.* v. *Yale Todd* (1794), discussed in a note to *U.S.* v. *Ferriera*, 13 Howard 40 (1851).

[8] There can be no doubt that the Dred Scott case seriously damaged the prestige of the Supreme Court. Warren, *op. cit.*, II, pp. 279–319. During the War the federal courts were practically defied by the President. *Ex parte Merryman*, Fed. case no. 9487 (1861). During the Reconstruction period, Congress went so far as to remove a case from the docket of the Supreme Court. *Ex parte McCardle*, 7 Wall. 506 (1869). For its own part, the Supreme Court displayed no great eagerness to grapple with the issues either of the War or the Reconstruction. *Ex parte Vallandigham*, 1 Wall. 243 (1864); *Mississippi* v. *Johnson*, 4 Wall. 475 (1867); *Georgia* v. *Stanton*, 6 Wall. 50 (1867); *Texas* v. *White*, 7 Wall. 700 (1869).

Beginning in the post-Civil War period, however, there was a more frequent use of the judicial power against congressional acts. Whether the constitutional justifications advanced were adequate does not for the moment concern us, nor does the fact that the development profoundly affected the balance of power not only between the Congress and the courts but also between the various governments in the United States and between the people and the federal government. For the present, however, it is important to note that from that particular time a latent power became increasingly active, and the courts became an increasingly important factor in the total governmental scheme.[9] As opposed to the pre-1860 record of four federal statutes found unconstitutional, the period between 1860 and 1937 saw over fifteen times that number.[10]

Together with the increased willingness of the courts to impose the judicial veto on congressional acts, a broadening of judicial control over state legislation can be noted. This development is more complicated since, as noted above, the function of checking state legislation involves somewhat different issues from those involved in the invalidation of congressional statutes, and also because the practice of judicial review over state laws was continuous from the early days of the Republic.[11] Nevertheless, a survey of the leading cases in which state statutes were held unconstitutional prior to the

[9] From some points of view it can almost be said that the courts by themselves restored the federal balance in opposition to the nationalizing tendencies of the Reconstruction Congresses. Following the decision in *Texas* v. *White, supra,* that "The Constitution, in all its provisions, looks to an indestructible Union, composed of indestructible States" (p. 725), the Court turned back a series of congressional attempts to interfere in what had theretofore been regarded as the police functions of the states. *The Civil Rights Cases,* 109 US 3 (1883); *U.S.* v. *Harris,* 106 US 629 (1883); *U.S.* v. *Reese,* 92 US 214 (1876); *U.S.* v. *Cruikshank,* 92 US 542 (1876). For a discussion of these cases see Robert K. Carr, *Federal Protection of Civil Rights* (Ithaca, 1947), pp. 40–47. These cases turned on the extent of the granted power to enforce the Thirteenth, Fourteenth, and Fifteenth Amendments. At the same time, the Supreme Court gave evidence of its willingness to find in the federal system an implied limitation on congressional powers, a limitation which Marshall had applied against the states, *McCulloch* v. *Maryland,* 4 Wheaton 316 (1819), but which was novel as a limitation upon the federal government, *Collector* v. *Day,* 11 Wall. 113 (1871).

[10] Lawrence B. Evans, *Cases on Constitutional Law,* ed. Fenwick (5th ed.), pp. 61–62. For discussions of cases in which congressional statutes have been found unconstitutional, see Henry W. Edgerton, "The Incidence of Judicial Control over Congress," 22 *Cornell Law Quarterly* 299 (1937), 1 *Selected Essays,* 793; Charles G. Haines, "Judicial Review of Acts of Congress," 45 *Yale Law Journal,* 816 (1936), 1 *Selected Essays,* 844.

[11] *Ware* v. *Hylton,* 3 Dallas 199 (1796); *Fletcher* v. *Peck,* 6 Cranch 87 (1810).

Civil War indicates that in nearly every case the holding of uncon-
stitutionality was based upon some fairly definite constitutional provision, although it is admitted that in some of the cases broad references to natural law, the spirit of our institutions, and the like,
can be found.[12]

This situation was radically changed by the adoption of the
Fourteenth Amendment and the interpretation subsequently put upon
it. This story is sufficiently familiar so that it need not be rehearsed
in detail. It is enough to say that the courts departed from the
narrower interpretation of "due process of law," as laid down in
Murray v. *Hoboken Land and Improvement Co.,* 18 Howard 272
(1856), but refused to assign to the phrase a definite meaning,
Davidson v. *New Orleans,* 96 US 97 (1878). There was at hand,
therefore, a constitutional doctrine capable of displaying an amazing
versatility and one ideally suited to permit the entrance of extracon-
stitutional notions into constitutional interpretation.[13] Mr. Justice
Holmes's well-known attitude toward this development epitomizes
the enhancement of the position of the courts that was involved:

> I have not yet adequately expressed the more than anxiety that I feel
> at the ever increasing scope given to the 14th Amendment in cutting
> down what I believe to be the constitutional rights of the States. As the

[12] Two outstanding exceptions to this generalization are *Calder* v. *Bull,* 3 Dallas
386 (1796) and *Fletcher* v. *Peck, supra.* In the former, however, although Mr. Justice Chase used some very broad language, his decision actually appears to turn upon
the definition of ex post facto legislation, and it should also be recalled that Mr. Justice Iredell took Chase to task for his dicta. In *Fletcher* v. *Peck,* Marshall also in-
dulges in some broad constitutional speculation about the nature of legislative power,
but in the end finds the Georgia statute in question to be in violation of the prohibition against state laws impairing the obligations of contract and, possibly, the prohibition against ex post facto legislation. As is sometimes the case, Marshall gives so
many reasons that it is difficult to decide which was actually governing.

[13] For the development of "due process" as a substantive concept, see E. S. Corwin, *Liberty Against Government* (Baton Rouge, 1949). The phrase first operated
as a substantive limitation on federal power in *Dred Scott* v. *Sanford, supra.* It re-
appeared in *Hepburn* v. *Griswold,* 8 Wall. 603 (1870). "Due process" did not, of
course, constitute a limitation on the states enforceable in the federal courts until
the adoption of the Fourteenth Amendment in 1868. The development of the broader
interpretation of "due process" was at first resisted, *Slaughter House Cases,* 16 Wall.
36 (1873); *Munn* v. *Illinois,* 94 US 113 (1877), but gradually emerged, *Allgeyer*
v. *Louisiana,* 165 US 578 (1897). Professor Frank R. Strong criticizes the Corwin
interpretation of the history of "due process," but his conclusion that there was "early
identification of the concept with substantive rights," *American Constitutional Law*
(Buffalo, 1950), does not disturb the general conclusion that the "due process" idea
was considerably broader in 1900 than it had been in 1850 (see particularly, pp. 307–
10).

decisions now stand I see hardly any limit but the sky to the invalidating of those rights if they happen to strike a majority of this Court as for any reason undesirable. I cannot believe that the Amendment was intended to give us carte blanche to embody our economic or moral beliefs in its prohibitions.[14]

Together with the revival of judicial review of federal legislation and the expansion of judicial control over state laws, a third institutional development of significance can be noted. This was the development of judicial control over the administrative commissions and boards that were coming into increasing prominence as governmental mechanisms.

There is no need to examine the full development of administrative law in the United States. The administrative board or commission is a fairly old device, but appears with greater frequency after the Civil War.[15] Such agencies were found to be useful in dealing with problems which none of the traditional branches of government could handle satisfactorily. This was especially true in the field of public utility regulation, although the growth of these agencies was by no means confined to that area.

The amount of supervision to be exercised by the judiciary over these agencies has always been a major problem. It is of some significance that there is agreement in dating what Jackson calls the "era of negation" from a case involving railroad rates set by a state commission,[16] in which the United States Supreme Court ruled, over a strong dissent, that

> The question of the reasonableness of a rate of charge for transportation by a railroad company, involving as it does the element of reasonableness both as regards the company and as regards the public, is eminently a question for judicial investigation, requiring due process of law for its determination. If the company is deprived of the power of charging reasonable rates for the use of its property, and such deprivation takes place in the absence of an investigation by judicial machinery, it is deprived of the lawful use of its property. . . .[17]

[14] Dissenting in *Baldwin* v. *Missouri,* 281 US 586, 595 (1930).

[15] *Report of the Attorney General's Committee on Administrative Procedure,* Senate Document no. 8, Seventy-seventh Congress, 1st Session (1941), pp. 7 ff.

[16] Robert H. Jackson, *op. cit.,* pp. 50 ff.; Charles M. Hough, "Due Process of Law—Today," 32 *Harvard Law Review* 218 (1919), 1 *Selected Essays* 302, 311.

[17] *Chicago, Milwaukee and St. Paul Railway Co.* v. *Minnesota,* 134 US 418, 458 (1890). Hough remarks, ". . . reason is another of those words as to which inclusion and exclusion are more appropriate than definition." *Loc. cit.*

This decision had many ramifications. As Jackson indicates, "Judicial review of all of the facts entering into rates set by utility commissions . . . [became] an effective process for slowing down and obstructing effective regulation of public utilities." [18] For us, the particular use which the judiciary made of their power, and whether their treatment of administrative agencies was friendly or hostile, are not so important as the fact that administrative agencies had been brought under judicial supervision.

The expansion of judicial control having been examined, we can now consider briefly the uses made of it during the latter part of the nineteenth century and the first third of the twentieth. That the cases reflect the nature of our growing industrial economy is to be expected; that they display generally a hostility to governmental interference with that economy is equally not surprising. It is, however, of great interest to note the ingenuity which went into producing the result and the resourcefulness with which restrictions were found within a constitution initially intended to establish a government with power to govern.[19]

The American legal system has always been sensitive to any threat to property.[20] Prior to the Civil War, however, the protections accorded to property by the federal Constitution were, as we have suggested, relatively specific in nature, the broader protections of the Bill of Rights were not available against state action,[21] and, at least after 1835, the federal courts were willing to allow considerable headway to state interventions in the economic sphere.[22] Although the state

---

[18] *Op. cit.,* p. 51. He also cites *Smyth* v. *Ames,* 169 US 466 (1898), in which the requirement of a fair return on investment was imposed, with the result that the courts became super-factfinding agencies and were led into all sorts of intricate valuation problems. Even the determination of the facts upon which the jurisdiction of a commission depended became a most complex affair. *Crowell* v. *Benson,* 285 US 22 (1932).

[19] *The Federalist,* No. 51. The complete statement is: "In framing a government which is to be administered by men over men, the great difficulty lies in this: you must first enable the government to control the governed; and in the next place oblige it to control itself." (Modern Library ed.), p. 337.

[20] The citation of cases might be multiplied almost indefinitely. A few of the principal ones which might be mentioned are: *Fletcher* v. *Peck, supra,* *Terrett* v. *Taylor,* 9 Cranch 43 (1815); *Dartmouth College* v. *Woodward,* 4 Wheaton 518 (1819); *Sturges* v. *Crowninshield,* 4 Wheaton 122 (1819); *Craig* v. *Missouri,* 4 Peters 410 (1830); *Bronson* v. *Kinzie,* 1 Howard 311 (1843). For an excellent discussion of the subject see E. S. Corwin, *Liberty against Government.*

[21] *Barron* v. *Baltimore,* 7 Peters 243 (1833).

[22] *Charles River Bridge* v. *Warren Bridge,* 11 Peters 420 (1837); *West River Bridge Co.* v. *Dix,* 6 Howard 507 (1848); *The License Cases,* 5 Howard 504

courts had succeeded in developing a protection for vested rights on the basis of the "law of the land" and "due process" clauses of the state constitutions, this doctrine did not receive federal approval as a limitation against state action until some time after the adoption of the Fourteenth Amendment.[23]

The fertility of the doctrine as a source of limitations was amazing. By the end of the century, the Supreme Court had in effect reversed its initial restricted interpretation of the Amendment [24] and had succeeded in making of it a protection to property and liberty of contract which was used with increasing vigor to hamper state legislative activity in the interests of the economically less fortunate.[25] The bearing of such a change in doctrine upon the constitutionally permissible relations between government and business is obvious.

(1847). Some of these doctrines were, of course, anticipated by the later Marshall court which, although very alert to find any impairment of obligation of contract, nevertheless did temper some of its concepts with the doctrine of the state police power. *Providence Bank* v. *Billings,* 4 Peters 514 (1830); *Ogden* v. *Saunders,* 12 Wheaton 213 (1827). See also *Willson* v. *Blackbird Creek Marsh Co.,* 2 Peters 245 (1829), in which the police power was allowed to prevail although a state regulation of interstate commerce was thereby sustained. For discussion of the extent and persistence of governmental regulation of business in the public interest prior to the Civil War see Louis Hartz, *Economic Policy and Democratic Thought; Pennsylvania 1776–1860* (Cambridge, 1948); Oscar Handlin and Mary Handlin, *Commonwealth; A Study of the Role of Government in the American Economy: Massachusetts, 1774–1861* (New York, 1947).

[23] E. S. Corwin, *Liberty against Government,* chap. III, discusses the pre-Civil War state decisions. He concludes that the state courts had worked out the doctrine of due process as a protection to property fairly early and that the doctrine was at hand when Field *et al.* finally succeeded in swinging the Court to their interpretation of the Fourteenth Amendment. See also Strong, *op. cit.*

[24] *The Slaughter House Cases, supra; Davidson* v. *New Orleans, supra.*

[25] *Allgeyer* v. *Louisiana, supra,* establishes liberty of contract as part of due process of law. *Lochner* v. *New York,* 198 US 45 (1905), invalidates a maximum-hours law for bakers because it interfered with liberty of contract. In a similar vein is *Coppage* v. *Kansas,* 236 US 1 (1915). See also *Adkins* v. *Children's Hospital,* 261 US 525 (1923), which applied the same doctrine to a federal regulation of hours and wages in the District of Columbia. The same tendency can be seen in the treatment accorded the doctrine of "business affected with a public interest." The doctrine makes its entry into the law in *Munn* v. *Illinois, supra,* as a justification of a legislative setting of rates for certain grain elevators and was used to justify regulation of railroad rates, *Smyth* v. *Ames, supra;* banking, *Noble State Bank* v. *Haskell,* 219 US 104 (1911); insurance, *German Alliance Insurance Co.* v. *Lewis,* 233 US 389 (1914), etc. Ultimately, however, it became a restriction which prevented regulation of ticket brokers, *Tyson* v. *Banton,* 273 US 418 (1927); employment agencies, *Ribnick* v. *McBride,* 277 US 350 (1928); and labor relations in the meat-packing business, *Wolff Packing Co.* v. *Industrial Court,* 262 US 522 (1923). The Supreme Court has now given up the doctrine as a test of the power to regulate. *Nebbia* v. *New York,* 291 US 502 (1934).

The implications so far as the judicial function is concerned are also important. That a phrase which had supposedly limited the federal government since 1791, but which had never been given more than a narrow significance, should display such fecundity warns against discounting the judicial branch.

Nor was "due process" the only section of the Amendment which expanded its meaning at the expense of the police power of the states. Despite the original interpretation of the Amendment as applying only to the newly freed Negroes or similarly situated groups,[26] within a few years, the Court, apparently without extensive consideration of the matter, included corporations within the meaning of the word "persons." [27] Subsequently, despite an early holding that corporations had no right to do business under any conditions in states other than that of their incorporation,[28] it was found that there were certain "constitutional" rights which states might not deny to out-of-state corporations.[29] Thus, not only were property and certain economic freedoms brought under the protection of the Fourteenth Amendment, but also the protections of that amendment were extended to a particular legal form of business organization which became increasingly important in the American economy as the nineteenth century turned into the twentieth.[30]

The late nineteenth and early twentieth centuries were more than a period in which state power was denied. It was a time also in which certain types of governmental power were protected and expanded. Illustrative of this latter development is *Truax* v. *Corrigan* [31] in which the United States Supreme Court struck down as contrary to the Fourteenth Amendment an attempt on the part of the state of Arizona to *deny* to its courts the power to issue injunctions in certain labor disputes. The total result was, therefore, to deny the state the privilege of withdrawing from intervention in the field of labor relations.

It is both interesting and significant that during this period one finds little judicial solicitude for personal, as contrasted with eco-

[26] *The Slaughter House Cases, supra.*
[27] *Santa Clara County* v. *Southern Pacific Railroad Co.,* 118 US 394 (1886).
[28] *Bank of Augusta* v. *Earle,* 13 Peters 519 (1839).
[29] *Terral* v. *Burke Construction Co.,* 257 US 529 (1922).
[30] For a discussion of the increased use of the corporate form see Adolphe A. Berle, Jr., and Gardiner C. Means, *The Modern Corporation and Private Property* (New York, 1932), pp. 13–15.
[31] 257 US 312 (1921).

nomic, liberty. While the courts were protecting liberty of contract, they were permitting the compulsory sterilization of congenital mental defectives.[32] The Fourteenth Amendment prevented the restriction of the labor injunction, but not the abolition of indictment by grand jury,[33] or trial by jury in both civil [34] and criminal cases.[35] When at last the federal courts began to use the Fourteenth Amendment to protect civil liberties, it is interesting that the tendency was to liken civil liberties to economic liberties, not vice versa,[36] and in the field of civil liberties the legislative judgment was accorded a deference that did not obtain in cases involving economic regulation.[37]

The resources of the federal Constitution for the protection of property against adverse state action were not exhausted with the Fourteenth Amendment. The interstate commerce clause also provided solace for groups seeking to escape state regulation. The question whether the grant of power to the federal government to regulate interstate commerce acted of its own force to bar state action affecting that commerce adversely had proved a troublesome one before the Civil War,[38] and the Court had finally arrived at a "solution" of the problem by dividing interstate commerce into categories and holding that in those types of commerce which admitted only of uniform national regulation the grant of power to the federal government precluded state regulation.[39] The question then became one of determining whether the subject matter which the states were seeking to regulate fell within the category of those admitting only of uniform regulation. It developed, for example, that although a state might prevent the sale of intoxicating liquor within its area,[40] and might even prohibit the manufacture of liquor in the state,[41] it could not for-

[32] *Buck* v. *Bell*, 274 US 200 (1924).
[33] *Hurtado* v. *California*, 110 US 516 (1884).
[34] *Walker* v. *Sauvinet*, 92 US 90 (1875).
[35] *Maxwell* v. *Dow*, 176 US 581 (1900).
[36] *Meyer* v. *Nebraska*, 262 US 390 (1922).
[37] Compare *Gitlow* v. *New York*, 268 US 652 (1925) with *Jay Burns Baking Co.* v. *Bryan*, 264 US 504 (1924).
[38] *Gibbons* v. *Ogden*, 9 Wheaton 1 (1824); *Brown* v. *Maryland*, 12 Wheaton 419 (1827); *Mayor of New York* v. *Miln*, 11 Peters 102 (1837); *The License Cases, supra; The Passenger Cases*, 7 Howard 283 (1849); *Groves* v. *Slaughter*, 15 Peters 449 (1841).
[39] *Cooley* v. *Board of Wardens*, 12 Howard 299 (1851).
[40] *Bartelmeyer* v. *Iowa*, 18 Wallace 129 (1874).
[41] *Mugler* v. *Kansas*, 123 US 623 (1887).

bid the importation of intoxicating liquors because to do so would interfere with interstate commerce.[42] Similarly, the commerce clause acted to bar the states from regulating railroad rates for interstate transportation.[43] The apparent choice in these cases between state regulation and federal regulation is deceptive. It is true that the era of federal rate regulation begins with these decisions, but when the early federal regulation cases are surveyed, the actual result was that for some twenty years effective regulation of the railroads was made more difficult.[44]

The courts' interpretation of federal powers during this period broadly parallels the rulings on state powers. There was the same tendency to restrain governmental power in some fields while releasing it in others. Again, a logical basis for the decisions is more difficult to find than is the social policy of the decisions. Granting, for example, the federal power to regulate interstate commerce, that power did not extend to the regulation of manufacturing because manufacturing was not commerce,[45] nor could that power be used to exclude from interstate commerce the products of child labor because that constituted an indirect regulation of a subject reserved to the states.[46] At the same time the power could be used to exclude lottery tickets from interstate commerce [47] and included authority to forbid the interstate transportation of women for immoral purposes.[48] While the regulation of interstate railroad rates was a matter of exclusive national concern, that power did not extend to the outlawing of "yellow-dog contracts" in railway employment.[49] The result was,

---

[42] *Leisy* v. *Hardin,* 135 US 100 (1890). It should be noted that this substantially overrules the License Cases, *supra.* The subsequent difficulties involved in trying to work out a system of joint federal-state regulation of the liquor traffic can be seen in *In re Raher,* 140 US 545 (1891) and *Clark Distilling Co.* v. *Western Maryland Railway Co.,* 242 US 311 (1917).

[43] *Wabash, St. Louis and Pacific Railway Co.* v. *Illinois,* 118 US 557 (1886). Cf. *Peik* v. *Chicago and Northwestern Railway Co.,* 94 US 164 (1877).

[44] Although this decision undoubtedly added impetus to movements for federal regulation of railroads, it was some time before the courts allowed the Interstate Commerce Commission scope for really vigorous action. *Counselman* v. *Hitchcock,* 142 US 547 (1892); *Cincinnati, New Orleans, and Texas Pacific Railway Co.* v. *ICC,* 162 US 184 (1896). See in this connection Carl B. Swisher, *American Constitutional Development* (Cambridge, 1943), chap. XVIII.

[45] *U.S.* v. *E. C. Knight Co.,* 156 US 1 (1895).

[46] *Hammer* v. *Dagenhart,* 247 US 251 (1918).

[47] *Champion* v. *Ames,* 188 US 321 (1903).

[48] *Hoke* v. *U.S.,* 227 US 308 (1913). [49] *Adair* v. *U.S., supra.*

therefore, that the federal government could use the Army to break strikes that halted interstate commerce,[50] but it could not legislate to remove one of the grievances that led to the strikes.

Equally instructive results appear from a survey of the holdings under the taxing power. Despite rulings of long standing that apparently justified an unapportioned income tax,[51] in 1895 it was suddenly found that a tax on the income from property was equivalent to a tax on the property itself and therefore subject to the requirement of apportionment.[52] When the country by constitutional amendment gave the Congress the power to levy taxes on "incomes, from whatever source derived, without apportionment," [53] the amendment was interpreted to preserve the intergovernmental immunities developed from the implications of the federal system.[54] Further, despite holdings that a federal excise tax was subject only to the requirement of uniformity [55] and that no one had sufficient interest to contest a governmental expenditure,[56] a combination of a tax and an expenditure for the purpose of assisting agricultural recovery was found to exceed federal powers.[57]

Examples could be drawn from other fields, but these are sufficient to illustrate the tendency against which much of modern American jurisprudence protests. Of the development as it has been outlined, several things can be noted. Of great importance is the central governmental position assumed by the judiciary. Given the constitutional powers of our courts, any legal change on whatever level will depend on the willingness of the courts to accept it. Further, enough has been said to indicate the extreme difficulty of explaining the development under the orthodox nonlegislative conception of the judicial function. The development was too recent and the social orientation of the trend was too obvious to encourage the belief that the courts were merely applying the law in a mechanical fashion. Finally, not only the increase in the number of laws invalidated but also their subject matter indicated a deep-seated divergence between the courts

[50] *In re Debs,* 158 US 564 (1895).
[51] *Hylton* v. *U.S.,* 3 Dallas 171 (1796) ; *Springer* v. *U.S.,* 102 US 586 (1881).
[52] *Pollock* v. *Farmers Loan and Trust Co.,* 157 US 429 (1895).
[53] Sixteenth Amendment.
[54] *Brushaber* v. *Union Pacific,* 240 US 1 (1916).
[55] *Knowlton* v. *Moore,* 178 US 41 (1900), saving, of course, *Indian Motorcycle* v. *U.S.,* 283 US 570 (1931).
[56] *Frothingham* v. *Mellon,* 262 US 447 (1923).
[57] *U.S.* v. *Butler,* 297 US 1 (1936).

and the people generally and rendered it essential that some way out of the impasse be found.

American reactions to judicial review of legislation have varied, as might be expected from the importance of the subject and the diversity of interests that the institution can be made to serve. Men have for differing reasons opposed it altogether, have attempted to set up some mechanical corrective, and have tried to redirect it in such a fashion as to preserve its positive values and at the same time to prevent its obstructing the operation of government.

Judicial review has been attacked, for example, because of its inconsistency with majoritarian democracy. A strong proponent of this viewpoint was the late J. Allen Smith who contended that the framers of the Constitution had deliberately set up judicial review as a counterweight to democracy. This move involved, he thought, an assumption of legislative functions by the courts, and was made with that purpose in mind.[58] The result was more than a minority check on the majority, it was minority government against the majority.[59] Under the influence of arguments drawn from English experience, we had tried to make the courts independent. We succeeded only too well, but with the result that we achieved "an independent legislative and judicial body combined." [60]

[58] ". . . it must be remembered that the Federal judiciary in assuming the exclusive right to interpret the Constitution has taken into its keeping a power, which, as we have seen, was not judicial in character when the Constitution was adopted, and is not even now considered judicial in any other important country. In declaring a legislative act null and void it is exercising a power which every sovereign lawmaking body possesses, the power to defeat any proposed legislation by withholding its assent. The mere fact our Supreme Judges and our legal writers generally have called it a judicial power does not make it such. That it is in reality a legislative and not a judicial power is amply confirmed by the uniform and time-honored practice of all other nations, even including England, whose institutions until a century and a quarter ago were our own." *Spirit of American Government*, p. 108.

[59] "The Constitution is and was intended to be rigid only in the sense that it effectually limits the power of the majority. The founders of our government were not averse to such changes in the system which they established as would promote or at least not interfere with their main purpose—the protection of the minority against the majority. Indeed, they intended that the Constitution as framed should be modified, amended and gradually molded by judicial interpretation into the form which they desired to give it, but which the necessity of minimizing popular opposition prevented them from accomplishing at the outset. Amendment by judicial interpretation was merely a means of conferring indirectly on the minority a power which the Constitution expressly denied to the majority." *Ibid.*, p. 167.

[60] *Ibid.*, p. 103. Smith was not content with merely a theoretical opposition to judicial review. "A study of our political history shows that the attitude of the courts has been responsible for much of our political immorality. By protecting the

Smith's opposition to judicial review was shared by Brooks Adams, although his constitutional analysis differed markedly from that of Smith. As opposed to the thesis that the courts were inevitably the instruments of minority rule, Adams concluded that ultimately courts were forced to accede to the dominant social pressures of the time. He also differed from Smith in believing that the judicial review to which objection was being made at the beginning of the twentieth century was much broader than the narrow type of judicial review justified by Marshall in *Marbury* v. *Madison*. Since it was his theory that the American Constitution was tending to approximate the unwritten British constitution,[61] he was not able to say that this broadening of the judicial power was unconstitutional. He did, however, fear that the position the courts occupied had forced them into legislative action which was outside the field of their particular competence.[62] That they undertook to decide what were essentially legislative questions by the traditional method of the law only served to enhance the difficulties and disadvantages of their position.[63] Further, the burden thus put upon the courts doomed them to defeat:

Even since Hamilton's time, it has been assumed as axiomatic, by conservative Americans, that courts whose function is to expound a written

capitalist in the protection and enjoyment of privileges unwisely and even corruptly granted, they have greatly strengthened the motive for bribery and other corrupt means in securing the grant of special privileges." *Ibid.,* pp. 329–30.

[61] "A hundred years have gone: the work is done; the nation has outgrown the shell that protected it in infancy. Modern America is ruled like England, by means of a mass of custom and tradition which silently shapes itself to the changing wants of the people. It would be impossible, even were it desirable, to bind the country by unaltering laws a century old. It is of little moment whether the meaning of our great charter is slowly construed away by the ingenuity of lawyers, or whether it is roughly thrust aside by force; its fate is sealed; it must yield where it obstructs. . . . in our country and our age that which the majority of the people want will be the law, and the President and Congress, who represent the people, will see that the work is done. Our destiny will be accomplished, and the men or the tribunal that would bar the way must fall like the Supreme Court." "The Consolidation of the Colonies," 55 *Atlantic Monthly* 302 (1885), pp. 307–08.

[62] "When the Supreme Court . . . undertook to determine the reasonableness of legislation it assumed, under a somewhat thin disguise, the position of an upper chamber. . . . The courts vote on the reasonableness of the use of the Police Power, like any old-fashioned town meeting. There is no rule of law involved. There is only opinion or prejudice, or pecuniary interest. The judges frankly admit that this is so." *The Theory of Social Revolutions* (New York, 1913), p. 105.

[63] "For the court of last resort having once declared the meaning of a clause of the Constitution, that meaning remains fixed forever, unless the court either reverses itself, which is a disaster, or the Constitution can be amended by the states, which is not only difficult, but which, even if 'it be possible, entails years of delay." *Ibid.,* p. 83.

constitution can and do act as a "barrier to the encroachments and oppressions of the representative body." I apprehend that courts can perform no such office and that in assuming attributes beyond the limitations of their being they, as history has abundantly proved, not only fail in their object, but shake the foundations of authority, and immolate themselves.[64]

Any continuation of the attempt to impose upon the courts duties essentially alien to their function as courts could result only in the loss of those services which as courts they were equipped to perform.

A court to be a fit tribunal to administer the municipal law impartially, or even relatively impartially, must be a small body of men, holding by a permanent and secure tenure, guarded from all pressure which may unduly influence them.[65]

But it is also true that:

The progress has been steady and uniform, each advance toward an assumption of the legislative function by the judiciary having been counterbalanced by a corresponding extension of authority over the courts by the people.[66]

Adams saw but one solution: the courts must retreat.

The fear, that under the guise of reviewing the constitutionality of statutes the courts were in reality legislating, has led to periodic attempts to arrive at some constitutional control over judicial review. These are in addition to the existing constitutional power of impeachment which, at least on the federal level, has never successfully been used as a means of controlling decisions.[67] The actual proposals made have varied considerably, from a constitutional amendment to forbid judicial review [68] to suggestions that a special agency be set up to deal

[64] *Ibid.*, p. 111.

[65] *Ibid.*, p. 76.

[66] *Ibid.*, p. 127.

[67] Only nine federal judges have been impeached and of these only four have been convicted. Frederick A. Ogg and P. O. Ray, *Essentials of American Government* (5th ed.; New York, 1947), p. 337 n. The test case seems to have been the failure of the impeachment of Mr. Justice Chase in 1805. It is interesting to note that Marshall himself was sufficiently worried by the Chase impeachment to suggest "A reversal of those legal opinions deemed unsound by the legislature . . ." Letter to Chase, January 23, 1804. Quoted in Albert J. Beveridge, *Life of John Marshall* (New York, 1919), III, p. 177. Beveridge's comment is: "Marshall thus suggested the most radical method for correcting judicial decisions ever advanced, before or since, by any man of the first class." *Ibid.*, p. 178.

[68] On the subject of constitutional attempts to solve the problem of judicial review see Katherine B. Fite and Louis B. Rubenstein, "Curbing the Supreme Court—State Experiences and Federal Proposals," 35 *Michigan Law Review* 762 (1937).

with social and economic legislation.[69] Somewhere in between these two might be listed the recall of judges,[70] the recall of judicial decisions,[71] and Senator Lafollette's proposed amendment to allow the Congress by a two-thirds vote to override Supreme Court decisions that invalidated legislation.[72] There have also been proposals, accepted in some states, to require an extraordinary majority of the bench to invalidate a statute.[73] President Franklin Roosevelt's plan to rejuvenate the federal bench is too recent to require discussion.[74]

Neither attempts to do away with judicial review nor devices to correct its results, however, represent the main tendency of American legal theory on judicial review. The principal effort has been rather to regard judicial review as an impregnable element of the Constitution, to preserve it where it serves a useful purpose,[75] and to guide the courts away from those areas where the exercise of the judicial veto has proved harmful.

Although none of the advocates of the theories discussed below wishes to abolish judicial review, they are united in a number of assumptions that are unorthodox in their implications. All are concerned with the political problems arising out of the development of

[69] Harrison S. Smalley, "Nullifying the Law by Judicial Interpretation," 107 *The Atlantic Monthly* 452 (1911).

[70] President Taft vetoed the proposed Arizona constitution because it subjected judges, along with other elected officials, to popular recall. The people of Arizona promptly reinserted the clause after the admission of the state. John M. Mathews, *The American Constitutional System* (New York, 1940), p. 54.

[71] This was a feature of the Bull Moose Platform, 1912. For the story of that campaign see Henry F. Pringle, *The Life and Times of William Howard Taft* II (New York, 1939), pp. 815 ff.

[72] The issues involved are discussed in Felix Frankfurter, "The Red Terror of Judicial Reform," *New Republic,* October 1, 1924, also in Frankfurter, *Law and Politics* (New York, 1939), p. 10 and in Robert L. Hale, "Judicial Review versus Doctrinaire Democracy," 10 *American Bar Association Journal* 882 (1924); also 1 *Selected Essays* 783.

[73] K. B. Fite and L. B. Rubenstein, *op. cit.*

[74] R. H. Jackson, *op. cit.*

[75] Compare Mr. Justice Holmes's remark, "I do not think the United States would come to an end if we lost our power to declare an act of Congress void. I do think the Union would be imperilled if we could not make that declaration as to the laws of the several States." "Law and the Court," *Collected Legal Papers,* p. 296. It has been strongly argued that judicial review of congressional statutes serves no useful purpose. Henry W. Edgerton, "The Incidence of Judicial Control over Congress," 22 *Cornell Law Quarterly* 299 (1937); also 1 *Selected Essays* 793; Charles G. Haines, "Judicial Review of Acts of Congress and the Need for Constitutional Reform," 45 *Yale Law Journal* 816 (1936); also 1 *Selected Essays* 844; Henry Steele Commager, *Majority Rule and Minority Rights* (New York, 1943).

the American economy. Basic to all is the rejection of the unsophisticated picture of the judicial veto as a device for preventing governmental action. There is a common insistence that the judicial veto is in itself governmental action, and in exercising it the courts are not deciding whether governmental power will be used but rather at which points and for what purposes that power will be brought to bear upon the social system. There is an increased awareness that the courts of the United States, by virtue of their peculiar constitutional position, are not arbiters of the Constitution so much as they are active agents in the governmental process. There is, therefore, the greatest necessity that the courts be guided by the empirical, pragmatic attitude that the situation demands. Finally, these writers agree both in rejecting the judicial process as the most appropriate agency for dealing with the problems of the modern state, and in reasserting the primacy of the legislative process as the principal method of defining the relationship between government and the economic system.

In the course of the twentieth century there has been fairly widespread adoption of this position. It should be understood, therefore, that in referring to the writing of Goodnow, Thayer, and Frankfurter, it is not intended to imply that they are unique in holding these views. Statements of equal cogency might be taken from the works of C. G. Haines, E. S. Corwin, Thomas Reed Powell, as well as a number of others. The statements set forth below are therefore examples merely.

The constitutional situation as these men analyzed it and the purposes they intended to achieve were set forth by Professor F. G. Goodnow:

> It is . . . [my] purpose . . . to state in the first place what is the program of political and social reform proposed by the most modern progressive countries which have been called upon to solve the problems the American people will soon be called upon to solve; in the second place, to inquire what is the attitude of American courts towards the concrete measures contained in such a program, and finally to consider what methods there are by which pressure may be brought to bear upon the courts to induce them either to abandon or not to adopt the conception that our constitutions postulate a fixed and unchangeable political system and a rigid and inflexible rule of private right . . .[76]

[76] *Social Reform and the Constitution* (New York, 1911), pp. 5–6.

The particular point at which the argument centered was the proper mode of interpreting the broad phrases of the Constitution, whose meanings were largely a judicial product. That this implied a fundamental shift in philosophical outlook was candidly admitted by Professor Goodnow:

> . . . at the present time thoughtful men are coming more and more to the conviction that a static society is all but impossible and that absolute political ideals are incapable of realization. More and more political and social students are recognizing that a policy of opportunism is the policy most likely to be followed by desirable results and that adherence to general theories which are to be applied at all times and under all conditions is productive of harm rather than good.[77]

The means by which he proposed to accomplish this change was a constant and informed criticism of the courts—a remedy which illustrates the difficulties faced by the reformer dealing with an institution both self-defining and final in its power.

Similar considerations underlay the theory of Professor James B. Thayer, one of America's great students and teachers of constitutional law. Professor Thayer was willing to accept the institution of judicial review, but he was especially concerned to indicate its limits. To him there was a grave danger that in failing to observe the limits that ought to guide them, the courts would usurp the functions of other branches of the government—"the courts must not, even negatively, undertake to legislate."[78] Therefore, it was necessary to remember that courts were not empowered under the Constitution to sit as revisory bodies over the legislatures. Thayer laid great emphasis upon the fact that the only way in which judges could speak on questions of constitutionality was by passing judgment in cases brought before them. Since this might never happen or be long delayed, he argued, the initial determination of the meaning of the Constitution was a legislative function. The courts therefore were not to conceive their duty to be that of announcing the true meaning of the Constitution, but rather it was that of considering the reasonableness of a legislative determination of the meaning of the Constitution. In performing this function, the task of the courts was not merely that of a mechanical comparison of words, a technique that tended to pervert judicial review into a "pedantic and academic treat-

[77] *Ibid.*, p. 3.
[78] *Legal Essays* (Boston, 1923), p. 28.

ment of the texts" and to effect a wrongful exclusion of the consideration of possible grounds of legislative action. Rather the court's task should be that of determining whether in the circumstances the legislature could reasonably have considered the act in question to be within its constitutional powers, and every reasonable doubt ought to be resolved in favor of the legislation. A judge should sustain a legislative determination of constitutionality about which there was room for disagreement even though he would have concluded against the constitutionality of the act were he a legislator or responding to a request for an advisory opinion.

This is the famous Thayer "Rule of Administration." It does not exclude judicial invalidation where a reasonable and well-informed man would be forced to conclude that no basis for legislative action existed.[79] The Rule, however, removes from the courts many of the questions that they had come to consider on the basis of their expansion of the Fourteenth Amendment. The Rule of Administration expresses the attitude that pervades the constitutional decisions of Holmes, Brandeis, Stone, and, to a greater or lesser degree, other judges in the same tradition. Professor Thayer's whole theory of judicial review, including its advantages and limitations, is admirably set forth in his essay on John Marshall:

> To set aside the acts of such a body, representing in its own field, which is the very highest of all, the ultimate sovereign, should be a solemn, unusual, and painful act. Something is wrong when it can ever be other than that. And if it be true that the holders of legislative power are careless of evil, yet the constitutional duty of the court remains untouched; it cannot rightly attempt to protect the people by undertaking a function not its own. On the other hand, by adhering rigidly to its own duty, the court will help, as nothing else can, to fix the spot where responsibility lies, and to bring down on that precise locality the thunderbolt of popular condemnation. The judiciary today, in dealing with the acts of their co-ordinate legislators, owe to the country no greater

[79] It is perhaps significant, that Professor Thayer chose ex post facto legislation, a fairly definite constitutional provision, as an illustration. (*Ibid.*, p. 28.) It should be recognized, however, that Thayer's rule does not exclude decision on reasonableness to the extent of forcing the court to accept any legislative determination as reasonable. He appears to approve, for example, the decision in *Chicago, Milwaukee and St. Paul Railway Co.* v. *Minnesota*, 134 US 418 (1890), which invalidated a statute providing for the determination of railroad rates by a commission and which did not allow appeal to the courts. (*Ibid.*, p. 26 n.) Note by way of comparison, Mr. Justice Black's position in *Polk* v. *Glover*, 305 US 10, 16–18 (1938) which seems to be that the fact of passage is of itself evidence of the reasonableness of legislation.

or clearer duty than that of keeping their hands off these acts wherever it is possible to do it. For that course—the true course of judicial duty always—will powerfully help to bring the people and their representatives to a sense of their own responsibility. There will still remain to the judiciary an ample field for the determinations of this remarkable jurisdiction, of which our American law has so much reason to be proud; a jurisdiction which has had some of its chief illustrations and its greatest triumphs, as in Marshall's time so in ours, while the courts were refusing to exercise it.[80]

The attitude underlying the work of Goodnow and Thayer finds expression also in the theoretical writings and in the opinions of Felix Frankfurter, Associate Justice of the United States Supreme Court. During his long career as a member of the Harvard Law Faculty, Frankfurter was a close student of the Supreme Court. His work deals for the most part with that institution. Although his tendency has been to focus his attention upon a single court, many of his remarks can, of course, be given a broader application.

In so far as Frankfurter restates the objections to judicial legislation through judicial review, there is no reason to discuss his theory in detail. In Frankfurter's terms, the Supreme Court is pre-eminently a law court.[81] By this, he does not mean that the Supreme Court is not important,[82] nor does he imply that its position is an

---

[80] *Legal Essays,* p. 41.

[81] Frankfurter was led to remark on one occasion, "After all, this is the Nation's ultimate judicial tribunal, not a super-legal aid bureau." *Uveges* v. *Pennsylvania,* 335 US 437, 449–50 (1948). He seems, on occasion, to pay more deference to the legal niceties than do some of his brethren. The Uveges Case is an example. *Screws* v. *U.S.,* 325 US 91 (1945) might be another. Here Frankfurter pressed the point that the state courts ought to try the case in a situation involving the killing of a prisoner by a deputy sheriff, although the state was displaying no eagerness to proceed. He is, however, very alert to abuses of trial and police procedure. *McNabb* v. *U.S.,* 318 US 332 (1943); *Haley* v. *Ohio,* 332 US 596 (1948). He has also been comparatively eager to protect the judicial process from outside pressures. *Bridges* v. *California,* 314 US 252 (1941). At the same time he has consistently upheld the right of the states to alter their judicial procedure within the limits of the "fair trial" concept. *Hysler* v. *Florida,* 315 US 411 (1942); *Carter* v. *Illinois,* 329 US 173 (1946). Frankfurter's tendency to emphasize the legal issues is for him an attempt to keep the Court within what he considers its special competence. This is open to some variation in interpretation. See W. H. Hamilton, "He [Frankfurter] operates best when weaving crochet patches of legalism on the fingers of the case." 56 *Yale Law Journal* 1459–60 (1947), quoted in Samuel J. Konefsky, *The Constitutional World of Mr. Justice Frankfurter* (New York, 1949), p. xv. See, further, Professor Rodell's somewhat similar reference to "legal needlepoint." 121 *New Republic* 11, 13 (1949).

[82] "Law is essentially legalistic in the sense that observance of well-recognized procedures is, on balance, socially desirable." *Uveges* v. *Pennsylvania, supra,* p. 449.

easy one. On the contrary, the proper performance of the Supreme Court's function calls for statesmanship of high order—statesmanship that is highly aware of the limitations imposed on it by the requirements of a functioning democratic order.[83] Frankfurter, therefore, returns to another position stated by Thayer: [84] that the judicial function is not the most appropriate instrument for the achievement of democracy.[85]

This attitude would probably occasion little comment were it confined to the sustaining of economic and social legislation. Frankfurter's faith in the democratic process leads him, however, to apply it in the civil liberties area. This aspect of his theory is shown most strongly in his two famous flag-salute decisions, where he voted to sustain a compulsory flag salute as a condition of obtaining a public education. The rationale seems to have been this statement:

And, further, "the Supreme Court is the final authority in adjusting the relationships of the individual to the United States, of the forty-eight states to one another, and of the states to the United States." Felix Frankfurter and James M. Landis, *The Business of the Supreme Court* (New York, 1928), pp. 307–8.

[83] "Justices of the Court are not architects of policy. They can nullify the policy of others, they are incapable of fashioning their own solutions for social problems." *Mr. Justice Holmes and The Supreme Court* (Cambridge, 1938), pp. 25–26. The only exception seems to be in cases involving the federal balance between the nation and the states. Here he admits an historic mandate for the judicial formulation of policy, although he insists that it should not be a personal policy: "In all governments there must be organs for finality of decision. In a federated government like ours, with powers distributed in necessarily broad terms, a free court is the most dependable instrument for adjusting controversies between the constituent states and the nation, and between individual states . . . The simple truth of the matter is that decisions of the Court denying or sanctioning the exercise of federal powers . . . largely involve a judgment about practical matters, and not at all any esoteric knowledge of the Constitution. Therefore it is that the decisions of the Court must be subjected to relentless scrutiny to save them from pedantry and sterility, as the unconscious rationalizations of the economic and social biases of individual justices . . ." *Law and Politics*, pp. 11–12. Interestingly enough, in this instance Frankfurter seems to allow to the Supreme Court a more active role in policy formation than would Thayer. Cf. Thayer, *Legal Essays*, pp. 36 n., 37 n.

[84] "It [Supreme Court] cannot rightly attempt to protect the people, by undertaking a function not its own." *Legal Essays*, p. 41.

[85] "Even where the social undesirability of a law may be convincingly urged, invalidation of the law by a court debilitates popular democratic government. Most laws dealing with economic and social problems are matters of trial and error. That which before trial appears to be demonstrably bad may belie prophecy in actual operation. It may not prove good, but it may prove innocuous. But even if a law is found wanting on trial, it is better that its defects should be demonstrated and removed than that the law should be aborted by judicial fiat. Such an assertion of judicial power deflects responsibility from those on whom in a democratic society it ultimately rests—the people." Separate concurring opinion in *American Federation of Labor* v. *American Sash and Door Co.*, 335 US 542, 553 (1949).

To fight out the wise use of legislative authority, in the forum of public opinion and before legislative assemblies rather than to transfer such a contest to the judicial arena, serves to vindicate the self-confidence of a free people.[86]

It can be said in perfect fairness to all concerned that Frankfurter's position is not a simple one. No one is more explicit than he in expressing his dislike for judicial legislation, even when it serves "humane ends."[87] At the same time he is not willing to relinquish altogether the power of judicial review. When he feels, for example, that the "historic liberties" of the Constitution are imperiled, he is perfectly willing to strike down legislation.[88] It would seem that Frankfurter, therefore, suggests history as the source of constitutional definition sufficiently precise to prevent judicial review from degenerating into judicial legislation. Whether he has here a standard that satisfies the demands of his own conception of the judicial function is open to question. Does "history, through the Constitution, [ever] speak so decisively as to forbid legislative experimentation"?[89] When one surveys the clash of opinion in a case such as *Adamson* v. *California*,[90] where Justices Black and Frankfurter locked horns over precisely what history, speaking through the Fourteenth Amendment, does say, it is difficult to suppress the thought that once again a purported solution to the problem has turned instead into a restatement of it.[91]

[86] *Minersville* v. *Gobitis*, 310 US 586, 600 (1940). See also *West Virginia* v. *Barnette*, 319 US 624 (1943) for a restatement of this position. These opinions occasioned some surprise among those who had taken Frankfurter's activities in behalf of Sacco and Vanzetti to indicate a wholehearted commitment to the civil liberties position. There is reason to doubt that such surprise was justified. See *Law and Politics*, p. 195. Here, in an editorial that appeared in the *New Republic*, June 17, 1925, Frankfurter argues that the gains resulting from the cases of *Meyer* v. *Nebraska*, 262 US 390 (1923), and *Pierce* v. *Society of Sisters*, 268 US 510 (1925), were too expensively bought when it is considered that they were achieved by the use of the same power that was developed in the invalidation of state social welfare measures as in *Lochner* v. *New York*, *supra*. In fairness to Frankfurter's critics, it should be indicated that since in the *New Republic* article he was apparently making an empirical evaluation, he might have used his votes on the Court to tilt the balance a little more strongly in favor of civil liberty. Actually, however, to him the balance is not exclusively an empirical one.

[87] *American Federation of Labor* v. *American Sash and Door Co.*, *supra*, p. 556.

[88] *Everson* v. *Board of Education*, 330 US 1 (1947)—the New Jersey School Bus Case; *McCollum* v. *Bd. of Education*, 333 US 203 (1948)—the Illinois Released-Time Decision.

[89] *American Federation of Labor* v. *American Sash and Door Co.*, *supra*, p. 550.

[90] 332 US 46 (1947).

[91] In some cases, Frankfurter turns to "impersonal standards of society" as the criterion of decision. For a discussion of the difficulties faced by recent and present

In the area of constitutional law, the legal theory of the modern state has resulted in a return of the judicial function to the narrowest possible boundaries. Although there appears to be no tendency to relinquish the right of judicial review, the tendency has been to solve the problem of judicial legislation by eliminating it. This marks a return to the original conception of the judicial function. The possible difference is that modern judges, more aware of the dangers of their position, will be less likely than their predecessors to read their unconscious predilections into the law.

Broadly considered, this means that the legislature again becomes the principal agency of change in adapting government to the problems of modern society. Whether the principle of judicial withdrawal will hold in the face of what appears to be legislative efforts to act in the civil liberties field, it is not at present possible to say. Even now, however, it can be said that the Constitution has in the past few years fundamentally changed from a judicially defined Constitution to one that is in important areas to a far greater degree an instrument of legislative definition. Once again the nature of our institutions has changed. But, as has been the case in the past, that change has been brought about by the use of the judicial power.

---

members of the Court in their search for standards of decision, see George D. Braden, "The Search for Objectivity in Constitutional Law," 57 *Yale Law Journal* 571 (1948).

Chapter 4

SOCIOLOGICAL JURISPRUDENCE

I

The turn of the century inaugurated a period of increasing activity among American legal theorists. The growing legal tensions of the time and dissatisfaction with the insularity of the traditional theory of law and of the judicial function prompted an extensive reconsideration of both the foundations and the actual operation of our legal system. During this period also American juristic theory achieved a marked degree of self-consciousness. There resulted a broad variety of analyses of the judicial function and proposals for its modification which went far beyond the narrower problems of constitutional law and took the form of a general re-examination of the position and function of the courts in our governmental system.

One of the most important of these newer theories was sociological jurisprudence, which will be discussed here as it appeared in the works of three men: Roscoe Pound, Benjamin N. Cardozo, and Harlan F. Stone. Like many modern American jurists they resembled Holmes in rejecting either the possibility or desirability of judicial action along the lines indicated by the traditional theory. They are to be distinguished from others of Holmes's followers, however, by their tendency to adhere to the concept of legal rules and systems as elements in the process of decision. They differ from the group of constitutional theorists discussed in the preceding chapter primarily in that their interest tended to focus on those aspects of the judicial function not directly concerned with the invalidation of legislation, although their views on constitutional problems were substantially similar to those of Thayer and Holmes.

Before turning to a more detailed discussion of the theories of judicial legislation put forward by Pound, Cardozo and Stone, however, it should be made plain that in choosing to look at sociological jurisprudence through the work of these men there is no implication that there are not other sociological jurists of great merit.[1] Reference will be made from time to time to other writers in the same general group. It should also be noted that, as a term, "sociological jurisprudence" presents many difficulties, not least among which is defining the sociology to which it refers. Actually, the term is not accurate as a description. There are jurists, equally "sociological" in their approach, who differ from Pound and Cardozo on almost every important point. Despite efforts to substitute the term "functional jurisprudence,"[2] however, "sociological jurisprudence" is so well-established in the literature that to avoid it would be an unnecessary affectation.

II

ROSCOE POUND: THE JUDICIAL FUNCTION AS "SOCIAL ENGINEERING"

Roscoe Pound was outstanding for his early attempt to apply sociological theory directly to the study and formulation of legal theory. Not only did he develop a sociological theory of the growth of law, but he attempted to set up sociological analysis as a guide for legal development. In so doing, he encouraged a tendency in legal scholarship that is still of the greatest importance in American legal theory. So aware was he of the claims of sociology, that he made the phrase "sociological jurisprudence"[3] a permanent fixture in our language.

[1] The problem of "classifying" modern American jurists is as difficult as it is unrewarding. Among those, however, who tend to accept the concept of legal rules and who seek to moderate some of the excesses of the later "realists" are Morris R. Cohen and John Dickinson. Arthur L. Corbin also seems to follow a fairly well defined sociological analysis.

[2] Carleton K. Allen, *Law in the Making* (4th ed.; Toronto, 1946), p. 29; George W. Paton, *A Text-book of Jurisprudence* (Oxford, 1946), p. 18.

[3] It may be well to repeat that there are as many types of sociology as there are types of jurisprudence, and that it is not possible to be too specific. When Mr. Justice Holmes, for example, said, "The Fourteenth Amendment did not enact Mr. Herbert Spencer's *Social Statics*" (*Lochner* v. *New York, supra*), he was not accusing the majority of being nonsociological, but rather of using the wrong sociology. What Pound meant, however, is fairly explicit: "In the past fifty years the development of jurisprudence has been affected profoundly by sociology. The older mechanical sociology affected the science of law by its insistence upon thinking about groups. Thus it had much to do with bringing us to give up the abstract individual as the central point in juristic thought. Also this insistence upon a social theory led jurists to seek to relate law more critically to other social phenomena. Later the biological sociology brought about more thorough study of primitive legal institutions and gave impetus to the unification of the social sciences by establishing con-

His principal significance here lies in his extensive reliance on the judicial function in the process of legal change.

Underlying Pound's legal theory is an emphasis upon the society in which law is a controlling force, but of which it is also a reflection.[4] The result is a concept, not unlike that already noted in Holmes, of the legal order "in which law results and for which it exists." [5]

The problem that Pound was attempting to solve by this concept can best be seen by looking briefly at his theory of legal history. As his acceptance of the idea of law as a societal institution implies, he was less interested in the development of legal doctrine than in the relationship between the legal system and the society of which it is a part. He was therefore concerned both with offering a scheme by which the development of legal systems can be presented,[6] and, even more importantly, with showing the societal necessities which impel the process. Legal development, according to his theory, resolves itself into a series of adjustments which are interactions between societal demands and the legal system and are made necessary by

---

nections with anthropology and ethnology. Still later the psychological sociology gave us a more adequate account of the traditional element in legal systems, turned attention to the problem of judicial and juristic method, and made us aware of the traditional art of the lawyer's craft as an element in law and a factor in legal development." "Sociology and Law," *The Social Sciences and Their Interrelations,* ed. W. F. Ogburn and A. A. Goldenweiser (Boston, 1927), p. 324.

[4] Edward A. Ross, whose work appeared at about the same time that Pound was formulating his basic concepts, appears to express Pound's notion rather better than did Pound. He also provides a good example of the type of sociology that had so much influence on Pound. ". . . Law-originating impulses became socialized and rationalized. Inwrought with other motives, they come to express the will of the Social Personality. The just settlement of disputes, from a private need, becomes a public function. When we consider the transformation of law by jurisconsults and judges, the enlargement of it by the action of the legislator, and the renovation of it in the name of the principle of social utility, it is plain that jurisprudence cannot hope to be more than a feudatory state in the realm of sociology." *Foundation of Sociology* (New York, 1905), pp. 22–23.

[5] "A New School of Jurists," *Essays in Jurisprudence,* 4 Univ. of Nebraska Studies 3 (July, 1904). The emphasis upon the legal order is reminiscent of Rudolf von Jhering to a considerable degree. See his *Struggle for Law* (Chicago, 1879) ; *Law as a Means to an End* (Boston, 1913), esp. pp. 231, 330.

[6] He outlined five stages: (1) the stage in which the principal concern was the keeping of the peace; (2) the stage of "strict law," characterized by a high degree of formality and rigidity and separation from morals; (3) equity or natural law, in which the excessive formalism is relieved and liberalized; (4) maturity, in which equality and certainty are prominent and stress is laid upon individual rights; and (5) the last stage in which the opposition between law and morals again becomes prominent and social interests are emphasized. "Legislation as a Social Function," 8 *Proceedings, American Sociological Association* 148 (1912).

the function of law as a controlling and therefore stabilizing force in a society constantly tending to change.

> Law must be stable and yet it cannot stand still, hence all thinking about law has struggled to reconcile the conflicting demands of the need of stability and of the need of change. The social interest in the general security has led men to seek some fixed basis for an absolute ordering of human action whereby a firm and stable social order might be assured. But continual changes in the circumstances of social life demand continual adjustments to the pressure of social interests as well as to new modes of endangering security.[7]

The law therefore cannot be regarded as a closed order, although there is always an attempt to make it so.

Legal history also includes, however, the development of ideas about law as well as of law itself, for, to Pound, ideas of what law ought to be played a large part in determining, or at least influencing, what law actually becomes.[8] It was, he felt, a common error to build a more or less complete theory of law upon the phase of the cycle that happened to be temporarily ascendant, and it was to avoid this error, that he tried to comprehend the antithetical notions of stability and change in the more inclusive idea of the legal order. This concept serves, therefore, as an attempt to include the conflict between the two opposing principles of law, but also to achieve a statement capable of accounting for both.

The concept of a dynamic societal legal order further provides an explanation for the legal system of a particular period and at the same time sets up the context within which the legal system could be criticized. The purpose of law is to control society, but it cannot do this without satisfying basic social needs. Knowledge of what those needs are depends again upon sociological analysis, and Pound contended that there was a manifest need for legal thinking to be broadened to include a wide and continuing knowledge of the actual effect of law upon social life.

The necessity for this new type of legal analysis arose from the difficulties with which the courts adapted themselves to the growth of social legislation. The philosophy of government that underlay the conservative decisions of the courts had as its primary end, in Pound's view, the protection of the individual from the government.

[7] *Interpretations of Legal History* (London, 1923), p. 1.
[8] See, e.g., *Introduction to the Philosophy of Law* (New Haven, 1922), p. 145.

Admitting that the dominance of this type of thought was historically explicable, he nevertheless believed that its day had passed. In a democracy, the frequent judicial invalidation of measures demanded by the people meant that the courts were trying to set the people up against themselves.[9] There was need for a theory that would permit the courts to sustain social legislation and to conserve their judicial effort for fields in which they could be more useful.

The sociological principles upon which Pound based this new legal analysis involved a shift of focus from individuals to groups, and he was willing to accept the corollary that such a shift in emphasis required a shift in legal values.[10] Society was to be seen in terms

[9] Pound was much disturbed by what seemed to him to be a growing distrust of law and lawyers. The growing divergence between public desires and those of the legal profession was damaging to the legal order. The idea recurs in several of his writings: "While to the lawyer law is above and beyond all will, to the people it is but a formulation of the general will. Hence it often happens that when the lawyer thinks he is enforcing the law, the people think he is overturning the law. While the lawyer thinks of popular action as subject to legal limitations running back of all constitutions and merely reasserted, and not created thereby, the people think of themselves as the authors of all constitutions and limitations and the final judge of their meaning and effect." "The Law and the People," 3 *Univ. of Chicago Magazine* 1 (1910), p. 12. In another place he said: "When it [the Court] assumes to stand between the legislature and the public and thus again to protect the individual from the state, it really stands between the public and what the public needs and desires, and protects individuals who need no protection against society which does need it." "The Common Law and Legislation," 8 *Columbia Law Review* 382, 403 (1908).

[10] "Juristically the change [i.e., in the legal interpretation of rights] began with the recognition of interests as the ultimate idea behind rights. It began when jurists saw that the so-called natural rights are something quite distinct in character from legal rights; that they are claims which human beings may reasonably make, whereas legal rights are means which the state employs in order to give effect to such claims within certain defined limits. But when natural rights are put in this form it becomes evident that these individual interests are at most on no higher plane than social interests, and, indeed, for the most part get their significance for jurisprudence from a social interest in giving effect to them. In consequence the emphasis comes to be transferred gradually from individual interest to social interests. Such a movement is taking place palpably in the law of all countries today. Its watchword is satisfaction of human wants, and it seems to put as the end of law the satisfaction of as many demands as we can with the least sacrifice of other demands. This new stage of legal development may be called the socialization of the law." "The End of Law as Developed in Legal Rules and Doctrines," 27 *Harvard Law Review* 195 (1914), pp. 225–26. It is interesting to note that not only the conceptions of interests as the basis of social analysis but the term itself seems to have come from Albion W. Small. Compare the following: "In brief, then, the form in which we must try to think all social experience is this: individuals in large numbers, each representing such and such combinations or specific interests, and working by means of, or in spite of, such and such operations of social function, directing their efforts toward such and such immediate aims, resulting in such and such episodes, incidental to conscious or unconscious endeavor of such and such nature to achieve such and such ultimate purposes. A science of the whole social process is

of the interests active within it. In these terms, "sociological jurisprudence" becomes almost synonymous with "socializing" the law.
Pound, therefore, accepted the doctrine that government is not inevitably an enemy of freedom, but is rather an instrument that can
be used to augment freedom.

Pound's theory of the legal order sets up the ability to adjust as
one of the important requirements of a satisfactory legal system.
The theory of group interests states the form in which problems are
presented to the legal system. Both concepts come from sociology
and, taken together, throw the emphasis of Pound's thought upon the
administration of justice as a process. It is in this frame of reference that his ideas concerning the judicial function assume significance.

The simplest way to approach Pound's theory of the judicial function is through his idea of the form of law. He reasserted the common distinction between statutes and judicial decisions. In most of
Pound's writings these are referred to as, respectively, the impera-
tive and traditional elements. Only in outline, however, does this
analysis correspond to the customary division of law. In asserting
that both were law, he separated himself, on the one hand, from the
historical jurists, to whom statutes were merely expressions of the
law [11] and, on the other hand, from the orthodox school, which did
not accept the idea that judicial utterances could be more than evi-
dences of law. Still more unorthodox was his assertion that judicial
activity is really the creative element in law.

That Pound considered judicial activity more creative than legislative activity is, perhaps, unusual, but, again, the explanation is
to be found in his theory of legal history. Depending upon circumstances, he thought, either of the two elements might predominate in
a legal system at a particular time. This does not mean, however,
that he accorded them an equal value. The preponderance of the
enacted element indicated to Pound a period of legal solidification

---

possible simply to the degree in which we become able to give a definite value to
each of those indefinite terms, through long series of social experiences." *General
Sociology* (Chicago, 1905), pp. 198–99. There are echoes of this concept in political
theory, e.g., the Pluralists. It also lies at the basis of the interest analysis in the
studies typified by Peter Odegard, *Pressure Politics* (New York, 1928). See also
Arthur F. Bentley, *The Process of Government* (Chicago, 1908).

[11] There are some intimations of this attitude in James C. Carter, The Province
of the Written and Unwritten Law, 24 *American Law Review* 1 (1890).

and organization. Attempts at codification are examples. But to Pound such activity also meant legal stagnation, a most undesirable condition in a dynamic social situation. For empirical verification, Pound turned to the state of the criminal law. Here was the prime opportunity for legislation, since in criminal law the requirements of uniformity and definiteness were basic. Yet the criminal law remained the most backward portion of our jurisprudence. Pound, however, went beyond merely demonstrating that legislation had failed to meet the requirements laid upon the legal system. He also asserted that the conditions of the legislative process render such failure almost inevitable. Given the complexity of modern life, it was inconceivable that legislation could be written that would foresee and provide for all cases. Of necessity, the filling of gaps and omissions would require continuous attention. The legislature, situated as it was in the center of the governing process, and necessarily pressed for time to consider even the most important projects, could scarcely devote to this task the attention it deserved and required. It was necessary therefore that such matters be left to other agencies of the government.

In the light of the pressing need for legal reform and the inability of the legislature to undertake it, Pound turned to the courts. His argument was strengthened by the fact that history demonstrated the futility of trying to prevent judicial legislation. The Prussian code of 1749 had failed in its attempt to prevent court-made additions. The adoption of codes in the United States had proved equally futile. Even in the France of the celebrated Code Napoléon there was a movement toward "free judicial decision," which to Pound indicated the inevitability of legal modification and creation through the judicial process. Assumed in the codes was a concept of the judicial function based upon untenable eighteenth-century notions of the separation of powers and natural law carried over into the analytical jurisprudence of the nineteenth century.[12] But neither the

---

[12] "In the nineteenth century the analytical jurist assumed a rigidly defined dogma of separation of powers. He assumed that judicial creative activity in modern states was at best a survival from a relatively primitive state of legal development before a separation of powers had been achieved. He assumed that until a complete system of legislative express commands had been set up, the deficiency would be eked out by a primitive device of judge-made rules which the state imposed *ad interim* till it got around to issue express commands." *The Formative Era in American Law* (Boston, 1938), p. 111.

eighteenth-century natural law school nor the analytical school had been successful in their attempt to suppress the judicial function.[13]

Pound granted the possibility that judge-made law might tend equally with legislation to become cumbrous and mechanical in operation. In fact, that it had become so was a major problem at the time he was writing. Nevertheless, its possibilities for the future were based upon its historically proved capacities to infuse ethical and moral values into the law. Provided that the judges were aware of their position and the requirements of the situation, the judicial process could be the superior instrument for achieving the continual adjustment demanded of a modern legal system.

Such a function could not, of course, be adequately performed if the judiciary were dominated by the old ideals of rational consistency, uniformity, and certainty. These had value, but not as exclusive ends; rather they were factors to be weighed along with others in achieving harmonious balance between law and life. The attitude most likely to produce such an adjustment was one of pragmatism, which Pound symbolized in the phrase "social engineering." More arresting than descriptive, the term is to be read as describing a mental attitude rather than any especial type of activity or body of learning:

> Engineering is thought of as a process, as an activity, not merely as a body of knowledge or as a fixed order of construction. It is a doing of things, not a serving of passive instruments through which mathematical formulas and mechanical laws realize themselves in the eternally appointed way. The engineer is judged by what he does. His work is judged by its adequacy to the purposes for which it is done, not by its conformity to some ideal form of a traditional plan. We are beginning, in contrast with the last century, to think of jurist and judge and lawmaker in the same way . . . We are thinking of how far we do what is before us to be done, not merely of how we do it; of how the system works, not merely of its systematic perfection.[14]

[13] Although the analytical jurists formally disavowed any reliance upon natural law, they managed to reach much the same result. Their assumption of universal harmony and their reliance upon reason provided a convenient bridge between their ideas and those of the natural law school. In the United States people were receptive to both sets of ideas because of the separation of powers, which comprised part of the constitutional system, and because of the reliance upon a written fundamental law, which according to the official theory resulted from a legislative act of the people.

[14] *Interpretations of Legal History,* p. 152. The concept of logic here involved is very similar to that held by John Dewey. Dewey says: ". . . either . . . logic must be abandoned or . . . it must be a *logic relative to consequences rather than to ante-*

The heavy burden of government which Pound placed upon the courts should be emphasized. While the circumstances in which Pound wrote supported the argument for legal change, his theory takes account of the need for stability as well. In those cases in which stability appears to be wise social engineering, it becomes the duty of the courts to lay down firm rules and to adhere to them closely. Whether there is a necessity for certainty in the law, is a problem of engineering to be solved pragmatically.

In admitting the possibility of stability in the law, Pound not only made reference to the two primary factors of stability and change, but he also indicated his position on the question of the·binding force of legal rules. Despite the generally dynamic quality of his theory, Pound was not willing to dispense altogether with the concept of "law as rule." In this, as in his acceptance of stability as a desideratum, he differs from a number of later American legal theorists. While he admitted that conceivably the judicial or administrative process might carry on the regulation of life without rules as guides to decision, he felt that the complexities of modern life require legal norms as "patterns or models of determination." [15] He was willing

---

cedents, a logic of prediction of probabilities rather than one of deduction of certainties." "Logical Method and Law," 10 *Cornell Law Quarterly* 17 (1924), p. 26. For the same thought see also *Experience and Nature* (New York, 1929), p. 27. In a more recent work, Dewey also uses the symbol of the engineer. "The crisis in democracy demands the substitution of the intelligence that is exemplified in scientific procedure for the kind of intelligence that is now accepted. . . . Approximation to the use of scientific method in investigation and of the engineering mind in the invention and projection of far-reaching social plans is demanded. The habit of considering social realities in terms of cause and effect and social policies in terms of means and consequences is still inchoate." *Liberalism and Social Action* (New York, 1935), pp. 72–73. In using the engineer as a symbol, both Pound and Dewey rely rather heavily upon their own definition. It can be argued that engineering has achieved a certain appeal as a symbol because it deals with principles which, within the limits to which the engineer employs them, are relatively definite and certain. An application of this phase of engineering to social problems is apt to lead to exactly the type of social thought which is the desire of Pound and Dewey and others of this group to avoid at all costs. It must be remembered that the mechanistic social theories of the late eighteenth century made a wide popular impression primarily because they seemed to be an application of the type of thinking that had proved so fruitful in physical speculation, as in Newtonian physics. Since much of Pound's social thought is predicated on the fact that the application of the mechanistic analogy to social affairs is limited, there are certain difficulties in his use of the term "engineer" except in the sense in which he was careful to define it. He might have used a happier metaphor. Success in ordinary engineering does not necessarily imply an empirical attitude in dealing with social and economic problems.

[15] *History and System of the Common Law* (New York, 1939), p. 6.

to concede that there are limits. to the field in which uniform rules can be laid down in advance, outside of which society must rely upon the trained reason of the magistrate,[16] but the area of certainty ought not to be unduly restricted. "If left to act freely in individual cases, without rule or standard, no will, either of king or people, is sufficiently set and constant to insure a uniform administration of justice. Law and caprice are incompatible." [17] And his tendency to try to retain the concept of rules, while at the same time lightening their weight as obstacles to change, can be seen in his definition of law as "general rules recognized and enforced in the administration of justice." [18] At the same time, the problem of when to use rules and when to rely on discretion is a judicial problem.

In the end, then, Pound's whole theory comes to rest upon the judicial function, and it becomes appropriate to ask what Pound offers to guarantee that the judicial function will produce the results that he desires. In general, he seems to offer three different answers to this problem. One is merely a postponement of the problem and is probably not to be taken too seriously, although it does indicate his fundamental pragmatism. He says:

> That an engineering interpretation might be put to ill use I shall not deny. But for a season the dangers are in another direction. We shall not outgrow the juristic pessimism of the immediate past easily or quickly, and lawyers . . . are not likely to be over-rash in outgrowing distrust of their power to do things.[19]

A second protection against the possibility of unbridled judicial discretion was a re-emphasis of the normative aspect of legal rules. Building perhaps on one of Pound's own suggestions,[20] later American writers came to emphasize the concept of the legal rule as an

---

[16] *Introduction to the Study of Law* (*Library of American Law and Practice,* 1912), p. 3.

[17] *Loc. cit.*

[18] "The Decadence of Equity," 5 *Columbia Law Review* 20 (1905).

[19] *Interpretations of Legal History,* p. 164. In the light of his reaction to what he considers the excesses of social jurisprudence, one can surmise that he regrets ever having said this.

[20] "Instead of these compounds resulting from the unfolding of an idea, they are oftenest the result of endeavour to provide for a concrete case, leading to the application of a concrete solution, behind which others proceed to put tentative generalizations until finally the more inclusive idea is worked out. Thus when we look back at it we say that an idea was realizing. But the idea served after the event . . ." *Ibid.,* p. 136.

empirical generalization from observed judicial behavior. To this Pound was heartily opposed:

> . . . the urge to make everything that was called a science conform in its method to experimental physical science, did nothing less than eliminate from the social sciences their real fundamental problem. For if the physical sciences have for their function to discover what is, the social sciences have for theirs to discover what ought to be and how to bring it about. If newly observed phenomena do not accord with the physicist's hypothesis, he must reject it and frame a new one. If particular facts of human conduct do not accord with some formula of justice or policies of law, the trouble may be with those facts, not with the formula, and conduct may have to be shaped to what-ought-to-be not formulas of what-ought-to-be shaped to facts of conduct which controvert the jural postulates of civilization. What-ought-to-be has no place in physical science. It has first place in the social sciences.[21]

That Pound again really fails to meet the problem is apparent. Granting that the legal rule, the legal "what-ought-to-be," may constitute a limitation on the judge, it is still open to question whether Pound ought to use the argument. It was he who pictured the good judge as the pragmatic "social engineer," and it was he who made the scope of legal rules a problem in social engineering. It is difficult to see how a legal rule that may or may not be used can constitute a limiting force. There would appear to be a misstatement either in the theory of judicial discretion or in the use of legal rules as a limiting factor; it is doubtful whether both can be correct. What Pound appears to be trying to set up is a sociological standard for sociological jurisprudence, and this is indeed to impose a burden upon an already heavily burdened judiciary.

In the end, Pound asserts that the legal process is in its nature self-limiting, and he comes to rely heavily upon the juristic tradition and the quest for certainty as the ultimate guarantees against abuse of the judicial power:

> The whole training of lawyers and judge, the tradition in which they were brought up, the criticism on the part of the profession which the judge has ever before him as something to fear, lead judges to act habitually not as if each action were a unique single instance, but as if it were, so far as they can make it such, an example of a general type of instances. They succeed in attaining a very high degree of uniformity

[21] *Contemporary Juristic Theory* (Claremont, Calif., 1940), p. 36.

and objectivity and impartiality in what they do. But no one does better than he tries to do.[22]

He goes on to say:

> We must not ignore the power of ideas. . . . In jurisprudence we are dealing ultimately with what ought to be. . . . We must make our pictures of what ought to be from our achievements rather than from our failures.[23]

These arguments are part of Pound's strong reaction to what he considered the destructive tendencies of legal realism, and his viewpoint will become more meaningful when some account of that development is available. Despite his vehemence, however, the basic question is left unresolved. It may be that the legal tradition is the principal reliance against what Pound calls "legal absolutism," but one wonders again if that argument is really available to Pound. After all, it was he who at one time led the attack on "scientific law," and it was he who sought to subordinate the influence of general ideas. He did much to destroy the tradition of judicial inactivity in the process of legal change. Has he not in reality destroyed his own defense, or if his defense is good, has he not jettisoned his analysis?[24] Or, if both his analysis and

---

[22] *Ibid.,* p. 48. See also: "The dogma of a complete body of rules to be applied mechanically was quite out of line with reality. It is just as unreal and unjustifiably dogmatic to refuse to recognize the function of the quest for certainty as contributing to the general security. It is just as dogmatic and unreal to be blind to the extent to which the administration of justice attains certainty through rule and form and the extent to which the economic order rests thereon. It is just as unreal to refuse to see the extent to which legal technique, with all its faults, applied to authoritative legal materials, with all their defects, keeps down the alogical or unrational element or holds it to tolerable limits in practice." "The Call for a Realistic Jurisprudence," 44 *Harvard Law Review* 679 (1931).

[23] *Ibid.,* p. 54.

[24] Morris R. Cohen deals with Pound's criticism of legal realism in the following terms: "On the one hand, we have a persistent opposition to mechanical jurisprudence of concepts or fixed rules, and a devastating criticism of our courts' uncritical reliance on such principles as the freedom of contract. On the other hand there is a naive clinging to the fiction of the division of power between the judiciary and the executive, against those who favor the fusion of judicial and administrative functions in commissions. He insists that only rules and principles interpreted by courts can stand between the citizen and official incompetence, caprice, or corruption, as if principles and rules could enforce themselves without human—all too human—judges. Courts, he insists, decide on principles. Yet no one has pointed so emphatically to the fact of judicial empiricism, that principles are empty and misleading unless we know all the relevant social facts to which they are to be applied. And how can any one doubt that our courts have less opportunity than commissions have to institute researches and factual inquiries even before disputes arise? He

limitation are true, does he not logically put himself in the position of advocating a doctrine that must in its nature remain the possession of only a few? [25]

Despite these difficulties, however, there can be no denial that Pound's influence on American jurisprudence has been very great. In his work there is an assertion that the traditional analysis of society in terms of individuals or social atoms has proved inadequate. He recognizes the fact that men naturally combine themselves in groups for the achievement of their desires and that social institutions are the results of these desires and of the combinations formed to achieve them. Law as a social organization must accommodate itself to these conditions. If, on balance, this means that some individual rights must be modified in order to make way for social interests, there is no alternative for the law but to adapt itself to that fact. He took the position, in common with the sociologists, that law is an institution, the product of a social demand, and should be considered in terms of its adequacy to the end for which it exists. As an institution, law is not more sacred or immune from judgment than any other institution.

Many of the reforms Pound favored cannot practicably be accomplished by legislation. Therefore he turned to the courts as the agency to accomplish the task. Since, upon the basis of history, he argued that the traditional method of legal progress has been through the courts, he is never entirely clear whether the need is for a new jurisprudence or merely a new sociology, but, in any event, he maintained that the judicial function held the best possibilities for future development. The courts should therefore be informed of the newer

denounced law without rules as cadi justice (which ignores the fact that in a simple community, governed by custom and the Koran, the rules are well known). Yet, in insisting on the element of judicial discretion and on the presence in the law of standards, he admits elements other than rules or principles." *Law—A Century of Progress,* II, pp. 298–99.

[25] Cf. "I confess that no light responsibility is laid upon the investigator who explores the mysterious processes that take place in the soul of a people, and dissects in public the ideals and affirmations elaborated in the social mind. The fact of control is, in good sooth, no gospel to be preached abroad with allegory and parable, with bold type and scare headlines. The secret of order is not to be bawled from every house top. The wise sociologist will show religion a consideration it has rarely met with from the naturalist. He will venerate a moral system too much to uncover its nakedness. He will speak to men, not to youth. . . . In this way he will make himself an accomplice of all good men for the undoing of all bad men." E. A. Ross, *Social Control* (New York, 1901), p. 441.

requirements placed upon the law and should assume their rightful task of bringing the law up to date.

The whole process is to be viewed pragmatically. The law, as is all life, is a process of adjustment. In these circumstances, the duty of the student of the law is to know "not only what the courts decide, but quite as much the circumstances and conditions, social and economic, to which these principles are to be applied . . ." [26] Pound thus expresses a central idea of modern American jurisprudence, and his tireless effort to expound that idea assures him a place as one of the major figures of American legal theory.

III

Benjamin N. Cardozo: The Method of Social Welfare

The position of Benjamin N. Cardozo in the development of sociological jurisprudence is equal to and possibly even greater than that of Pound. His expositions of the functions of the modern judge are classics of American juristic literature, and his great prestige as a judge adds support to the sociological view of the nature of law and of the creative theory of the judicial function. Although much that he said was not new, his statement of the sociological position undoubtedly contributed to a widened public appreciation of the role of the judiciary in modern government.

Writing principally in the mid-1920's, Cardozo's immediate concern was with the growing volume of criticism to which the courts were being subjected. In his view, much of this criticism was based upon the outmoded conception of law as a body of unchanging principles in some fashion beyond the reach of human agencies. This misconception both hampered and obscured the necessary functioning of the courts. In the first place, it prevented understanding of the courts' shifts in doctrine, and, second, to it could be attributed the widespread inability to appreciate the essential similarity of the legislative and judicial functions in the common task of legal development.

To the Blackstonian conception of law as fixed and immutable principles Cardozo opposed a definition based upon his own judicial experience. There are, he said, numerous precedents and principles embodied in the recognized body of legal literature, and there is a

[26] "The Need for a Sociological Jurisprudence," 19 *Green Bag* 607 (1907), pp. 611–12.

high probability that these will be drawn upon in the decision of cases. Further, it is reasonably certain that courts will defend these principles against attack. Since, taken together, these principles constitute a relatively well-defined body, there is a measure of predictability as to what courts are likely to do in certain situations, and to that extent judicial decisions are predictable. Even when a court unexpectedly relies upon principles other than those expected to form the basis of decision, in all likelihood these, too, will come from the recognized corpus of doctrines. This measure of certainty gives warrant for calling these precepts law.[27]

The courts employ this body of materials to decide cases justly. In so doing they perform two sorts of functions. In some cases, where the principles are sufficiently plain and established to remove any reasonable doubts as to what the court should do, the judge merely administers or applies the accepted principles. In other cases, the law is less definite. The law reflects the life it governs: "If life feels the tug of . . . opposing tendencies, so also must the law which is to prescribe the rule of life." [28] In this area, the function of the judge is truly "judicial." Where the law does not give clear guidance and where, upon analysis, the rules themselves become merely standards and degrees, the judge has no choice but to create his own rule. In so doing, the judges do only what judges have always done. The product, as well as the method, is legislative:

> We are told at times that change must be the work of statute, and that the function of the judicial process is one of conservation merely. But this is historically untrue, and were it true, would be unfortunate. Violent breaks with the past must come, indeed, from legislation, but manifold are the occasions when advance or retrogression is within the competence of judges as their competence has been determined by practice and tradition.[29]

[27] "What permits us to say that the principles are law is the force or persuasiveness of the prediction that they will or ought to be applied. Even when the conclusion upon a special state of facts is in doubt . . . there is little doubt that the conclusion will be drawn from a stock of principles and rules which will be treated as invested with legal obligation . . . This stock of rules and principles is what for most purposes we mean by law. We may not draw the same deductions from them as the court does in this case or in that. There will be little difference in our premises. We shall unite in viewing as law that body of principle and dogma which with a reasonable measure of probability may be predicted as the basis for judgment in pending or in future controversies." *Growth of the Law*, pp. 44–45.

[28] *Paradoxes of Legal Science* (New York, 1928), p. 7.

[29] *Ibid.*, pp. 7–8.

The essential modernity of Cardozo's outlook is reflected in his insistence upon this creative judicial choice as an essential part of the legal system. He was no more willing than Holmes or Pound to accept even the idea of an eternally perfect system of law. Even if a body of law adequate to its day could be conceived, changing social conditions would render it invalid in the future. The purpose of the law is to define relations, but the points of reference are not fixed:

> The acts and situations to be regulated have a motion of their own. There is change whether we will it or not . . . True constancy consists in fitting our statement of the relation to the new position of the objects and the new interval between them.[30]

Especially true in the field of constitutional law, where the method of "free decision" had come to prevail, it is also true in the common law, the legal formulation of the mores of the time.[31] He therefore

[30] *Ibid.*, pp. 11–12. It is significant that in this passage Cardozo referred to Einstein's theory of relativity. As Newton provided the scientific terminology for the eighteenth century, so also does Einstein for the twentieth. Cf. "This search for a static security—in the law or elsewhere—is misguided. The fact is that security can only be achieved through constant change, through the wise discarding of old ideas that have outlived their usefulness, through the adapting of others to current facts." William O. Douglas, "Stare Decisis," Eighth Annual B. N. Cardozo Lecture, 49 *Columbia Law Review* 735 (1949), p. 735.

[31] Cardozo's use of the Sumnerian term "mores" suggests the wide influence of the developmental concept as a method of legal analysis. The Sumnerian influence is even more apparent in Arthur L. Corbin of the Yale Law School. Corbin starts from a concept of the courts as agencies for the exercise of societal force. They display "uniformity of behavior" which allows us to speak of laws. "The common law consists of this uniformity and consistency." "The Restatement of the Common Law by the American Law Institute," 15 *Iowa Law Review* 19, 26 (1929). The analogy with physical laws is not to be pressed too far, however, since societal laws and uniformities of judicial conduct are not given in the nature of things. Rather, they "represent the prevailing *mores* of the time, and with the *mores* they must necessarily be born, survive for the appointed season, and perish." Preface, *Anson on Contracts* (3rd ed.; New York, 1919), p. v. The judge is therefore a legislative official in much the same sense as a legislator: ". . . the difference between the legislature and the judge in their process of 'making' law is merely in the mode and rapidity of their procedure. That of the judge is piecemeal, the generalization that constitutes the rule usually being the result of a series of decisions, occurring perhaps over a long period of time. The legislature can fulminate generalizations without a single precedent and in short order by a majority vote, though the effectiveness of this legislation in its application to living facts depends chiefly upon the courts." Review of C. K. Allen, "Law in the Making," 38 *Yale Law Journal* 270 (1928), p. 274. In the circumstances, Corbin argues, the judges should be held politically responsible. See "Law and the Judges," 3 *Yale Review* (new series), p. 235 (1913). Corbin did not, however, support the Roosevelt Court Plan. See his "Letter to Volunteer Citizens Committee of Boston," 23 *American Bar Association Journal* 411 (1937).

could admit openly what J. C. Carter a generation before had indignantly rejected as an "impeachable offense."

> I take judge-made law as one of the existing realities of life. There, before us, is the brew. Not a judge on the bench but has had a hand in the making. The elements have not come together by chance. *Some* principle, however unavowed and inarticulate and subconscious, has regulated the infusion. It may not have been the same principle for any judge at all times. But a choice there has been, not a submission to the decree of Fate . . .[32]

Although Cardozo warned against overemphasis upon the "waste spaces of the law," [33] he was nevertheless willing to defend lawmaking of this type as peculiarly judicial. Granted both that there is no assurance that the judge will be able to perform this function adequately, and the dependence of the judge upon other agencies of government, particularly the legislatures, he still must undertake a leading role in translating popular ways of thought and action into rules of law enforced by the power of society. Despite the theoretical neatness of trying to assign the whole of the creative function to the legislature, what assurances can there be that such an arrangement would be any better in result? Cardozo, like Pound, believed that legislation is better handled by those familiar with the problems, and he did not believe that legislatures are superior to courts either as to *expertise,* method, or in the form of the result.[34] In any event, the question is no longer open. The custom of the constitution and our governmental practice have vested the power in the judges. The exercise of this power is necessary to the fulfillment of the judicial function.

There is some echo here of the common lawyer's traditional distrust of the legislative product, but it is an echo merely. Rather,

---

[32] *The Nature of the Judicial Process* (New Haven, 1921), pp. 10–11.

[33] See particularly his "Address before the New York State Bar Association, January 22, 1932," *New York State Bar Association Report,* 1932, p. 263.

[34] "If legislation is to take the place of the creative action of the courts, a legislative committee must stand back of us at every session, a sort of super court itself. No guarantee is given us that a choice thus made will be wiser than our own, yet its form will give it a rigidity that will make retreat or compromise impossible. We shall be exchanging a process of trial and error at the hands of judges who make it the business of their lives for a process of trial and error at the hands of a legislative committee who will give it such spare moments as they can find amid multifarious demands. Even if we could believe that the amateurs would be wiser than the professionals, their remedy would be prescribed too late to help the patient whose disease they had observed." *Growth of the Law,* pp. 133–34.

Cardozo was interested to assert the claim of the courts as coopera-
tive agencies in the accommodation of the legal system to social demands—there was no thought of the use of the judicial power to
hamper a coordinate body of government or to usurp its functions.
"One department of the government may not force upon another its
own standards of propriety." [35] And while not denying the power of
the courts to invalidate legislation, to him their real importance was
as instruments "in making vocal and audible the ideals that might
otherwise be silenced, in giving them continuity of life and of expression, in guiding and directing choice within the limits where choice
ranges." [36]

Cardozo realized the delicacy of the judicial task as he depicted it.[37]
Having made the judge squarely responsible for the development of
the law, he offered a guide for the performance of the judge's work.
His premise is that no one method of decision is sufficient for all
places and at all times. He therefore outlined four methods, each to
be used in its appropriate place. These are: the method of philosophy, in which the logical element predominates; the method of history, which looks to the development of the community as a guide for
the law; the method of custom, which derives guidance from the
actual practices of the community; and the method of sociology,
which introduces the concepts of "justice, morals and social welfare."
Of these, the last is the most important. Not only does it guide the
development of principle when logic, history, and custom prove inadequate, but it also guides the judge in his choice of method. "In a
sense it is true that we are applying the method of sociology when
we pursue logic and coherence and consistency as the greater social
values." [38] And it is also the method that must, in the ultimate,
prevail over all of the others when the results produced by them
conflict.

Like other members of the sociological group, Cardozo assigned
his own definition to "sociology," which he used as roughly synonymous with "social welfare" or "social justice." His position is that
in the interstitial area where judgment is not mechanically deter-

[35] *Nature of the Judicial Process*, p. 90.
[36] *Ibid.*, p. 94.
[37] He quotes from Thomas Reed Powell, ". . . there is no gospel that will save
us from the pain of choosing at every step." *Growth of the Law*, p. 65.
[38] *Nature of the Judicial Process*, p. 75.

mined, the judges are capable of weighing the considerations grouped under the heading of "social welfare" as well, or better, than the legislatures; and if the method of sociology seems indefinite as a guide for the one, it is equally indefinite for the other. The possibilities of clear gain warrant opening the judicial process to the considerations heretofore thought solely appropriate for legislative consideration:

> In the present state of our knowledge, the estimate of the comparative value of one social interest and another, when they come, two or more of them, into collision, will be shaped for the judge, as it is for the legislator, in accordance with an act of judgment in which many elements co-operate. . . . his experience of life; his understanding of the prevailing canons of justice and morality; his study of the social sciences; at times, in the end, by his intuitions, his guesses, even his ignorance or prejudice . . .[39]

In outlining his theory and its method, Cardozo was aware that many would accuse him of urging ex post facto legislation. His defenses against this possibility were several. Granting the force of the objection, much of the difficulty could be prevented, he argued, by the practice of the court's announcing in advance the rule to be followed, although refraining from applying it in advance of such an announcement. Having thus disposed of the difficulties attendant upon a change in a settled rule, he went on to argue that in those cases where there is no settled rule, the real law is that doubtful cases will be decided by an impartial judge. A fair trial having been had, neither side can claim that a decision was ex post facto. Even in such cases where the judge is forced to devise his own rule, Cardozo said, usually the judge does no more than to enforce reasonable expectations. The judge's guide should be the accepted moral sense of the community, neither an impossibly high standard nor the standard followed by the least desirable elements. In such a case, a judgment can scarcely upset established interests.

"Wide enough in all conscience is the field of discretion that remains," [40] as he said. But, if his analysis is true, it is rather a regularization than an actual broadening of the scope of judicial legislation.

[39] *Growth of the Law,* pp. 85–86.
[40] *The Nature of the Judicial Process,* p. 141.

IV

Harlan Fiske Stone: Sociological Jurisprudence and Constitutional Law

Although it is logically possible to distinguish sociological juris-prudence from the modern liberal school of constitutional interpre-tation, the work both of Frankfurter and of Cardozo suggests the tendency for the two theories to appear together. The likelihood that those who hold the developmental view of the law will be sympathetic to legislative attempts to modify the legal system is further illus-trated in the work of Harlan Fiske Stone.

Stone came to accept the sociological position only after a rather vigorous rejection of its assumptions. The change in his views can be seen by comparing two of his books that are separated in time by some twenty-two years. In his *Law and Its Administration*,[41] al-though he agreed with some of the basic assumptions of sociological jurisprudence, the limits of his acceptance are clearly indicated. He concurred in the idea that law is justified only in terms of its ends:

> The law is pre-eminently a practical system administered by human agencies. The only justification for its existences is the accomplishment of its ends—social order and well-being.[42]

He even went so far as to say that the common law is a product of the judicial process:

> To summarize the matter, the law is what the judges having jurisdiction of the case declare it to be. The sources of the law are statutes, prece-dents, custom, the opinion of experts, and public policy tempered and judged in the light of experience.[43]

And he accepted the doctrine that without a remedy, there is no right, with all of its implications for enhancing the importance of the judicial process.[44]

Stone refused to go the whole way with those who advocated judicial legislation, however, and clung to the notion that judges "discover" the law:

> . . . the term discover when used in connection with the process or method by which law is formulated by the just and capable judge has a

---

[41] New York, 1915.
[42] *Ibid.*, p. 8.

[43] *Ibid.*, p. 19. And see p. 16.
[44] *Ibid.*, p. 52.

descriptive quality which commends its use; for example, if the choice of words lay between *discover* and *invent,* I should say unhesitatingly that the former was preferable. The judge, in formulating the role of law, is guided by the principles of the common law. In determining those principles by the method which we have described, the duty of the judge should be that of the patient investigator and seeker for scientific truth. To that extent, at any rate, he is a discoverer, and the rule which he discovers is a rule which is profoundly influenced, if not controlled, as it is in the great majority of cases, by established principles of law.[45]

To Stone, sociological jurisprudence was not a theory of judicial decision. As he put it:

. . . the basis of the so-called sociological jurisprudence [is:] 'legal science ought to be founded upon generalizations from a descriptive sociology.' As a principle of judicial decision consciously adopted and applied, certainly nothing could be more foreign to the spirit of the common law, and certainly nothing could be more destructive of its essential qualities. Sociological jurisprudence, as thus defined, is really a theory of legislation, since it is an attempt to formulate law on the basis of the legislator's view of what is sound public policy based upon his observation of social conditions, his prediction of what social conditions will be in the future, and his particular theories for improving them.[46]

It was not the function of the judge to listen for the " 'newest thing' in social welfare." The judge has no way of determining social welfare—to base his decisions on it would be merely to give the advantage "to those who cry the loudest." [47] And, finally, even the election of the judiciary would not make the judge the representative of the popular will in such matters.[48]

[45] *Ibid.,* p. 23.

[46] *Ibid.,* pp. 41–42.

[47] *Ibid.,* p. 46. Stone here hits upon a very fundamental problem in sociological jurisprudence: how to get the facts to the judiciary. On the constitutional level, the effort to accomplish this took the form of the "Brandeis Brief," which marshalled social and economic facts for the consideration of the courts. The Brandeis technique can work both ways, however, as is shown by *Jay Burns Baking Co.* v. *Bryan,* 264 US 504 (1924), and is not needed when the proper presumptions in favor of the constitutionality of legislation are indulged. *O'Gorman and Young* v. *Hartford Insurance Co.,* 282 US 251 (1931); *U.S.* v. *Carolene Products Co.,* 304 US 144 (1938).

[48] "The judge, although elected in most states, unfortunately so I believe, is not elected to inaugurate or carry out legislative programs. He is, or should be, appointed because of his expert knowledge, experience, and integrity to apply an existing system of law to the settlement of controversies as they arise. That system of law is the accumulated wisdom and experience of our whole civilization, not lightly to be trifled with or overturned. Its history demonstrates that it is capable of progress and expansion, and that it has, in fact, by reason of its own essential qualities,

In the course of time, however, Stone seems to have adopted a different emphasis. The stress came to be laid upon the element of choice in the making of a judicial decision and a recognition that this involved a weighing of social values. The skill with which the judge was able to do this was a measure of the vitality of the common law system. There was still a recognition that great changes must come through statutory law, but this is because judge-made law necessarily lags behind social development. In the last analysis, however, the judicial decision must depend strongly upon considerations of social advantage, determined by investigation into economic and social data. The whole shift of emphasis was summed up in Stone's own words:

> I shall state succinctly what I think is the resulting tendency of our legal thinking. We are coming to realize more completely that law is not an end, but a means to an end—the adequate control and protection of those interests, social and economic, which are the special concern of government and hence of law; that that end is to be attained through the reasonable accommodation of law to changing economic and social needs, weighing them against the need of continuity of our legal system and the earlier experience out of which its precedents have grown; that within the limits lying between the command of statutes on the one hand and the restraints of precedents and doctrines, by common consent regarded as binding, on the other, the judge has liberty of choice of the rule which he applies, and that his choice will rightly depend upon the relative weights of the social and economic advantages which will finally turn the scales of judgment in favor of one rule rather than another. Within this area he performs essentially the function of the legislator, and in a real sense makes law. . . . We realize that this is in fact nothing more than the method which, consciously or unconsciously, the great judges have employed.[49]

Stone's name is associated with several of the most interesting developments in our constitutional doctrine after 1937.[50] Although these are not all of equal value for a study of the judicial function, of particular interest is the problem involved in expanding "due

---

progressed and expanded to meet the reasonable needs of every age. Its progress and expansion have been caused in every instance by the pressure of facts proven in court, and rarely, if ever, by political agitation or by theories of social progress formulated outside the court room." *Ibid.*, p. 48.

[49] *The Common Law in the United States* (Cambridge, Mass., 1937), pp. 140–41.

[50] See Samuel J. Konefsky, *Chief Justice Stone and the Supreme Court* (New York, 1945).

process of law" in the Fourteenth Amendment to include protection of civil liberties from adverse state action. The issues involved have already been discussed in connection with the judicial theory of Felix Frankfurter.[51] Stone's interest in this question was great. He was not of the view that the justices of the Supreme Court should under guise of interpretation read their private ideas into either the Constitution or statutes,[52] and he consistently objected to the use of the Fourteenth Amendment as a barrier against economic and social legislation.[53] At the same time, he was very much interested in the protection of civil liberties.[54] The tendency of the courts to find widened protection for civil liberties within the contours of the "due process clause," [55] however, raised serious questions whether the Court was not legislating under the Fourteenth Amendment in the same fashion as previously, although perhaps in the service of more humane ends. The problem was well stated by Judge Learned Hand in his appreciation of Stone's work on the Supreme Court, although it has been suggested that Hand more accurately indicated his own conclusions than those of Chief Justice Stone.[56] Said Judge Hand:

> He [Stone] could not understand how the principle which he had all along supported, could mean that, when concerned with interests other than property, the courts should have a wider latitude for enforcing their own predilections, than when they were concerned with property itself. There might be logical defects in his canon, but it deserved a consistent application or it deserved none at all; at any rate it was not to be made into an excuse for having one's own way in any given case.[57]

[51] *Supra*, pp. 67 ff.

[52] See his dissent in *U.S.* v. *Butler, supra.* For his views on statutory interpretation see his dissent in *Girouard* v. *U.S.*, 328 US 61, 70 (1946), where he protested against the reversal of earlier interpretations of the citizenship oath, although in the original cases he had favored the interpretation subsequently adopted. See his dissents in *U.S.* v. *Mackintosh*, 283 US 605 (1931) ; *U.S.* v. *Bland*, 283 US 636 (1931).

[53] *Ribnick* v. *McBride, supra.* See also Konefsky, *op. cit.*, chap. V.

[54] See his dissent in the first flag-salute case, *Minersville* v. *Gobitis, supra.*

[55] The widespread interest aroused by this development will perhaps excuse the multitudinous citations that a full illustration would require. For an excellent and brief outline see Robert E. Cushman, *Leading Constitutional Decisions* (8th ed.; New York, 1946), pp. 101–3; 111–14; 120–24. See also Robert K. Carr, *Federal Protection of Civil Liberties* (Ithaca, 1947), chap. I.

[56] Charles E. Clark, "The Dilemma of American Judges," 35 *American Bar Association Journal* 8, 11 (1949).

[57] Learned Hand, "Chief Justice Stone's Conception of the Judicial Function," 46 *Columbia Law Review* 697, 698 (1946).

Stone's famous Carolene Products footnote [58] has been suggested as Stone's solution to the problem. There Stone said:

> There may be narrower scope for operation of the presumption of constitutionality when legislation appears on its face to be within a specific prohibition of the Constitution, such as the first ten amendments, which are deemed equally specific when held to be embraced within the Fourteenth.

The difficulty which later writers have had in interpreting what Stone meant by the footnote [59] indicate the grave difficulties that attend the whole subject, but it can be suggested that Stone's appeal to the "definiteness" of the Bill of Rights indicates his desire to avoid judicial legislation on the constitutional level, even in the civil liberties area.

V

The emergence of sociological jurisprudence marks the formulation of a general legal theory for the modern state in America. Its emphasis on judicial legislation, together with the concurrent attempt to state a theory by which to mitigate the rigors of judicial review, indicates the increasing acceptance of positive governmental action in economic and social affairs. The power of government, whether exercised through the legislature or through the judiciary, is to be used consciously to effect the adaptation of the legal system.

In brief statement, the central ideas of sociological jurisprudence seem obvious. Not directly interested in many of the standard questions of jurisprudence, the sociological jurists concentrate their at-

---

[58] *U.S.* v. *Carolene Products Co., supra,* p. 152 n. "It is unnecessary to consider now whether legislation which restricts those political processes which can ordinarily be expected to bring about repeal of undesirable legislation, is to be subjected to more exacting judicial scrutiny under the general prohibitions of the Fourteenth Amendment than are most other types of legislation. . . . Nor need we enquire whether similar considerations enter into review of statutes directed at particular religions, . . . or national, . . . or racial minorities, . . . whether prejudice against discrete and insular minorities may be a special condition, which tends seriously to curtail the operation of those political processes ordinarily to be relied upon to protect minorities, and which may call for a correspondingly more searching judicial inquiry."

[59] This footnote has been the subject of considerable comment. See G. D. Braden, "The Search for Objectivity in Constitutional Law," 57 *Yale Law Journal* 571, 580 (1948) ; Lewis Lusky, "Minority Rights and the Public Interest," 52 *Yale Law Journal* 1 (1942) ; Clark, *op. cit.* See also Mr. Justice Frankfurter, concurring in *Kovacs* v. *Cooper,* 336 US 77 (1949).

tention on the interactions between law and society.[60] Their basic
concept is that law is a social institution, a product of the society
which it governs, and therefore subject to the same influences and
measurable by the same criteria as other social institutions. Contrary
to the prevailing belief, the expansion of law was not achieved by the
logical development of assumed first principles, but rather through a
series of adjustments to new empirical situations. The proper
method of the law is therefore pragmatic. The universal solutions
of the past having failed, the sociologists accept the concept of "adjustment" as their final criterion. The concept of development in
its post-Spencerian form has become the basis of an important part
of American legal theory.

It is important to recognize the volitional element upon which sociological jurisprudence insists. Pound and Cardozo are not willing
to bow to any inevitable necessities cast in evolutionary form. This
is not to say that they assert complete freedom of action, but they do
insist that there remains a possibility of rational control of legal development. They are thereby permitted to lay down a goal for legal
development, a measure to gauge the quality of the "adjustment" they
seek, in the concept of "social welfare" or the "maximum satisfaction
of social wants."

Without precluding legislative action in its proper sphere, judicial
action is an important reliance in accomplishing this end. The sociological jurists emphasize the legislative aspects of the judicial function. They go beyond the statement that judges do legislate, to an
assertion that judges ought to legislate and that in many areas it is
socially advantageous for the judges, rather than the legislatures, to
undertake legal change. It is difficult at times to escape the impression that this choice is in part based upon an acceptance of legislatures
as they are and courts as they might become, but the preference for
judicial legislation is a deliberate and important part of the theory.

The fact that sociological jurisprudence marks a departure from
the orthodox American theory of law and the judicial function is
obvious. It must be remembered, however, that in the minds of the
sociological jurists this departure is not a wholesale affair. Both
Cardozo and Pound are at pains to indicate that it is only a limited
judicial discretion they contemplate. At the limits, perhaps, ad-

[60] Julius Stone, *The Province and Function of Law* (Cambridge, Mass., 1950),
pp. 391–94.

judication becomes a species of arbitration without rule, but even here the discretion is not arbitrary since it is confined by received traditions and the necessity of observing established procedures. The position of the sociological jurists is, therefore, a moderate one, and, they have had the usual moderate's necessity to defend himself against attack from both sides.

The criticism directed against the sociological group has arisen only in part, however, from their attempt to maintain a central position. It is due in measure also to a certain vagueness of some of the basic concepts of the theory. Admitting that it may be inappropriate to impose an obligation of airtight definition upon a theory so basically pragmatic, it remains true, unfortunately, that Cardozo's "social welfare" and Pound's "maximum satisfaction of social wants" imply, rather than state, a standard. From such indefiniteness follow a number of difficulties, not least of which is the problem of method. Presumably, everyone accepts "social welfare" as a goal, but even so there is room for wide disagreement as to what it may be. And even if there were consensus on that point, there is still no necessary implication of agreement on how to accomplish it. It was, of course, a major departure from orthodox theory when the sociological group proposed that the judge should assume an active responsibility in achieving social welfare, but he is left in considerable doubt either to determine how to go about it or to know when he has succeeded. To the breadth of what appear to be the central conceptions of the group may also be attributed a certain flexibility in their position in criticizing other legal theories, particularly legal realism. The vigor with which Dean Pound, especially, undertook to criticize some of the later juristic developments which seem most easily read as attempts to follow out his own suggestions suggests that he had never succeeded in making his own meaning clear.

Some of the methodological problems left unsolved by the sociological group are reflected in their attitude toward "facts," a subject which they frequently discuss, but with an unstated assumption that the "facts" are both obvious and speak for themselves. It is a dubious thing indeed to assume that there is such general agreement on what "facts" are or what they say, if anything, or, most importantly, how the judge is to find out about them. Here is one of the great unexplored areas of sociological jurisprudence. Their basic interest in the interrelationships between law and society ought to have led the sociological jurists into an intensive search for some method of demonstrating those relationships. If the judiciary are to keep law in touch with life, we might hope for a clearer indication of how the judges themselves are to be kept in touch with life.

These aspects of sociological jurisprudence are in part explained, of course, by the fact that sociological jurisprudence began as a program of reform and received its strongest statement as a theory of dissent. In the circumstances, the major changes it tried to effect were sufficiently agreed upon, so that there was little need for discussing what must have seemed obvious. If the position is taken, however, that at least on the constitutional level most of these problems have been solved, the present usefulness of sociological jurisprudence appears somewhat limited. Further, it remains open to question whether sociological jurisprudence ought to be credited with more than an indirect influence in the solution of these problems. Although, therefore, the theory provided a strong basis for dissent, it remains to be seen whether it can sustain a more positive program. It is not the least of the paradoxes in the field of legal theory, that law joined the social sciences at about the time that the social sciences began to be measurably less sure of themselves, and it might be suggested that a good deal of the confidence in the social sciences displayed by the sociological jurists was the confidence of lawyers moving in relatively unfamiliar disciplines.

These reservations should not detract from the historical importance of the sociological jurists. If they did not solve all of these problems, it may well have been because so much of their time was consumed in fighting an uphill battle against an unsympathetic profession. Many of the assumptions of later American writers are possible because that fight was made. And many of the criticisms made of sociological jurisprudence apply equally, if less justifiably, to the theories that followed.

Chapter 5

LEGAL REALISM: THE BEGINNING

I

Although much of the American juristic writing of the 1920's and 1930's is in one way or another connected with "legal realism," the term itself defies definition. In part, it represents an extension of Holmes's dictum that law is "prophecies of what the courts will do in fact." [1] In part also it involved a vigorous attempt to broaden the study of law with the aid of borrowings from the other social sciences, and is, therefore, the development of an idea common to both Holmes and the sociological jurists. Beyond these resemblances, however, legal realism exhibits the greatest diversity as well in method as in conclusions.

There are several factors that may account for the heterogeneity that legal realism displays. Like sociological jurisprudence, legal realism developed as a protest against the orthodox theory of law and the judicial function. As such, its critical aspects are necessarily the more predominant,[2] and common disbeliefs do not necessarily support common affirmations. Then, too, the diversity of legal realism is in part symptomatic of the growing diversity of the social sciences. Legal realism is capacious enough to include several types of sociological jurists, a group of psychological jurists, several statistical jurists, and some who call themselves institutional jurists. As we have said, jurisprudence became a social science just at the time that it was becoming increasingly difficult to define the social sciences. In truth, legal realism is less a description than a slogan and carries emotional connotations rather than precise meanings.

---

[1] In some cases, as will be noted later, this is shifted to "what the courts do in fact," a significant alteration.

[2] "Authorized spokesmen" have pointed out that legal realists agreed principally in their negations. Karl N. Llewellyn, "Some Realism About Realism," 44 *Harvard Law Review* 1222 (1931); Jerome Frank, Preface to 6th printing, *Law and the Modern Mind* (New York, 1936 *et seq.*), p. viii; *If Men Were Angels* (New York, 1942), Appendix V.

"Realism" was used in the literary rather than the philosophical sense; and allegiance to "the facts" has proliferated into almost as many varieties of jurisprudence as there are observers of "the facts." In the end, legal realism comes very close to being what legal realists discussed.[3]

In the circumstances, therefore, a rigorous definition will not be attempted. In so far as legal realism represents a frame of mind, and there is much to favor such a description, it is more important to catch the mood of the juristic discussion of the 1920's and 1930's than to attempt a dissection. The theories that are discussed in the chapters to follow are therefore merely examples of the variety of legal theory bearing upon the issue of judicial legislation that has developed in the United States.

II

Diverse as modern American legal realism may be, however, it is not altogether without a certain common intellectual background. Setting aside the intricate question of deeper philosophical influences,[4] it is now proposed to examine the theories of four American legal and social theorists, whose work attained a certain currency among the legal realists. It is not possible to combine them to reconstruct the complete thought of any of the more modern writers, and the in-

[3] In this connection, it should be indicated that legal realism was largely an academic affair which resulted in an ever-increasing number of "legal realists," and this in turn contributed to the diversity so characteristic of later American legal theory. The student has some help here in the form of a semi-authoritative listing of legal realists in Karl N. Llewellyn, "Some Realism About Realism," *supra*. Llewellyn's position as apologist-elect is, however, somewhat qualified by the fact that he appears to have selected his own constituency. A comparison of Llewellyn's article with Pound's "A Call for a Realistic Jurisprudence," 44 *Harvard Law Review* 697 (1931), to which it was a reply, gives rise to the suspicion that neither of them was very clear on the point of dispute. Jerome Frank, in the Preface cited above, redefines his position and expresses a preference for dropping the term "realist." Some substantial differences between his list and Llewellyn's are apparent, although he assisted Llewellyn in the preparation of the article. In Frank's list, for example, some doubts are cast on Llewellyn's realism.

[4] Such an exploration would be an endless task and one of questionable worth. Although it occasioned considerable shock to professional philosophers, no one seemed more willing blithely to ignore the metaphysical implications of their work than were the legal realists. See, for example, Morton G. White, *American Social Thought—The Revolt Against Formalism* (New York, 1949); Sidney Hook, "The Folklore of Thurman Arnold," 5 *University of Chicago Law Review* 341 (1938); Mortimer G. Adler, "Law and the Modern Mind—A Symposium," 31 *Columbia Law Review* 82 ff. (1931).

fluence of these comparatively early writers must be seen as comple-
mentary to that of such figures as Holmes and Pound. Nevertheless,
the writings of Gray, Bingham, Bentley, and Dewey form an important part of the frame of reference within which legal realism
moves, and although their relation to the common tradition varies,
some consideration of their work is helpful to an understanding of
later developments. For this reason, attention will be given to
Gray's emphasis on the importance and uniqueness of the judicial
function, to Bingham's nominalism as an approach to the judicial
function, and to some of the methodological contributions of Bentley
and Dewey.

III

John Chipman Gray was one of those who early dealt with the
problem of judicial legislation. Interested, among other things, in
the conventional problems of jurisprudence, he chose as his point of
attack the orthodox distinction between "the law" and judicial decision, according to which a judicial decision was merely an exposition of the rules of law discovered by the judge.

In Gray's view "the law of the State or of any organized body
of men [was] composed of the rules which the courts, that is the
judicial organs of that body, lay down for the determination of legal
rights and duties." [5] Although this definition does not seem especially astonishing in itself, there is a certain significance in its development. An orthodox theorist could probably accept his statement with the substitution of the single word "follow" for the
phrase "lay down." Gray chose, however, to emphasize the latter
phrase, and in so doing, gave a new orientation to his legal theory.

Gray's theme comes from a sermon preached by Bishop Hoadly
before the king, a passage which appears with considerable regularity
in modern American writings on these subjects. The statement
is:

> Whoever hath an *absolute authority to interpret* any written or spoken
> laws, it is *he* who is truly the *Law-Giver* to all interests and purposes,
> and not the person who first spoke or wrote them . . .[6]

[5] *Nature and Sources of the Law* (2d ed.; New York, 1920), p. 84. See also p. 1.
[6] *Ibid.*, p. 102. Gray's fascination with the idea is shown by his quoting it three
times. See also pp. 125 and 172.

And despite the good bishop's rather obvious begging of the question in his use of the words "absolute authority," Gray chose to take it at face value. In point of fact, he took it at something more than face value, for not only does he accept Bishop Hoadly's dictum as saying that courts make law through the interpretive process, but he continues to the assertion that nothing which does not receive the imprimatur of judicial decision can be called law.

The development of the theme involved a sharp distinction in the Austinian manner, although only in manner, between "law" and "source of law." Under Gray's definition, anything except rules enforced by the courts is a source of law. As he puts it:

> The difference in this matter between contending schools of Jurisprudence arises largely from not distinguishing between the Law and the Sources of the Law. On the one hand, to affirm the existence of *nicht postivisches Recht,* that is, of Law which the courts do not follow, is declared to be an absurdity; and on the other hand, it is declared to be an absurdity to say that the Law of a great nation means the opinions of half-a-dozen old gentlemen, some of them, conceivably, of very limited intelligence.
>
> The truth is, each party is looking at but one side of the shield. If those half-a-dozen old gentlemen form the highest judicial tribunal of a country, then no rule or principle which they refuse to follow is Law in that country.[7]

Looked at in one sense, the idea is not very complicated, although at the time it was certainly unorthodox. Gray, like the legal positivists, is defining law as the product of a known process involving certain agencies that can be empirically identified. From this point of view, Gray would seem to be an Austinian one step farther along in the governmental process. Seeing, first, that even a legislative declaration goes through a further refinement before being brought to bear upon the settlement of a dispute and, second, that legislative rulings are not the only guides to the determination of controversies, he simply chooses an agency other than the legislature as his defining factor. And it must be admitted that his system has the advantage of obviating the fiction relied upon by the positivists—"What the Sovereign permits, he commands."

Gray's position becomes a little more difficult if it is taken to mean that anything a court says is law. But this he does not mean.

[7] *Ibid.,* p. 84.

Again to refer to his definition of law, it will be noted that he speaks of "general rules which are followed." [8] He does not say, nor does he believe, that judges are free to declare anything to be law; and so far as his definition is concerned, there is no necessity to suppose that a creative aspect is present in the judicial function. Up to this point, then, there is no necessary implication of judicial legislation at all.

Gray did, however, believe in considerable judicial creativeness, although he did not argue for it on the basis of the definition which we have been considering. His belief in judicial legislation depends rather upon his ideas that the primary function of the judge is not "to declare the Law, but to maintain the peace by deciding controversies" [9] and that the rules do not automatically decide controversies by themselves. Much is involved in what he read into Bishop Hoadly's phrase "to interpret." He points out that in interpreting a statute or other legal document the judge may merely have to give effect to what is there.[10] Frequently, however, the judge has to give effect to an "intent" that was obviously not there because the authors of the document did not have any intent on the precise question facing the judge. In some instances, the judge has to give effect to his own idea of what the intent should have been. There is, moreover, a degree of judicial freedom, which varies with the definiteness of the source of law with which the judge works. The latitude that the judge enjoys even in statutory interpretation is broadened as he deals with less definite sources of law. And where the sources of law are so indefinite as to give the judge complete latitude, Gray argues that the judge should enforce his own notions of what is right or wrong even when those notions run counter to those of the community.[11]

For present purposes, however, the actual amount of creativeness which Gray thought inherent in the judicial function is not important.

[8] Jerome Frank points to this as evidence of Gray's incomplete emancipation from the childish urge for the Father-as-Infallible-Judge sort of security. In the absence of more complete biographical data, the childish longing is reconstructed from Gray's acceptance of guiding rules. See *Law and the Modern Mind, passim.*

[9] Gray, *op. cit.,* p. 100.

[10] Gray believed that these were general principles and that they have a compulsive force on decision. He denies also that "wrong decisions" are law. *Ibid.,* pp. 116–17.

[11] Here he differed from Cardozo, who believed that the judge should in such cases enforce the community's notion of right or wrong. *Nature of the Judicial Process,* pp. 88–89.

The grounds upon which he justified judicial legislation are rather common and need not be pursued further, although it might be remarked that he found an inverse but close relationship between judicial lawmaking and legislative lawmaking and thereby closely related his theory to the American constitutional situation of his day. His idea of the centrality of the judicial act in giving the quality of law to a rule is, however, of great significance. In his paper on the *Common Law in the United States*,[12] the late Harlan Fiske Stone gave as one of the striking features of modern American jurisprudence the "fresh analysis of the judicial lawmaking function." Gray is surely in part responsible for this. His emphasis on the vital significance of the judicial function represents an important element common in recent legal thought.

IV

A second current in the stream that ultimately became "legal realism" was Joseph W. Bingham, Jr.'s attack upon the concept of generalization.[13] The problem of the existence and force of legal generalization is an important one for the advocate of the judge-as-legislator. If generalizations or legal principles exist and are binding upon the judges, then there is no way by which judges themselves can free the law from its reliance upon the past. One method of attack is to admit the existence of generalizations but to question the degree to which they are binding. Within limits, this would be Gray's position, since he spoke of rules, although at the same time he pointed to a considerable area of freedom for the judge which was provided by the facts of the legal system. It is possible also to take another alternative and deny that it is possible for legal generalizations to have binding force, because they do not exist. Bingham was among the first to do this.

For reasons known best to himself, he chose to approach his problems by means of a broad and rigorous nominalism. He went so far as to assert that it was impossible for two persons to hold the same idea. To him, an idea was a mental reflection of something outside the mind. The same object might be reflected in the minds of two

---

[12] *Supra,* p. 91.

[13] Llewellyn hails Bingham as the first legal realist. "Some Realism about Realism," 44 *Harvard Law Review* 1222, 1244 (1931).

different persons at the same time, but the result would be two separate reflections or ideas. The same thing would be true of ideas induced by words. One person might use words to express something in his mind, and a second person might hear or read those words. The two might have a similar mental state, but it could not be said that they had the *same* idea. Certainly, it could not be said that the idea had any existence of its own.

The application of this theory to the law focuses attention wholly upon what goes on in the mind of the individual judge deciding an individual case. The legal generalization has no existence or force except in terms of the judicial mind. In Bingham's words:

1 . . . The law does not consist of generalizations.
2 . . . Rules and principles of law are only mental tools used in discussing and deciding legal problems.
3 . . . Sequences of legal phenomena are always concrete.[14]

It would follow that the judge is not engaged in applying generalizations to facts and arriving at an automatic conclusion, but rather "is engaged in the act of government. He is making law . . ."[15]

Bingham felt that the time had passed when the people would accept decisions based solely upon precedent. Theoretical soundness would no longer suffice to justify actually unjust decisions. The judge could no longer shelter himself and his unpopular decisions behind the doctrines of the law.[16] Especially would this be true when it was realized by the people that generalizations and doctrines could not in themselves provide checks on the governing power of judges. Rules not only do not prevent the entry of individual bias in the process of decision, but actually encourage it, since they provide a screen "to conceal the real motives or incapacity of the judge."[17] The remedy, according to Bingham, is to recognize the real nature of the judge's act. Thereby the judge will be forced to justify his decisions on grounds open to public discussion and criticism. Freeing the judge from the notion of generalization is really a method of preventing arbitrariness.

Therefore, although Bingham urged the necessity of recognizing the fact of judicial legislation, in reality he was trying to reduce it.

[14] "What Is the Law," 11 *Michigan Law Review* 1 and 109 (1912), p. 121 n.
[15] *Ibid.,* p. 10.
[16] *Ibid.,* p. 114 n.
[17] *Ibid.,* p. 113 n.

"The judicial function of the courts is not legislation but the orderly settlement of litigation between parties."[18] There was objection equally to the attempt to project decisions into the future and to the overruling of a settled doctrine. To do the first is to decide moot cases, to do the second is to legislate ex post facto. In either case, the court exceeds its constitutional powers. The paradox is that the very doctrines which were thought to prevent judicial legislation had led the courts into most obnoxious types of legislative practices. That the traditional theory leads to such results permits Bingham to conclude that he is advocating no increase in judicial power but merely urging that judges recognize the situation as it exists. The theory has not prevented that which it was designed to prevent; nothing but gain can result from relinquishing it.[19]

In general, later developments seem to indicate that Bingham's conclusions are more popular than his premises. The attack upon the concept of legal generalization has continued, and Bingham has been recognized as an early leader in the fight. But the discussion has continued without much reference to the nominalism which he considered basic to his conclusions. If modern realistic jurisprudence really depends upon such a metaphysical underpinning, it is notably reticent about it.

V

We have already noted that there is in legal realism a strong tendency to base jurisprudence upon sociological analysis and that an important part of legal realism is primarily an extension of certain assumptions implicit in sociological jurisprudence. In this connection, the work of Arthur F. Bentley is of considerable interest. His most important work, *The Process of Government,*[20] is roughly contemporaneous with Pound's early writing, although Bentley never achieved the prominence of Pound and only somewhat belatedly has received recognition.[21] Bentley did not develop an elaborate legal

[18] *Ibid.,* p. 18.

[19] "My theory of the law does not propose an addition to the power of judges over the substantive law." "Legal Philosophy and the Law," 9 *Illinois Law Review* 98 (1914), p. 102. See also p. 103.

[20] Chicago, 1908.

[21] For a discussion of the neglect of Bentley, see Bertrand M. Gross, "Review" of *The Process of Government,* XLIV *American Political Science Review* 742 (1950). It is interesting to note that Bentley does not appear in Llewellyn's first

theory; he devised a scheme of social analysis and broadly indicated its application to law. Therein he differs from Pound who concentrated on the legal application to such an extent that he never made altogether clear his scheme of social analysis.[22]

The subtitle of Bentley's book, *A Study of Social Pressures,* indicates his primary thesis that the truth about social phenomena can be found only by considering the "activities" of men. To study the course of ideas without recognizing that ideas have significance only as they are reflected in social activities is to omit the study of the vital element in political and social life.

> The raw material can be found only in the actually performed legislating-administering-adjudicating activities of the nation and in the streams and currents of activity that gather among the people and rush into these spheres.[23]

And again:

> If we start with a theory about ideas and their place in politics, we are deserting our raw material even before we take a good peep at it. We are substituting something else which may or may not be useful, but which will certainly color our entire further progress, if progress we can make at all on scientific lines.[24]

Social problems result from conflicts among activities and are solved by bringing activities into such balance that the conflict is no longer acute. The accurate study of social problems, therefore, depends upon devising a method of measuring the forces that come to bear upon any point. The method of measurement varies with the type of problem and between types of societies. Underlying this analysis is the premise that governmental and legal problems are social in nature and are open to the same type of analysis as other social problems. Bentley states his principal aim as follows:

> There is no political process that is not a balancing of quantity against quantity. There is not a law that is passed that is not the ex-

---

lists of legal realists. See "A Realistic Jurisprudence—the Next Step," 30 *Columbia Law Review* 431 (1930); "Some Realism About Realism," *supra.* Llewellyn's discovery of Bentley in "The Constitution as an Institution," 34 *Columbia Law Review* (1931), p. 1 n, is noted by Gross.

[22] Pound's study, "The Administration of Justice in Cleveland" (Cleveland, Ohio, 1922) is, of course, an outstanding exception to Pound's more characteristic generality. Cf. the criticism of Pound in Jerome Hall, "Concerning the Nature of Positive Law," 58 *Yale Law Journal* 545 (1949).

[23] *The Process of Government,* p. 180.

[24] *Ibid.,* p. 181.

pression of force and force in tension. There is not a court decision
or an executive act that is not the result of the same process. Understanding any of these phenomena means measuring the elements that
have gone into them.[25]

Men group themselves in activities around their common desires.
Analysis of these groups is the only way to get at the ideas operative
in a society at a given time:

> Indeed the only reality of the ideas is their reflection of the groups, only
> that and nothing more. The ideas can be stated in terms of the groups;
> the groups never in terms of the ideas.[26]

The law does not differ from any other type of activity:

> It is possible to take a Supreme Court decision, in which nothing ap-
> pears on the surface but finespun points of law, and cut through all the
> dialectic till we get down to the actual groups of men underlying the
> decisions and producing the decisions through the differentiated activity
> of the justices.[27]

Bentley thought this process especially evident when the Court deals
with a relatively new problem, in which the traditional or legalistic
element is less obvious.

Bentley did not come to the point of asserting that this activity on
the part of judges involves conscious alteration of the law in response
to social pressures. His analysis led him only to the position that,
despite assertions to the contrary, social pressures are able to force
themselves upon the attention of the law. Speaking of a case of interest at the time, he said:

> I do not mean that the justices consciously forced the law to fit the case,
> nor that they showed any traces whatever of demagogism or of sub-
> serviency to popular clamor. Quite the contrary. I am convinced that
> they all, or at any rate most of them, acted with the most single-hearted
> desire—if one must use such phrasing—to render justice in strict ac-
> cordance with precedent. What I do set forth about them is that so far

[25] *Ibid.*, p. 202. He continues: "If we can get our social life stated in terms of
activity, and of nothing else, we have not indeed succeeded in measuring it, but we
have at least reached a foundation upon which a coherent system of measurements
can be built up. Our technique may be very poor at the start, and the amount of
labor we must employ to get scanty results will be huge. But we shall cease to be
blocked by the intervention of unmeasurable elements, which claim to be themselves
the real causes of all that is happening, and which by their spook-like arbitrariness
make impossible any progress toward dependable knowledge." *Loc. cit.*

[26] *Ibid.*, p. 206.

[27] *Ibid.*, p. 205.

from being a sort of legal machine, they are a functioning part of this
government, responsive to the group pressures within it, representatives of all sort of pressures, and using their representative judgment to
bring these pressures to balance, not indeed in just the same way, but
on just the same basis that any other agency does . . .[28]

Changes in the law, although unconsciously achieved, illustrate the
place of legal theory. A case is a conflict between different interest
groups, each of which exerts pressure to get the support of the law.
These interests are represented in court by advocates, whose particular type of social activity is the forwarding of claims by the use of a
general body of legal theory. To all general appearances, the case is
decided solely in accord with the dictates of the theory of the legal
system. The theoretical activities of the bar, including the bench,
are, nevertheless, a reflection of the more fundamental pressures
underneath. Legal theory becomes a secondary statement of this
process.[29]

To picture the courts as responding to pressures solely from the
outside is, however, to present an incomplete analysis. The law itself
is also an activity capable of exerting pressure in conflict with other
interests.

There is one other phase of this court process to consider; that is the
judiciary presenting itself as an organization with specified interest lines
of its own, which must be looked upon at times, not merely as process
for the interest content that is functioning through it, but as content over
against content . . .[30]

Here Bentley appeared to have in mind something similar to the juristic tradition upon which Pound ultimately came to rely as his principal defense against arbitrariness. Later writers, such as Thurman
Arnold and Fred Rodell, also recognize the force of the law interest

[28] *Ibid.,* p. 393.
[29] "The theory of course is most often put before us as though it were a purely
psychic phenomenon abstracted from the action to which it relates. It is never that,
but always itself an activity, reflecting in a particular way the underlying activities.
The courts make this theorizing a dignified portion of their work. But they do not
decide cases purely in the highly rarified [sic] atmosphere of such theorizing. They
decide them by letting the clash of the underlying interests work itself out, and then
making the theorizing follow suit (not crudely, remember, but as a representative
process). Within fairly broad limits theories will be found available for either apparent alternative of activity. When this theorizing activity gets away from the
lawyers and away from the judges, it works itself up into a philosophy of law which
is still more remote from the underlying interests . . ." *Ibid.,* pp. 294–95.
[30] *Ibid.,* p. 398.

as an independent factor in the social equation, although they go beyond Bentley's impartial analysis to assert that curbing it would tend to increase the social good.

Bentley's principal aim, as has been said, was to devise a system of social study. Although his actual influence is uncertain, interest group analysis has come into increasing acceptance among students of legal and social problems. More recent writers go beyond him, of course, in developing the implications for the judicial function of his analytical scheme. The enthusiasm with which later writers accepted his work indicates, however, the congeniality of his theory with modern jurisprudence.

VI

The growth of philosophical-pragmatism as an important factor in undermining the intellectual foundations of the traditional theory of the judicial function has already been discussed. The close relation between the pragmatic philosophy and the development of the newer legal theories is made explicit, however, in the work of John Dewey, who occupies an almost official position as philosopher for the legal realists. Dewey is more than a source of ideas for the modern American legal theorist; he is himself one of the modern legal theorists. His influence is therefore double, although there is little to indicate that the community of conclusions between Dewey and many of the legal realists in all cases implies a community of premises.

Although the problem of presenting Dewey's philosophy as it bears upon his legal theory is not simple,[31] perhaps the most convenient point of departure is his conception of the nature of thought. Dewey starts with the idea that man is an organism which in order to live must be constantly active. This activity involves a reciprocal influence between the organism and the environment. This reciprocal influence is, according to Dewey, experience, out of which arise thought and knowledge.

> . . . the interaction of organism and environment, resulting in some adaptation which secures utilization of the latter, is the primary fact, the basic category. Knowledge is relegated to a derived position, sec-

---

[31] For an excellent discussion of Dewey's role in the development of American thought, see M. G. White, *Social Thought in America—The Revolt Against Formalism* (New York, 1949).

ondary in origin, even if its importance, when one is established, is over-shadowing.[32]

Accordingly, thought arises when the organism faces a problem. It is an instrument employed in the solution of the problem and cannot be separated from the experience out of which it arose. Reason and logic are instruments by which thought operates.

Thinking involves facing the facts from which the problem came. It is in this fact-situation that the individual finds the truth for which he seeks. Dewey, like James, adopts a pragmatic definition of truth. Truth is what works in the circumstances. It is not something external to experience or to the individual, but whatever is successful in providing answers for the questions that are faced. Since conditions are constantly changing, and new relations continually demand formulation, there can be no eternal truths. It is true that there are some relatively constant ideas which are revealed to us in the history of thought. Their truth comes, however, from their present quality of appropriateness. There is no other test:

> Instead of a closed universe, science now presents us with one infinite in space and time, having no limits here or there, at this end, so to speak, or at that, and as infinitely complex in internal structure as it is infinite in extent. Hence it is also an open world, an infinitely variegated one, a world which in the old sense can hardly be called a universe at all; so multiplex and far-reaching that it cannot be summed up and grasped in any one formula. And change rather than fixity is now a measure of 'reality' or energy of being; change is omnipresent. The laws in which the modern man of science is interested are laws of motion, of generation and consequence. . . . He does not try to define and delimit something remaining constant *in* change. He tries to describe a constant order *of* change.[33]

That this theory has much to say in opposition to traditional legal thinking is clear. According to that theory, thinking begins with the principle as the major premise, the facts provide the minor premise, and the conclusion follows as a matter of logic. Dewey was highly critical of this explanation:

> As a matter of fact, men do not begin thinking with premises. They begin with some complicated and confused case, apparently admitting of

[32] *Reconstruction in Philosophy* (New York, 1920), p. 87. With this epistemology, Dewey would undoubtedly have difficulty with Bingham's "reflective" theory of knowledge. Note, however, that both of them arrive at approximately the same legal point.

[33] *Ibid.*, pp. 60–61.

alternative modes of treatment and solution. Premises only gradually
emerge from analysis of the total situation. The problem is not to draw
a conclusion from given premises; that can best be done by a piece of
inanimate machinery by fingering a key board. The problem is to *find*
statements, of general principles and of particular fact, which are worthy
to serve as premises. . . . Thinking may be defined either as a development of premises or development of a conclusion; as far as it is one
operation it is the other.[34]

He held that the logical method of the law was largely a question
of the form in which decisions were delivered. "The mental operations involved therein [in exposition] are somewhat different than
those involved in arriving at a conclusion." [35] The purpose of the
exposition is to show that the decision was not arrived at arbitrarily.

The traditional method of the law was not productive of good results. It not only encouraged thought to rise above the empirical
problem that demanded solution, but it also became identified with
forces blocking reform:

Here is where the great practical evil of the doctrine of immutable and
necessary antecedent rules comes in. It sanctifies the old; adherence to
it in practice constantly widens the gap between current social conditions and the principles used by the courts. The effect is to breed
irritation, disrespect for law, together with virtual alliance between
the judiciary and entrenched interests that correspond most nearly to
the conditions under which the rules of law were previously laid down.[36]

The answer was to substitute the new theory of logic:

. . . either . . . logic must be abandoned or . . . it must be a logic
relative to consequences rather than to antecedents, a logic of prediction of probabilities rather than one of deduction of certainties. For the
purposes of a logic of inquiry into probable consequences, general principles can only be tools justified by the work they do. They are means
of intellectual survey, analysis, and insight into the factors of the situation to be dealt with. Like other tools they must be modified when they
are applied to new conditions and new results have to be achieved.[37]

Dewey often uses the metaphor, reminiscent of Pound, of the
scientist in the laboratory, and, like Pound, he urges the adoption of
the scientific attitude on the solution of social problems:

[34] "Logical Method and Law," 10 *Cornell Law Quarterly* 17 (1924), p. 23.
[35] *Ibid.*, p. 24.
[36] *Ibid.*, p. 26.
[37] *Loc. cit.*

The crisis in democracy demands the substitution of the kind of intelligence that is exemplified in scientific procedure for the kind of intelligence that is now accepted. The need for this change is not exhausted in the demand for greater honesty and impartiality, even though these qualities be now corrupted by discussion carried on mainly for purposes of party supremacy and for imposition of some special but concealed interest. . . . Approximation to the use of scientific method in investigation and of the *engineering mind* in the invention and projection of far-reaching social plans is demanded. The habit of considering social realities in terms of cause and effect and social policies in terms of means and consequences is still inchoate.[38]

Despite Dewey's obvious interest in reform, it should not be thought that he opposes everything on the score of age alone. He accepts the value of institutions and general rules. He is, however, concerned both to prevent their dominating men's attempts to solve their current problems and to demonstrate that such factors are always subject to contemporary re-evaluation. Whether an institution is to be preserved or the general rule is to prevail over the particular instance is a choice to be made by those faced with the problem. These choices are to be made on the basis of present need and a calculation of future need. There is nothing sacrosanct about institutions or rules, and, if they do not fit the present situation, they should be discarded.

The conclusions arrived at by Dewey are similar to those of Pound, Holmes, and Cardozo. They may be said to reinforce certain factors already present in the legal tradition. There can be no question, however, that the influence of Dewey on modern legal writers has been very great. His theory of truth as an hypothesis until it is tested in terms of the formulated problem, his attack upon the syllogistic method of reasoning, together with the apparently scientific foundation of his theories, have given him great appeal in an age which is vastly impressed with the success of the physical sciences.

Although the four writers here considered do not supply the whole of the intellectual background of legal realism, each has contributed ideas important to the understanding of modern American juristic thought. Bentley's analysis of group interests in relation to law and of law itself as a group interest seems to adumbrate several of

[38] *Liberalism and Social Action* (New York, 1935), p. 73. (Emphasis supplied.)

the more important legal realists. Gray's development of law as the product of the judicial function is widespread in later juristic theories, as is Bingham's attack on the concept of legal generalizations. Dewey's instrumentalism is an obviously influential factor as well in juristic thought as in other American intellectual developments. Clearly, not all the ideas of all of these men can be true, and to develop a coherent theory from these sources will require a high degree of selectivity. Whether this selective process has actually been successful is a major question in the development of legal realism.

Chapter 6

LEGAL REALISM: THE EXPOSITION

I

The third and fourth decades of the twentieth century mark the emergence of a group, increasingly dominant in the critical tradition in American jurisprudence, to which the label "legal realists" has been attached. As has been noted, the term carries no precise denotation beyond indicating a certain deep skepticism about traditional legal theory, a skepticism characteristic in some degree of nearly all of the theorists thus far discussed. In relation to the broader tendency in American jurisprudence as it has developed, the realists stand principally for a vigorous and intensive application of ideas and methods suggested in the work of Holmes, the sociological group and the writers whose theories have just been surveyed. We are therefore in an area in which distinctions fade into matters of degree, and it is perhaps this fact above all others that has made the disagreements and controversies within the critical tradition itself so difficult to understand.

Before proceeding further, it will perhaps save possible confusion later if we stop to indicate broadly some of the problems that concerned the various legal realists. Generally speaking, there appear to have been two matters that occupied their attention. The first was the establishment of a "science of law." This involved, at the very least, shaking off the myths of the traditional theory and resurveying traditional legal materials and the functioning legal system in a new and more "realistic" fashion. In so far as this "science of law" involved an effort to find uniformities of legal behavior, it could not directly result in any new theory of the judicial function. Most of, if not all, the realists, however, were also greatly interested in the subject of legal reform. This usually involved some notion of judicial freedom, although the realists are notably less interested than the sociological group in the judicial formulation of general rules and seem to emphasize the satisfactory disposition of individual cases at the expense of more systematic considerations. Very few of the realists, of course, were wholly occupied with either of these two issues, and it is not always clear which was uppermost in a particular writer's mind at a given time. Further, neither of these two categories appears completely relevant to certain theorists who were led by their "realism" to attempt to step outside the juristic tradition altogether and to consider the legal system in such terms that their work is seemingly more akin to social psychology or anthropology than to anything traditionally recognizable as jurisprudence.

It may bear repetition, however, that little in the realist "movement," if it can be called that, was so novel as to justify the tremendous furor that featured American jurisprudence after about 1931. The vehemence of the criticism heaped upon certain of the realists obscured rather than clarified their points of difference with the sociological group. In the circumstances, even to indicate where attitudes tend to diverge is by no means a simple undertaking.

II

As a theory of legal analysis, legal realism can be viewed as an attempt to apply Holmes's dictum: "The prophecies of what the courts will do in fact, and nothing more pretentious, are what I mean by the law." The statement implies, and the work of Gray reinforces the implication, that the court decision is the proper focus of legal study. Legal realism seeks to isolate the factor or factors upon which court decisions actually rest in order to provide the student and the practitioner with an accurate method of forecasting what the courts actually do. The ideal is a "science of law."

The notion of a "science of law" is, of course, not new. Every legal scholar, Blackstone as well as Jerome Frank, who tries to be accurate about the nature of the law or of the legal system, develops a "science of law," although Blackstone and Frank would agree neither with one another nor with Herman Oliphant, for example, upon what the science includes or how to achieve it. The factor that distinguishes the "science of law" idea as it developed in certain realistic writings was, therefore, not the ideal, but rather the approach of these writers to the methods and scope of such a science.

In considering these conceptions, it is helpful to bear in mind that legal realism has always been primarily an academic movement and that the "science of law" group were frequently law teachers. The leading law schools in the United States have usually been attached to the universities. They have had the responsibility of supplying the legal profession with personnel. At their best, however, they have always been something more than merely technical schools, and their connection with other academic disciplines has opened them to the influence of the several social and physical sciences. That this connection has been close is suggested by the parallels between the developments in legal theory and those in economics, sociology, and psychology, not to mention the physical sciences. And, it should not be forgotten, for many years the outstanding figure in American jurisprudence was Roscoe Pound, whose position as Dean of the Harvard Law School encouraged acceptance of his idea that law should be receptive to the findings of other branches of knowledge. In the circumstances, it is not surprising that a group composed in the main of teachers of law, desirous at the least of improving their teaching should turn to other disciplines for helpful suggestions in improving their analytical and predictive techniques.[1] It is also not

---

[1] Although not strictly germane to a study of the development of theories of judicial legislation, it may well be that the area of greatest influence for the newer legal theories has been in the field of legal education. It is exceedingly difficult, of course, to verify such an influence statistically, and at the outset certain baffling questions are encountered. What changes in legal education are discernible? Are such changes the cause or the result of changes in legal theory? How does one distinguish between a real change and merely a change in a course description?

There are several rough indices that can be used to indicate what is involved here although, admittedly, the changes may be more apparent than real. The "aim" of the Columbia Law School, for example, as stated in its *Bulletin* for 1911–12 was oriented toward the training of barristers and law teachers. The Yale Law School *Bulletin* for the same year emphasized training for the bar and in the "science of law." By 1931, the Columbia Law School included in its statement of purpose its desire to "encourage research and the nonprofessional study of law in order that the nature and function of law may be comprehended, its results evaluated, and its development shaped to meet the needs of modern life." *Bulletin,* 1931–32, p. 6. In the same year the Harvard Law School's statement of purpose included "the investigation of problems of legal adjustment of human relations and how to meet them effectively." *Bulletin,* 1931–32, p. 4. Noteworthy, also, over the same period of time is the proliferation of law courses, the introduction of seminar methods of teaching law and the encouragement of student research. In 1910–11, Yale, Columbia, and Harvard had fairly restricted law curricula centering around traditional legal subjects. Twenty years later, not only were more law courses taught, but new subjects, difficult to reconcile with the older curricula, were listed. There was a growth, for example, of courses in Public Regulation of Business, which had apparently absorbed the older courses in Railroad Law. One notes at Yale, which probably led in this activity, the presence of a course in Methods of Social and Legal Research, taught by a sociologist (Dorothy Thomas). Courses in Business Units appear to have replaced the older courses in Corporations and Partnerships, and the Yale

to be wondered at that their model was generally the physical sciences, whose analytical and predictive methods were most conspicuously successful.

These tendencies are clearly illustrated in some of the theoretical writings of Karl N. Llewellyn. To him, the law constitutes a body of objective data to be studied and described by the legal student as the material world is an object of study to the physicist. This concept has important implications for the attitude of the legal student:

> The temporary divorce of Is and Ought for purposes of study. By this [they] mean that whereas value judgments must always be appealed to in order to set objectives for inquiry, yet during the inquiry itself into what is, the observation, the description and the establishment of relations between the things described are to remain as largely as possible

---

Institute of Human Relations appeared in the Yale Law School *Bulletin* for 1931–32 in connection with a listing of research projects, most of which had both legal and sociological aspects.

Interesting, also, is the change in the descriptions of courses over the same period. In 1911, the Yale Law School courses on Property carried the following description: "The course covers the entire field of estates in real and personal property, rights incident to ownership, powers, trusts, rights to the use or profits of another's land, and fraudulent disposition of property." In the second year, the subject included "the entire field of title by private grant . . . and title by devise . . . prescriptive rights, mortgages, and liens both equitable and statutory." In 1950–51, the Property 1A course in the Yale Law School dealt with: "Property, the individual, and the community in a capitalist, federal state; resource allocation by private volition (vendor and purchaser, possessory estates and future interests, leases, concurrent interests); patterns of anarchy in land use; planning and community; land-use planning by private agreement (rights in land); the planning and development of metropolitan communities; state and regional planning (from water law to public corporations); national planning for an efficient physical environment; resource planning and development in the world community."

Although the examples given are from only three law schools, it should not be forgotten that at each of these there has been emphasis upon the training of law teachers, so that a widening of the tendencies noted can be anticipated in other schools as well. For a skeptical analysis of the actual results of these and other changes, see B. Currie, "The Materials of Legal Study," 3 *Journal of American Legal Education* 331 (1951). Mr. Currie, after asserting the primacy of the Columbia Law School in the development of the new legal education, says: "Within a few years the pace of reform moderated at Columbia, and, while other schools have attempted to put similar reforms into operation, the course of development has been decidedly irregular. The main stream of legal education flows on much as before. The typical casebook, although its banner now reads 'Cases and Materials,' is essentially like its predecessors. There are still courses in Contracts, Torts, Property, and Trusts, retaining their old names and shapes; and even in those courses which have been revamped and renamed the appellate decision is the focus of study still. Law and the social sciences remain unintegrated." *Ibid.*, p. 337. For a similar judgment, see Julius Stone, *op. cit.*, p. 14.

uncontaminated by the desires of the observer or by what he wishes might be or thinks ought (ethically) to be.[2]

Among many of this group, there is a further deep skepticism as to the accuracy with which traditional methods of legal study are useful in discovering the realities of the legal system. The emphasis upon legal rules as traditionally conceived is rejected,[3] and there is a reassessment of the uses of logic as the principal juristic method.[4] These attitudes are accompanied by a re-examination of the institution of stare decisis.[5]

[2] "Some Realism About Realism," 44 *Harvard Law Review* 1222, 1236 (1931).

[3] "There has been an asserted or tacit assumption that there exist certain general principles of inherent and abiding validity, and that, therefore, a new case can be properly decided by deducing from some general principle the particular rule applicable to the case at hand. The invalidity of the method is, of course, fundamental. It is found in the fact that all of our so-called general principles are but experimental rationalizations of our previous experiences and, therefore, they cannot contain the inevitable solution of *new* problems, which of necessity form no part of the experience rationalized. By the bare fact of stating the 'general principle' as the major premise of a syllogism with the new problem as the subject of its minor premise, the applicability of the 'general principle' is predestined. This method is valid only for establishing the most obvious relations of identity. There it is needless and hence useless." Herman Oliphant, "Current Economic and Social Problems," 10 *Proc. Acad. of Political Science* (1923) pp. 325–26.

[4] ". . . the naive belief that men think in syllogisms and that new truth about the world can be deduced from general laws arrived at by induction, still persists in much of the thinking that goes on in the field of the social sciences. It is a curious paradox that when men are confronted with situations still more complex than those found in the physical and biological sciences, as is the case in economics, sociology, ethics, and law—situations which therefore are more difficult to deal with by scientific technique—the more insistent do they become as to the prior existence of fixed and universal principles or laws which can be discovered and directly applied and followed . . . they are prone to assimilate the problems in these fields to those of mathematics. As a result they either fail to discover what their problems are or to deal adequately with them if they do." Walter W. Cook, "Scientific Method and the Law," 13 *American Bar Association Journal* 303 (1927), p. 307. Similar statements by Cook are to be found in "The Present Status of the 'Lack of Mutuality' Rule," 26 *Yale Law Journal* 397 (1927); "The Logical and Legal Bases of the Conflict of Laws," 33 *Yale Law Journal* 457 (1924); Review, 31 *Columbia Law Review* 725 (1931); "A Scientific Approach to the Study of Law," *Essays in Honor of W. W. Willoughby*, eds. J. M. Mathews and J. Hart (Baltimore, 1937).

[5] Llewellyn argues that the judicial technique includes the ability both to narrow and to broaden precedents. *The Bramble Bush*, p. 65. In "The Normative, The Legal, and the Law Jobs: The Problem of Juristic Method," 49 *Yale Law Journal* 1355 (1940), he classifies judicial handling of precedents as "law-waver," that is "an incipient practice . . . unpredictable in detail" (pp. 1358–59). He also stresses that the multiplicity of precedents frees the judge from the burden of conformity to precedent. "Legal Tradition and Social Science Method—A Realist's Critique," *Essays on Research in the Social Sciences* (Washington, 1931), p. 108 n. Herman Oliphant argues that in actual practice stare decisis tends to become *stare dictis,* that is, attention to what courts say, rather than to what they do. "A Return to Stare Decisis," 14 *American Bar Association Journal* 71, 159 (1938). In so far as

Having demonstrated the inadequacies of certain of the basic elements of traditional legal theory, the legal realists then proposed to base their "science of law" upon the observed facts of judicial behavior, in effect to substitute a new sort of rule. Again to quote Llewellyn:

> The main thing is what officials are going to *do* . . . the main thing is seeing what officials do, do about disputes, or about anything else; and seeing that there is a certain regularity in their doing—a regularity which makes possible prediction of what they and other officials are about to do tomorrow.[6]

Finding out "what officials do" is not, of course, an easy process. Basically, it involves extracting from the total process some factor or factors that appear to correlate with the actual outcomes of cases. Although this does not necessarily imply a total rejection of the relevance of legal rules, it does involve an insistence that they are only one of several factors that go into the decision of a case.[7] Therefore, although there is an insistence on "facts," it would be inaccurate to suppose that there is a total reliance on facts.[8]

The effort to find a more scientific basis for legal study led to a number of attempts to redefine the scope and methods of legal re-

---

dicta constitute a check upon what courts do, the implications of his argument appear to run counter to the implications of Llewellyn's argument.

[6] *The Bramble Bush* (New York, 1951), p. 13.

[7] There are many instances in which Llewellyn, for example, recognizes the importance of legal rules. "He [the judge] can throw the decision this way or that. *But not freely.* For to him the logical ladder, or the several logical ladders, are ways of keeping himself in touch with the decisions of the past . . . This, as a judge, he would have to do even if he did not wish . . . And while it is possible to build a number of divergent logical ladders up out of the same cases and down again to the same dispute, *there are not so many that can be built defensively* . . . Thus unless the result raises the hair . . . and forces a different outcome so to speak at the muzzle of a gun, the judge will never get as far as inquiring into justice. He will decide by 'law' and let it go at that." *Loc. cit.* Similarly Edward W. Patterson seeks to reduce the theoretical importance of the rule, but still insists that legal rules have their place. "Legal rules mark the boundary of the judicial function; they guide thinking toward possible solutions. . . . Professional training and experience limit and condition the scientific imagination which casts up experimental hypotheses, and the experimentation that leads to choice between them." "Can Law Be Scientific?" 25 *Illinois Law Review* 121 (1930), p. 136.

[8] The legal realist's attitude toward facts subsequently became a bone of contention between Roscoe Pound and Llewellyn. Discussing Pound's "queer blindness or willful perversity," Llewellyn says, "The misconception lies in conceiving that anyone thinks facts are all that jurisprudence is concerned with, merely because he cries out for needed facts or in a particular preliminary study tries to report facts as objectively as possible . . ." "Through Title to Contract and a Bit Beyond," 15 *New York University Law Quarterly* 159 (1938), p. 162 n.

search. Among the most elaborate of the efforts in this direction was
the establishment in 1928 of the Johns Hopkins Institute of Law,
which had a strong research orientation and emphasized the "scientific
study of law." [9] Financial considerations caused the later abandon-
ment of the project. A further interesting example of this trend is to
be found in the work of the late Professor Underhill Moore of the
Yale Law School, who attempted to apply the scientific method to a
segment of the law in order to demonstrate his general thesis that a
broader view of the facts surrounding cases would produce correlations between facts and decisions that would provide a basis for predictability. The facts as they are reported in the opinions failing to
provide an adequate basis,[10] the student or practitioner must carry his
investigation further:

> It is proposed that the field of the lawyer's attention be extended to in-
> clude not only the relation between judicial behavior and the "facts of
> the case," but also the relation between judicial behavior and institutional
> (frequent, repeated, usual) ways of behaving (e.g., doing business) in
> the contemporary culture of the place where the facts happened and the
> decision was made. If such a relation is found to be significant, a step
> toward more reliable prediction will be made.[11]

[9] The breadth of the approach at the Institute is reflected in its basic statement:
". . . the activities of the Institute shall include not only a study of law in a narrow sense, but also a consideration of such other branches of science and philosophy
as may be necessary in order that the operation and effects of law in all its relations
to human life may be effectively studied." The "General Plan" of study included:
"1. Concentration upon research as contrasted with traditional instruction. 2. Provision for training in legal research. 3. Recognition of the need of scientific investigation along both theoretical and practical lines. 4. Emphasis upon the need
of developing methods for and stimulating the observation and collection of comparable data as to legal phenomena. 5. Integration of legal research with inves-
tigations in other fields of knowledge and in cooperation with those engaged in allied
branches of science. 6. Comparative study by reference to foreign thought and experience." "The Institute of Law," *Johns Hopkins University Circular,* New Series
1932 #6 (June, 1932).

[10] "In greater part, however, the lawyer's limited success in formulating laws of
judicial behavior is probably to be accounted for by his failure to attempt to correlate judicial behavior with any event except the 'facts of the case.' His persistent
pursuit of his laws in the 'facts of the case' may be explained by the fact that the
judges and administrators themselves in their opinions began quite irrelevantly and
ambiguously to say that their behavior was the necessary consequence of these laws.
From logical deduction to necessary behavior was an easy step and the transformation of scientific generalizations into Law was complete. Whether this new and
puissant being was the daughter of God, of nature, or of the state, her will had been
ascertained by correlating judicial behavior with the facts of the case, and should
therefore continue to be so ascertained." Underhill Moore and Theodore S. Hope,
Jr., "An Institutional Approach to the Law of Commercial Banking," 38 *Yale Law
Journal* 703 (1929), p. 704.

[11] *Ibid.,* p. 705.

As Moore rather dryly remarked, by the use of his method the social sciences might attain the same degree of accuracy as meteorology.[12]

The attempt to widen the empirical base of legal study led also to a number of scientific studies of the actual administration of justice in selected areas or fields. Although, formally, these studies are merely objective measurements of the efficiency of legal institutions, they have important implications for law itself.[13] One of the more elaborate of these studies, and one that relies heavily upon the use of the quantitative method, is the survey of the administration of justice in Connecticut carried out by Judge (formerly Professor) C. E. Clark and Professor H. N. Shulman, then both of the Yale Law School. The major purpose of the study was to provide objective data upon which to base reforms in the administration of justice,[14] and the position occupied by such studies in the general trend of social studies is made explicit by the authors themselves:

[12] U. Moore and G. Sussman, "Debiting Direct Discounts," 40 *Yale Law Journal* 555 (1931).

[13] One of the pioneer efforts was the *Cleveland Survey of Criminal Justice* (Cleveland Foundation, 1922), carried out under the direction of Roscoe Pound. The wide discretion there demonstrated to rest in the hands of the prosecuting attorney points to both a theoretical and a practical problem. The Wickersham Commission's Report on the Enforcement of the Prohibition Laws (Washington, 1931) indicated the difficulties of enforcing law against the wishes of substantial portions of the population. Mention can also be made of the *Study of the Business of the Federal Courts,* 2 vols. (American Law Institute, Philadelphia, 1934). This study began at the Yale Law School, was continued under the Wickersham Commission, and was finally completed under the auspices of the American Law Institute. It was very influential in the development of methods of reporting judicial statistics. Other studies have pointed out the desirability of establishing special agencies to handle certain types of legal problems: Ben B. Lindsey and Harvey J. O'Higgins, *The Beast* (New York, 1910); Katharine F. Lenroot and Emma O. Lundberg, *Juvenile Courts at Work* (Washington, 1925); Bernard Flexner, Reuben Oppenheimer, and Katharine F. Lenroot, *The Child, The Family and the Court* (Washington, 1933). It is interesting to note that this book opens with a discussion of "social jurisprudence," pp. 1–5. For a general discussion, see William F. Willoughby, *The Principles of Judicial Administration* (Washington, 1929), especially chaps. III, IV, and V.

[14] "The ultimate results upon the community of the adoption of certain legal principles rather than others has been but imperfectly understood. Definite data have been lacking as to what business and social habits, practices and customs were actually in vogue and as to their interrelation with current legal rules. In default of such definite information, the courts have at times taken the opinions of experts, have at other times used supposed authorities under the application of the doctrine of judicial notice, but have perhaps more often made deductions based upon knowledge of a limited kind. Often, however, they seem distinctly harmful, for they tend to assume as settled fact something which is either unproven, or at times even presumptively untrue . . ." Charles E. Clark, "Fact Research in Law Administration," 2 *Connecticut Bar Journal* 211 (1928), p. 211.

. . . [the] need as felt in the law for more adequate social data as to
the administration of justice is but part of a general movement in the
social sciences to substitute for the vague generalizations of the older
economists and philosophers concrete information based upon adequate
statistical information.[15]

That studies of this type might also have somewhat broader implications for both the practice and enforcement of the law was at one
time suggested,[16] but in general the attempt to derive norms of decision from studies of actual practice has not continued.[17]

Another result of the tendency toward empirical study of legal
questions can be noted. This is the increased interest in the functioning of trial courts, as opposed to appellate tribunals, that features
the work of a number of the realist group. As Clark puts it:

[15] *Ibid.*, p. 212.

[16] "To the bench and bar actively engaged in law administration they [statistics]
tell much in the way of averages and hence in the way of predictability. I will mention a few facts which, now that we have seen them, appear obvious although I must
admit that we had not thought of them before. Thus most judgments are plaintiff's
judgments. . . . Is it not of value to a trial judge to know that as a case comes
before him the chances are three out of four or greater that a judgment should be
entered for the plaintiff?" C. E. Clark, "Some of the Facts of Law Administration,"
3 *Connecticut Bar Journal* 161 (1929), p. 164. Such reliance on correlations, unless
they are perfect, is open to objection. Since a judge deals with only one case at a
time, it is scarcely enough for him to know that three out of four cases are decided
for the plaintiff unless he has some other way of knowing which out of the four is to
be the defendant's decision. He would, of course, be right more often than not if he
decided all cases for the plaintiff. On the other hand, if perfect correlations in a
certain type of case could be found, this should serve to eliminate that type of case
altogether. In so far as there is any intimation that judicial statistics can be used as
a basis for decision, there is an underlying assumption that a given course of decision
is correct. In view of the general reformist tendency of the legal realists, this is a
strange assumption.

[17] In later publications Clark clarified the somewhat misleading statement quoted
above: "There developed an ambition and pretension about the objectives and values
of this kind of study which were misleading and unfortunate. It almost came to be
believed that from the trial-court records statistical data could be collected on all
phases of judicial administration and all manner of sociological problems involved in
litigation, and that the statistical data could be the open sesame to solutions. It can
be truthfully said that the authors and workers on this project never regarded the
study with such excessive optimism or gave utterance to claims more extensive than
shrewd as to results." C. E. Clark and Harry Shulman, *Law Administration in Connecticut* (New Haven, 1937), p. 200. It is also to be noted that Charles H. Pritchett
is careful to qualify his use of the quantitative method in his study of judicial dissents, *The Roosevelt Court* (New York, 1948). After statistical demonstration of
the fact of a considerable division on the Supreme Court and the discussion of possible explanations, he says: "For an answer to these similar questions, it is necessary
to move on from statistics to semantics, from counting dissent to analyzing the issues
causing dissents, from charting judicial alignments to discovering judicial attitudes,"
p. 45.

The trial courts are the backbone of our judicial system, the closest to the economic and social order, and well or ill they decide most of the cases. From the standpoint of social welfare we want to know how and what they are doing; equally from the standpoint of private profit it is essential to be able to predict lower court trends more accurately than can be done from appellate decisions.[18]

Jerome Frank has on several occasions emphasized his belief that the trial courts, particularly in their finding of facts, are the source of much of the unpredictability in the administration of justice, and goes so far as to use skepticism about the adequacy of the fact-finding process as his own test for legal realism.[19]

III

In so far as legal realism accepts Llewellyn's separation of the Is and the Ought in the study of law, it does not necessarily involve a theory of judicial legislation. It must be remembered, however, that the separation of Is and Ought is only a temporary one. Although the reuniting of Is and Ought is not always perfectly achieved, legal realism is, like sociological jurisprudence, a theory of legal reform. In the accomplishment of that reform, it depends heavily upon judicial activity.

The theory of free judicial decision as it appears in the realist literature involves two concepts: the idea of the "marginal case" and, second, a widening of judicial cognizance to include more factors as relevant to the decision-making process. In both instances, the realists argue that greater predictability in law will be achieved. A conclusion of this sort from the premises given is admittedly somewhat startling. The reasons advanced to support it are various.

The idea that there is an inescapable judicial duty to legislate in cases that present the unsettled problems of society has already been considered in connection with the study of Benjamin N. Cardozo. The realists tend to accept his thesis and to give it greater emphasis. And, just as Cardozo distinguished between the "administration function" performed by judges and their "judicial function," so the realists insist that the real problem of jurisprudence is to formulate

[18] "Some of the Facts of Law Administration," p. 162.
[19] Preface to the Sixth Printing, *Law and the Modern Mind; Courts on Trial.* Additional discussion of the problems involved on the trial level can be found in Leon Green, *Judge and Jury* (Kansas City, 1930).

a theory of the judicial function for dealing with marginal cases. In Llewellyn's phrase, "Only *in* the penumbra do judicial problems lie. A theory to solve those problems must be a theory of the penumbra."[20] Here Llewellyn clearly reflects the influence of those philosophies that premise themselves on the concept of change. His general position is that in trying to deny change, we do not prevent it, we merely increase its apparent capriciousness.[21]

Llewellyn's concept of the importance of the marginal instance can be matched with similar statements by other realist writers. The criticism of traditional legal logic by both Cook and Patterson involves an assertion that logic cannot decide cases when the cases dealt with by a judge are *new* cases, that cannot by definition have been included in the old rules. Leon Green also shares this view,[22] of which the most adequate exposition is found in the work of the late Professor Max Radin:

> It is, therefore, not the common and usual situation but the marginal and exceptional one with which the law deals. Nor is it the law that has made it marginal by establishing a general and usual class which does not obviously contain the exceptional one. The general character of the class has been made by social custom, by people acting habitually in a certain way and acting in that way for reasons that have nothing to do with the law. When a marginal experience takes place, it is recognized as such by those who share it. If it were one of the common collisions of interest, the attitude that people adopt toward each other would be part of the experience itself . . . But when the situation is one that is outside the obviously general classification, when it can be called marginal or exceptional, the law is likely enough to be asked to judge it. And in this margin of life, it speaks with authority.[23]

The fact that a case is marginal, in the sense that it does not clearly fall within accepted categories, does not relieve the judge of the necessity of deciding it. The legal realists give no indication that they

[20] "The Constitution as an Institution," 34 *Columbia Law Review* 1 (1934), p. 32.

[21] "We have, moreover, a first attack upon the realm of the unpredictable in the actions of courts. That attack suggests strongly that one large element in the large incalculable consists in the traditional pretense or belief (sometimes the one, sometimes the other) that there is no such area of uncertainty, or that it is much smaller than it is." "Some Realism About Realism," 44 *Harvard Law Review* 1222 (1931), p. 1251.

[22] "The clear cases do not require rules. Even laymen can decide easy cases. Nevertheless it is in these that most of our rules find their parentage. We have them in abundance where we need them least." *Judge and Jury*, p. 214.

[23] *Law as Logic and Experience*, p. 28.

wish to take this burden from the judge. On the contrary, they are willing to argue that in a changing world, the only stability will be found in an harmonious legal change,[24] and, further, that it is a responsibility of the judiciary to accomplish such change.

In this aspect, therefore, legal realism is an assertion of judicial responsibility. The judge must employ more than "judgment" in the solution of human difficulties. The law offers few solutions to the problems that come before him; the judge must formulate his own solutions. In the end "[t]he only guarantee of judicial wisdom will remain the judge."[25]

The responsibility for legal change having been clearly placed on the judge, what then do the legal realists set up as guides for the judge's discretion? Their solution to this problem involves primarily a widening of the factors the judge is to consider in arriving at his decisions. And, it is well to note, the realists assert that, in so widening his field of cognizance, the judge performs an essential governmental function:

> . . . a sane theory would utterly disregard a Documentary text *if any relevant practices existed* to offer a firmer, more living basis for the ideal picture. The judge's first duty would be study not of the Text nor (though these are distinctly less obnoxious because influenced by life) of the decisions. His first duty would be study of the structure and func-

---

[24] "[In] a regime of change, certainty in law is attained whenever . . . [a] judge's ways move in step and pace with changes in the ways—and so in the expectations—of the relevant laymen." Llewellyn, "Law and the Modern Mind—A Symposium," 31 *Columbia Law Review* 82 (1931), p. 87. See also: "This search for a static security—in the law or elsewhere—is misguided. The fact is that security can only be achieved through constant change, through the wise discarding of old ideas that have outlived their usefulness, through the adapting of others to current facts. There is only an illusion of safety in a Maginot Line. Social forces like armies can sweep around a fixed position and make it untenable. A position that can be shifted to meet such forces and at least partly absorb them alone gives hope of security." William O. Douglas, "Stare Decisis," Eighth Annual B. N. Cardozo Lecture, 49 *Columbia Law Review* 735 (1949), p. 735.

[25] Llewellyn, "The Constitution as an Institution," *op. cit.,* p. 34. See also: "One objection to experimental thinking in law is that the judge is bound by the law, and has only to apply it, not to make it. As one irate practitioner put it, we are inviting the judge to commit an impeachable offense. This is all of a piece with the logical theory that there are pre-existing concepts which decide all particular cases. . . . Legal rules mark the boundary of the judicial function; they guide thinking toward possible solutions. Within these boundaries the only safeguard lies in the personality and training of the judge and of those superior judges and professional practitioners (not to mention law review editors) who control officially, or censor unofficially, his decisions. Professional training and experience limit and condition hypotheses, and the experimentation that leads to choice between them." Edwin W. Patterson, "Can Law Be Scientific?" *op. cit.,* p. 136.

tioning of going government. . . . Moreover, sane theory would approach the study of these matters with an outlook basically at odds with the rigid attitude inculcated by orthodoxy. For the major problem that sane theory must work out is the problem of *leeway* in government. No institutional structure can be made viable, save insofar as it contains within itself the wherewithal for give, for readjustment, . . .[26]

It is essential to recognize, however, that the immediate purpose of the broadening of the area of judicial discretion was to increase the predictability of the legal process. At this point, the theory of a "science of law" and the theory of legal reform come together: the Is and the Ought are reunited. Patterson very plainly exhibits the paradoxes involved when he says:

If law is to be scientific, we must prepare ourselves for the shock of having judicial decisions grounded upon reasons which do not even pretend to be axiomatic.[27]

In the end, therefore, the legal realists come back to the position stated by Holmes. The demand is not for an increase of judicial freedom

[26] Llewellyn, "The Constitution as an Institution," *op. cit.,* p. 31. In this article, in which, incidentally, Llewellyn explicitly acknowledges the "discovery" and the inspiration of Bentley, there is clear recognition of a difficulty which the sociological jurists never completely solved: Were they criticizing previous courts for being non-sociological or for being bad sociologists? Llewellyn adopts the second line, which is, it might be added, the more consistent. ". . . there is no quarrel to be had with judges *merely* because they disregard or twist Documentary language, or 'interpret' it to the despair of original intent, in the service of what those judges conceive to be the inherent nature of our institutions. To my mind, such action is their duty. To my mind, the judge who builds his decision to conform with his conception of what our institutions must be if we are to continue, roots in the deepest wisdom. I may differ with him in his choice of an idea. I may feel, say in the *Coppage* and *Abrams* and *Adkins Cases,* that he was quite misguided. But I cannot simultaneously defend the dissents in those cases and deny the implicit premise common to majority and to dissent: to wit, that certain fundamental features of our institutions need expression in the rulings of the Supreme Court of the United States, whatever be the language of the Document." *Ibid.,* p. 33.

[27] "Can Law Be Scientific?" p. 137. Llewellyn seems to assert much the same thing when he says: "To *recognize* that there are limits of the certainty sought by verbalism and deduction, to seek to define those limits, is to open the door to that other and far more useful judicial procedure: *conscious* seeking *within the limits laid down by precedent* and statute, for the wise decision. Decisions thus reached, *within those limits,* may fairly be hoped to be more certainly predictable than decisions are now—for now no man can tell when the court will, and when it will not, thus seek the wise decision, but hide the seeking under words. And not only more certain, but what is no whit less important: more just and wise (or more frequently just and wise)." "Some Realism about Realism," *op. cit.,* pp. 1251–52. See also *The Bramble Bush,* p. 71. For similar statements by other writers see Walter W. Cook, "Privileges of Labor Unions in the Struggle for Life," 27 *Yale Law Journal* 779 (1918), p. 785; Max Radin, *The Law as Logic and Experience,* p. 32: "Legal Realism," 31 *Columbia Law Review* 824 (1931), p. 824.

so much as it is for a consciousness of the fact of judicial freedom:

> Remembering always that the final choice for both judge and scholar in deciding a case or criticizing a decision is always a practical one, whether consciously or unconsciously so, the problem how a more conscious and methodical process can be substituted for an intuitive empiricism in making that choice, transcends in importance all other problems of legal education. Until its solution is attempted, a socialized jurisprudence will continue to be a mere aspiration and social engineering will be the profession of many but the occupation of none.[28]

Although the realists thus far considered may seem to have displayed a tendency to carry their emphases further than would the sociological group, they have nevertheless remained within the general lines of the American juristic tradition. The differences between realists and the sociological jurists are matters of more or less; both groups have been concerned with the development of a legal system which, although differing in important ways from the orthodox tradition, would nevertheless be both systematic and legal.

The writers discussed above, although perhaps the more representative, do not, however, constitute the whole of the realist tradition. Their very moderation sets them off from a group of realists, now to be considered, who hold that the study of law must be governed by entirely different, and extralegal, considerations, and who maintain that the legal practitioner and judge must be trained to a different set of attitudes from those accepted by the writers already studied.

Of the principal exponents of this point of view, four have been selected: Edward S. Robinson, Thurman W. Arnold, Jerome Frank, and Fred Rodell. These men, gifted writers, succeeded for a time in identifying the whole "realist movement" with themselves, and much of the conservative criticism of the "realist" approach was directed at their work. There are close connections among them, although these are not necessarily ideological. Robinson, before his death, conducted a joint seminar in the Yale Law School with Mr. Arnold, who subsequently became Assistant Attorney General of the United States. Judge Frank, who is presently a judge of the United States Court of Appeals, Second Circuit, has upon occasion taught in the Yale Law School, where Rodell is Professor of Law. Before proceeding with an examination of their theories, however, it is neces-

[28] Herman Oliphant, "A Return to Stare Decisis," *supra,* p. 160.

sary to enter a note of caution. As has been the case with many, if not most, of the jurists studied, this group was interested in many aspects of legal theory other than judicial legislation. Frank, for example, has on several occasions reiterated that his principal concern has been with the administration of justice on the trial level. Similarly, Thurman Arnold was concerned with broader governmental problems, and his theory of the judicial function should be seen as ancillary to his more general position. Nevertheless, as will be seen, there are implications for the judicial function in the more comprehensive theories of these jurists, who share in displaying a high development of the technique of viewing the law from the outside in the manner of the social psychologist or the cultural anthropologist rather than in that of the traditional jurist.[29]

Robinson's theory, which he described as "naturalistic jurisprudence," was based on the argument that "Every legal theory, insofar as it is more than the statement of an arbitrary statute or rule of procedure, is a theory about the human mind and human behavior." [30] In the absence of reliable data, jurists and lawyers had invented their own psychological concepts. We were, he thought, at a point where "every major legal problem will soon be worked over in terms of the psychology of today." [31]

In Robinson's argument, however, are the foundations for two lines of development which, although related, are not necessarily consistent. In the first place, he develops the thought that psychological data and methods might well replace traditional legal assumptions and methods in the handling of certain legal problems. Secondly, he suggests social control through psychological methods.

[29] It is recognized that Professor Llewellyn has made vigorous efforts to apply cultural anthropology to law. See "The Normative, the Legal and the Law-jobs: The Problem of the Juristic Method," *op. cit.* It is submitted, however, that Llewellyn's characteristic approach and conclusions are markedly more traditional than those of Frank *et al.* From Frank's criticism of Llewellyn (*Courts on Trial,* pp. 73-77) it is clear that Frank does not regard Llewellyn as in any marked degree emancipated from traditionalist misconceptions.

[30] *Law and the Lawyers* (New York, 1935), p. 50.

[31] *Loc. cit.* See also: "It is necessary to develop a positive science of social control which shall make constructive use of what is known about human interests and about the psychological processes through which they are realized. Psychological, sociological, and economic facts must be assimilated into legal learning as the basic materials of that science. If it be true that banking and railroading and marrying and racketeering and the thinking of the judges appear in a new light when examined statistically, economically, sociologically, psychologically, it would seem as though legal science must have to be renovated and first things put first." *Ibid.,* p. 70.

The first argument is not especially novel. It is a statement that jurisprudence should be psychological in the same sense that Pound sometimes [32] thought that jurisprudence ought to be sociological. Robinson merely says that psychology has data that indicate that traditional legal methods are wrong. The law relies, for example, upon the testimony of witnesses in circumstances that would indicate to a trained psychologist that the witness' memory is probably not reliable. Robinson goes on to suggest that trained penologists are better able to handle criminal law than are the lawyers. He does not, unfortunately, work out the details of this side of his argument and is willing to admit that the problem is not a simple one:

> The fact that there are few, if any, easy transfers from the general problems of the experimental psychology of memory to the specific issues of reliability of testimony in the court room does not mean that the law will do as well if it operates according to its own hunches and traditions. It may be important for the future judge or counsellor to know the time-honored arguments about the reliability of testimony as they have become habits of the court room, but a naturalistic jurisprudence will insist that knowledge of the reliability of memory as it is revealed by the most competent empirical investigation is even more important. [33]

Nevertheless, he insists that a critical knowledge of psychology is a necessary part of a lawyer's mental equipment:

> The student of jurisprudence will be required to throw himself into psychology completely enough to become his own competent critic on matters of psychological theory. There is no easy way. There are no official guides to lead him through the shifting controversies and to pick out for him just those elements of psychological theory which he can adopt with safety and a sense of permanence. [34]

As noted above, however, Robinson appears also to develop a second and somewhat different application of psychology to law. The difference is elusive, but perhaps it might be described along the following lines: whereas in his first argument Robinson proposes the use of psychology in the solution of legal problems, in his second he looks

---

[32] The qualification is necessary because Pound sometimes insisted that law should depend upon sociological data and sometimes looked at law as a sociological phenomenon. He used "sociological jurisprudence" to describe both views.

[33] *Ibid.*, p. 117. Cf. Roscoe Pound's contention that law has sufficient psychological data of its own upon which to rely. "The Call for a Realistic Jurisprudence," 44 *Harvard Law Review* 679 (1931).

[34] *Ibid.*, p. 111. This gives rise to the observation that apparently Robinson expected lawyers to be somewhat more discriminating about psychology than are the psychologists.

at law and the legal process as the solution to a psychological problem. In this sense his jurisprudence is psychological jurisprudence in the sense that Bentley's jurisprudence was "sociological." Both men assess law as a social phenomenon to be studied from the viewpoints of their particular disciplines.

At the extreme, this idea comes almost to the point of suggesting the manipulation of society by psychological devices, although it is difficult to be certain that Robinson would have gone so far. The suggestion, at least, is apparent in his discussion of legal fictions, where he says:

> . . . the judicial process is concerned with the resolution of conflicts that are emotional as well as intellectual. *It is one thing to be empirical in our examination of judicial deliberation and quite another to assume that good judges are those who neglect all values except those of truth and fact.* Successful adjudication requires the satisfaction of something more than merely logical men.[35]

Robinson here would seem to be imposing upon the courts an obligation that the natural scientist does not have, and he requires a psychological theory of law to take account of that fact:

> We . . . see how inadequate is that psychology which leads to a mere debunking of the law. Going on the simple assumption that the actual springs of action always lie in unconscious biological or economic cravings, such a psychology brushes aside as fictions juristic formulas and values. What is required as a basis for a naturalistic jurisprudence is a psychology capable of seeing that legal doctrines which are not to be taken literally are yet to be taken seriously.[36]

The "élitism" of the judge's function here suggested by Robinson goes beyond that found in the theories of the other legal realists yet considered. The obvious analogy is that of the physician who cures a patient by prescribing sugar pills. The analogy of the physician and the patient suggests Plato of course, and one wonders how far Robinson would have subscribed to Plato's "Royal Lie." That such a reading is not altogether fanciful is shown by the interpretation put

---

[35] *Op. cit.,* p. 231. (Emphasis supplied.)

[36] *Ibid.,* p. 147. Cf. "Perhaps one significant difficulty in teaching social, and particularly political, psychology is that it may analyze too clearly the methods of 'democratic' control. While this may be useful to the future politician, it may be dangerous for too many laymen to understand all of the methods whereby people are manipulated." John F. Markey, "Trends in Social Psychology," George A. Anderson, Nels Lundberg, Read Bain, and others, *Trends in American Sociology* (New York, 1929), p. 169.

upon Robinson's jurisprudence by Thurman W. Arnold, his col-
league and co-worker:

> He [Robinson] never denied the utility of legal concepts, or the neces-
> sity of using them when one appeared on the solemn judicial stage. He
> never denied that it was the function of the law school to teach that
> language. He asserted only that there was room for two sciences, one
> a science *of* law to be used within the little dramatic universe of the law
> and the other a science *about* law which was useful not on the judicial
> stage but in the conference room of the diagnostician of social insti-
> tutions.[37]

The second aspect of Robinson's theory, his "theory about law,"
is restated in a broader and more popular form by Thurman Arnold.
The general tone of Arnold's discussion can be gathered from the
following:

> The success of the play requires that an idea be made real to the au-
> dience. The success of the law as a unifying force depends upon making
> emotionally significant the ideal of a government of law which is ra-
> tional and scientific. . . . Functionally the primary purpose of the sci-
> ence of the law is to be a sounding board of both the prevalent hopes
> and the prevalent worries of those who believe in a government of laws
> and not of men, to reconcile those hopes and worries somewhere in the
> mists of scholarship and learning, and never to admit that this is what
> it is doing.[38]

To Arnold, law, like most of the institutions of society, is a cluster
of myths or folklore. People are dominated by such myths to the
extent that a realistic appraisal of a situation is exceedingly difficult.
People do not want to face facts; when the real forces that make institutions work are dragged into the light, they seem to "nice people"
to be "slightly obscene."

In his popular book, *The Folklore of Capitalism,* Arnold was concerned over the popular irrationalities that stood in the way of practical efforts to deal with the Depression of 1929. His remarks apply as
well, however, to the popular theory of law:

> To find peace, men denounced government by men, and sought relief by
> reciting principles. The fundamental assumption of the folklore about

---

[37] "The Jurisprudence of Edward S. Robinson," 46 *Yale Law Journal* 1282
(1937), p. 1286. Cf. Arnold: "Perhaps, in some future time which accepts 'Experimentation' as the source of knowledge and is willing to trust in the personal expertness of judges, as today we trust in the expertness of physicians, jurisprudence may
again be simple." *Symbols of Government* (New Haven, 1935), p. 50.

[38] "Apologia for Jurisprudence," 44 *Yale Law Journal* 729 (1935), p. 729.

government during the great depression was that principles could be more trusted than organizations. Organizations were dangerous because of their tendency to err and stray. Principles, provided that they were sound, endured forever, and could alone make up for the constant tendency of social groups to backslide.[39]

His objection to this phenomenon is that such illusions stifle action. "Formulas become more important than facts."

Arnold's ideal is the "fact-minded observer" or the "cheerful, practical technician." [40] Such a person realizes that people in general react emotionally. He will therefore present his plans as slogans, although to him they are tools, not matters of belief. Since he is free of the stultifying effects of the popular "religion of government," he will be able to deal with problems as they arise:

> Actual observation of human society . . . indicates that great constructive achievements in human organization have been accomplished by men who violated most of the principles which we cherish . . . Principles, once formulated into a logical system and accepted, seem to paralyze action in the actual arena of human affairs.[41]

Arnold, in common with other modern jurists, concludes by placing a heavy burden on the judiciary. His theory is complicated by his recognition of the symbolic value of legal systems and courts and his tendency to include legal theory (including legal realism) [42] among the social phenomena serving a symbolic purpose. In the end, however, he believes that a symbolic function need not paralyze action, and he dedicates his work to the hope that

> . . . a new public attitude toward the ideals of law and economics is slowly appearing to create an atmosphere where the fanatical alignments between opposing political principles may disappear and a competent, practical, opportunistic governing class may rise to power.[43]

[39] *Folklore of Capitalism* (New Haven, 1937), pp. 68–69.
[40] *Ibid.,* p. 120.
[41] *Symbols of Government* (New Haven, 1935), p. 5. See also *The Folklore of Capitalism:* "Everyone will not become a student of government. Most people will think in terms of a religion of government. For the public generally, all that is needed to make this point of view effective is that it be tolerated in those who manage and study governmental organizations," p. 162.
[42] "The fact that today as a necessary gesture toward a new habit of thought the 'Law' is dressed up to look like a 'science' does not change it as a way of thought. It means only that the earliest conception that the law came from God and the later conception that it arose from logic and reason have both been worn thin." *Symbols of Government,* p. 33.
[43] *Ibid.,* p. 271.

Jerome Frank shares Robinson's and Arnold's interest in law as a psychological phenomenon. Convinced that legal certainty and predictability are not only fictitious [44] but also on the whole undesirable, he is nevertheless impressed with the persistence of the belief in certainty and predictability among the lay public and also among the legal profession.

Approaching this phenomenon as a psychological problem, Frank finds a partial explanation [45] in the demand for security which is present in most human beings. Following Piaget's studies of child development, he allies the desire for certainty in law with the father-security demand of the child:

> . . . To the child the father is the Infallible Judge, the Maker of definite rules of conduct. He knows precisely what is right and what is wrong and, as head of the family, sits in judgment and punishes misdeeds. The Law—a body of rules apparently devised for infallibly determining what is right and what is wrong and for deciding who should be punished for misdeeds—inevitably becomes a partial substitute for the Father-as-Infallible-Judge.[46]

Security and predictability, therefore, persist as goals in legal thinking because men are immature and have not outgrown their childish longings:

[44] "Yet the layman errs in his belief that this lack of precision and finality is to be ascribed to the lawyers. The truth of the matter is that the popular notion of legal existence is based upon a misconception. The law always has been, is now, and will ever continue to be, largely vague and variable. And how could this well be otherwise? The law deals with human relations in their most complicated aspects. The whole confused, shifting, helter-skelter of life parades before it—more confused than ever, in our kaleidoscopic age . . . When human relationships are transforming daily, legal relationships cannot be expressed in enduring form." *Law and the Modern Mind* (New York, 1949), pp. 5–6.

[45] Frank is careful to point out at several places that his answer is only "partial." This device has certain obvious conveniences since it is nonquantitative and at the same time pervasive. It has the further advantage of explaining criticism in advance. In fairness to Judge Frank, it must be said that he offers some fourteen other explanations of the basic legal myth. *Ibid.*, p. 263. Of these, attention is directed to the "religious impulse," "the aesthetic impulse" (which Frank suggests may be related to infantile longings), "the human instinct to seek security and certainty," "inertia," "stupidity," and "language and word magic." One wonders whether the alternatives are much help. It is of interest to note that Llewellyn in his discussion of *Law and the Modern Mind*, 31 *Columbia Law Review* 82 ff. (1931), points out that the conclusions stand without the premises but then goes on to say that Frank more than half-believes them himself. This puts Frank somewhat in the position of being slain in the house of his friends. In his later work, *Courts on Trial*, Frank introduces several other psychological explanations to buttress the same conclusions. See also the work of Schroeder, a pioneer in this field (p. 134, below).

[46] *Law and the Modern Mind*, p. 18.

. . . The desire persists in grown men to recapture, through a redis-
covery of a father, a childish, completely controllable universe, and that
desire seeks satisfaction in a partial, unconscious, anthropomorphizing
of Law, in ascribing to the Law some of the characteristics of the Child's
Father-Judge. That childish longing is an important element in the
explanation of the absurdly unrealistic notion that law is, or can be
made, entirely certain and definitely predictable.[47]

Frank's theory, like Robinson's, is an example of a rigorous application of the conclusions of a nonlegal discipline to the study of
legal problems. He concludes, as might be expected, by suggesting
that the essential problem is not legal at all. It would indeed be extraordinary if, after finding a "partial" source of our legal ills in the
fundamental infantilism of the human race, the solution should be
other than psychological regeneration. His suggestions for the judicial process involve changes of considerable magnitude:

We need judges possessed of . . . [a] Shavian spirit who will enjoy
thinking as experimentation, to whom a wakeful attitude of intelligent
doubt will be a source of pleasure. Such men will not talk of 'rules'
and 'principles' as finalities while unconsciously using them as sopo-
rifics to allay the pains of uncertainty. They will treat rules and principles as shorthand expressions, ingenious abbreviations, metaphors,
short-cuts, figures of thought, intellectual scaffoldings, and the like; they
will find positive satisfaction in hypothetical, relative, fictional and provisional thinking.[48]

Although for the most part the realists have not gone so far,[49] a
recommendation such as Frank's indicates the wide departure of
American jurisprudence from its traditional moorings and the degree
to which modern American legal thinking looks upon the legal system

[47] *Loc cit.* In so far as Frank's fellow realists tried to improve the predictability
of law, they, of course, proved themselves as immature as the rest of the profession.
Frank does not leave this to inference. In *Courts on Trial,* he makes explicit his
disapproval of the "left wing adherents of the old magical tradition" and puts
Llewellyn, among others, in the "second class of legal wizards," p. 74. After their
rather hearty exchanges in 1931, Llewellyn must have been rather more surprised
than pleased to find himself bracketed with Dean Pound. Frank's standard is a
rigorous one, and the number of truly adult jurists is rather limited. Holmes is included, of course, but Cardozo does not give completely satisfactory evidence that he
enjoys insecurity.
[48] *Law and the Modern Mind,* p. 166.
[49] Llewellyn, reviewing Frank's book, said: "Law, in the sense of decision, is in
fact much more predictable, and hence more certain, than his treatment would indicate. In his enthusiasm for illusion-smashing he paints the illusion as somewhat
more illusive than it is." "Law and the Modern Mind, a Symposium," 31 *Columbia
Law Review* 82 (1931), p. 87.

as a process of adjudication rather than as it has been traditionally pictured :

> To do their intricate job well our judges need all the clear consciousness of their purpose which they can summon to their aid. And the pretense, the self-delusion, that when they are creating they are borrowing, when they are making something new they are merely applying the commands given them by some existing external authority, cannot but diminish their efficiency. They must rid themselves of this reliance on a non-existent guide, they must learn the virtue, the power and practical worth of self-authority.[50]

This survey of the more extreme group among the legal realists can be concluded with a brief glance at the development of the "myth idea" as found in the work of Fred Rodell. In his book, *Woe Unto You, Lawyers*,[51] he is ostensibly interested in the practicing legal profession. His general outlook appears in his opening remarks :

> In tribal times, there were the medicine-men. In the Middle Ages, there were the priests. Today there are the lawyers. For every age, a group of bright boys, learned in their trade and jealous of their learning, who blend technical competence with plain and fancy hocus-pocus to make themselves masters of their fellow men. For every age, a pseudo-intellectual autocracy, guarding the tricks of its trade from the uninitiated, and running, after its own pattern, the civilization of its day.[52]

[50] *Law and the Modern Mind*, p. 121. Frank is not the only American juristic theorist to attempt a more or less direct application of psychological theory to legal problems. An early example of the use of psychology in legal study is found in the work of Theodore Schroeder. Mr. Schroeder, like Frank, is influenced by the psychological concept of the subconscious. He is of the opinion that in judicial opinions can be found the outbreaking of the infantile lust for power. He says: "When we remember that our dominant impulse must be a defense against or for something which is in our subconscious feelings or in the actual phantasies back of the present conscious act, or perhaps the personal experiences still further back, which are essential to the creation of the precise character of these present desires, or impulses or phantasies. So may we read the life of the judge backwards. Thus it is that every opinion is unavoidably a fragment of autobiography for those who know how to read the impulses and experiences behind the words, unconsciously expressed in their choice, by methods that are not at the command of the ordinary reader. Every opinion thus amounts to a confession." "Psychologic Study of Judicial Opinions," 6 *California Law Review* 93 (1918) p. 94. He suggests that the judge check his "Infantile lust for power by more or less conscious and efficient coordination," p. 96. This, of course, has no particular bearing on the theory of the judicial function but is interesting as an early and little known example of the use of the same technique that Frank applies. It is to be noted, however, that the dominating impulse is opposite to that relied upon by Frank.

[51] New York, 1939.

[52] *Ibid.*, p. 3. Rodell is, it will be recalled, Professor of Law in Yale University. Perhaps he is boring from within.

In the remainder of his book, he develops an attack upon the concept of legal rules in a more or less customary manner. The judges make their decisions, then fit the ideas to them:

> No single fact is so essential to the life and lustiness of the legal racket as the sober pretense on the part of practically all its practitioners—from Supreme Court judges down to police court lawyers—that the Law is, in the main, an exact science. No pretense was ever more absurd. The basic assumption behind settlement of every legal dispute, whether it be settled by a judge's sacred words or out of court, is that according to the Law, there is only one right answer, one preordained answer, to the problem . . . They take a problem, any problem, push the buttons on the big machine that correspond to those symbols, and the right answer automatically pops out at the bottom.[53]

One thing, however, distinguishes Mr. Rodell from most of his contemporaries. His dislike for the whole process is fundamental; he is not willing to bother with petty remedies. Good decisions and bad fall into the same category:

> And it is worth repeating, and remembering, that the alleged logic of Constitutional Law is equally amorphous, equally unconvincing, equally silly whether the decisions the Court is handing down are "good" or "bad," "progressive" or "reactionary," "liberal" or "illiberal" . . . No matter in which direction the legal wand is waved, the hocus-pocus remains the same.[54]

Here there would seem to be a logical limit. Whether such a denial is to be considered the logical development of legal realism will remain a matter of choice. It is clear, however, that Rodell carries ideas that are common among the group beyond any bounds that might be set. What he appears to be advocating is a suppression of what is customarily regarded as the legal process in favor of a species of arbitration. His own argument appears in the following:

> Since certainty and consistency are impossible of attainment in the orderly control of men's affairs, the sensible thing to do would be to go straight after justice in the settlement of any specific question that comes up for solution. Now justice itself is concededly an amorphous and uncertain ideal. One man's justice is another man's poison. But that is where written laws come in. Wherever different people's different ideas about what is fair and what is right clash head on, written laws, enacted by democratic processes, should contain, in so far as possible, the

[53] *Ibid.*, p. 157.
[54] *Ibid.*, pp. 98–99.

answer. Wherever written laws cannot or do not contain the answer, *somebody* has to make a decision. And that decision might better be made on grounds of plain, unvarnished justice, fairness, humanitarianism—amorphous though it be—than on any other.[55]

One need only to remark that the remedy is in accord with the analysis.

IV

The materials thus far considered under the heading "legal realism" in many ways represent the earlier and more exuberant phase of the movement. It will be well, therefore, to refrain from any attempt at final judgment until some of the criticisms of the realists and the later attempts to restate legal realism have been surveyed.

At this point, it is possible to note, however, that whatever it may have been that held the realists together, it was not their theories of the judicial function. Granting that realism of the type we have been discussing placed no great premium on conformity, it is still noteworthy that the theories of the judicial function explicit or implicit in the materials studied range from the apparently discretionless notions of Underhill Moore, through the "interstitial legislation" ideas of Llewellyn, to Rodell's adjudication in the name of "justice" in those areas in which there can by definition be no "rule" to guide the process. Common negations do not, apparently, lead to common conclusions; nor does a common devotion to the "facts" produce either uniform analysis or similar deductions therefrom.[56]

The variety exhibited by the realists can, of course, be given a number of interpretations. The general lack of agreement might be

---

[55] *Ibid.*, pp. 251–52. The demand for codified law generally assumes, it will be recalled, that the technique of adjudication can be one of application merely. Professor Rodell's proposal is interesting in that it uses a denial of the possibility of certainty and consistency as an argument of increasing certainty and consistency through written laws.

[56] In this connection see Julius Stone, *The Province and Function of Law* (Cambridge, 1950), pp. 416–17: "Professor Pound's initial hypothesis is that law in books bears a close relation to law in action, and he then inquires in what respects the hypothesis requires qualification. The 'realist' initial hypothesis, on the other hand, is that what courts, legislators and administrative officers do is not controlled by law as it is found in the authoritative materials, but by factors extraneous to those materials. Both hypotheses perfectly tested, should yield the same results; but unfortunately few thinkers can do more than open up the field lying nearest to their initial hypothesis. That tends willy-nilly to mean the field presenting most support for the hypothesis."

taken to indicate that value judgments have somewhere entered the process and that, although the realists generally hold that value judgments ought to be explicit, they are something less than meticulous in following their own canon. Or, again, the variety of approaches to legal problems tested by the legal realists can be considered symptomatic of the general lack of unity among the social sciences which has been steadily developing and still characterizes the area of social studies. It would be, in such circumstances, more strange if the legal theorists did exhibit a unanimity of either method or conclusions. Finally, and this is perhaps the most likely, the incongruities in legal realism and the disagreements among the realists are inevitable offshoots of the vigor with which they attacked their problem and therefore are symptomatic of the depth of their dissatisfaction with the results and supposed methods of the traditional legal theory. And that this attack should have been appropriate and relevant so many years after doubts of the orthodox notion began to be expressed, is in its way a tribute to the strength of that theory.

Stronger in criticism than in constructive force, the early phase of the realist movement was one of the most active periods in American jurisprudence. There is no doubt that the realists opened themselves to criticism and were guilty of overstatement. Anxious to establish their individuality, there was a common overemphasis of difference among theorists whose ultimate goals were almost identical. Perhaps something of this sort was in Pound's mind when he wrote:

> The American realists of the moment . . . put universally a theory of the judicial function as it goes on in the United States today, in a time of transition, when ideals are in flux and there is little to guide the application of standards while there is a constantly increasing number of standards to apply.[57]

If this is true, and there is much to indicate that it is, it will be necessary to await the refining influence of time and criticism before the final contribution of the realists can be weighed.

[57] Roscoe Pound, "Law and the Science of Law in Recent Theories," 7 *American Law School Review* 1057 (1934), pp. 1059–60.

Chapter 7

LEGAL REALISM: THE CRITICISM
AND RESTATEMENT

The juristic argument precipitated by the legal realists was a vigorous one and had both theoretical and political overtones. Assailed on all sides, the realists responded with fervor, and neither the attack nor the defense managed at all times to maintain a completely impersonal tone. Of the outrage manifested in more conservative legal circles, nothing need be said; the traditionalist position has already been stated and by definition is incapable of change. More interesting, however, was the criticism leveled at the realists by such men as John Dickinson, M. R. Cohen and Roscoe Pound, none of whom adhered to the traditionalist viewpoint, but who were equally unable to accept the newer statements. There resulted a redefinition of the realist position, in which there was an attempt to take account of the principal objections. Although it cannot be said that the restatement answered all the problems raised by legal realism, there was at least a moderation of some of the excesses, and legal realism was brought closer to the main stream of American jurisprudence.

The criticism of legal realism centered around three points. First, the critics objected strongly to the scientific positivism of the legal realist's attempt to identify law with uniformity of behavior, either social or judicial. Second, there was strong resistance to the legal realist's attempt to discard logic. Finally, and as a consequence of the first two, there was a reassertion of the legal rule as a compulsive element in the process of decision. None of these points necessarily involved a return to the mechanical conception of the judicial function.[1] Since both the realists and their critics admitted discretion and

---

[1] This is not to say that the mechanical conception does not still have its champions. Of interest in this connection is a speech by Senator Bricker of Ohio, as reported in the *New York Times*, February 12, 1950. "Sounding the tocsin in the impending struggle between the court and Congress," the Senator invited "lawyers, regardless of political affiliation to line up against 'judicial legislation.'" He asserted that "the political philosophy underlying judicial law making is strikingly

the exercise of judicial will in the administration of justice, the differences between the two groups can be described as those of degree and purpose. Those who criticized the realists believed that the discretion of the judge should be directed toward the formulation of new general principles to guide the administration of justice, as opposed to the realist tendency to follow Bingham's emphasis upon the particular decision.[2]

In at least one of its aspects legal realism tended strongly to stress the desirability of a "legal science," in which the study of law would be analogous to the physical sciences. Legal realism of this type perforce emphasized observation of judicial behavior as the object of legal study. In so far as the statistical method or Moore's attention to the "facts of the case" were thought valuable as analytical devices leading to improved predictability, there was implied both a governing determinism and a uniformity of judicial behavior. The basic incompatibility of such assumptions with a theory of judicial legislation has already been suggested. The attempt to make legal rules comparable to physical laws was attacked also from the point of view that

---

similar to state socialism." The Senator singled out for special mention Justices Black and Douglas and the late Justices Murphy and Rutledge. Some of the Senator's specifications for the attitude to which he objects are of interest; for example, "1. A desire that state regulation be superseded by federal regulation." This raises certain questions about the Senator's reading of Justices Black's and Douglas' dissent against the extension of a federal excise tax to state-produced products in *New York* v. *U.S.* (Saratoga Springs Case), 326 US 572 (1946). The Senator also found "5. A conviction that labor organizations can do no wrong," which is interesting in the light of Mr. Justice Black's majority opinion upholding state anti-closed-shop laws. *Lincoln Federal Labor* v. *Northwestern Iron and Metal Company,* 335 US 525 (1949). The "irrepressible sympathy for the underdog in both economic and political activities" (item 3) is, of course, to be distinguished from the Senator's activities as Attorney General of Ohio when he appeared as *amicus curiae* urging the constitutionality of minimum-wage legislation, *West Coast Hotel Co.* v. *Parrish,* 300 US 379 (1937), although this might be an example of Llewellyn's "separation" of the "Is and Ought." The Senator concluded by predicting that the whole issue would be settled by the voters. This is either legal realism with a vengeance or a statement that the people will instruct the legislatures not to pass any laws for the courts not to declare unconstitutional. It is also of interest that the Senator's appeal was specifically directed to lawyers. On the influence of the Bar in the development of constitutional law, see Benjamin Twiss, *Lawyers and the Constitution* (Princeton, 1942).

[2] This is especially noticeable when John Dickinson is compared with Thurman Arnold. It will be recalled that Dickinson tried to limit the area of permissible administrative discretion by insisting upon the reference of individual cases to some general principle. *Administrative Justice and the Supremacy of Law in the United States* (Cambridge, Mass., 1927), pp. 118–19, 140, 150, 168. Note also his adoption of Pound's expression of the same distinction. *Ibid.,* p. 15 n.

whereas the latter are not normative, the legal rule necessarily includes normative elements. Critics of this aspect of legal realism emphasized that even for the legal student the problem of observing judicial behavior must be different from that of the physical scientist working with his materials. Even for purposes of study, one cannot anticipate a judge's decision in a case as he would anticipate "how a muscle will react when brought into contact with an electric current." [3] The element of conscious intent in the judge and his feeling that the rule of law must be followed destroy the analogy.[4]

Even were one to grant the propriety of the "scientific attitude" in the student of law, however, it does not follow that a similar attitude could be maintained by a judge. The function of generalizations in the physical sciences and in the judicial process is essentially different; in the one, the generalization is an instrument of anticipation and description, in the other, it is a tool of decision. Again to quote from Dickinson:

> The aim of science being discovery, its concern with its general formulations is primarily to test them for their conformity to future situations. The interest of a scientist in a scientific "law" is to determine the degree of accuracy with which it turns out to describe a future case, and if possible to supersede it with a new generalization which will make possible a description having a higher degree of accuracy . . .

> This whole procedure is radically different in intent and method from the kind of reasoning which is directed toward deciding controversies by the application of law . . . The goal of normative thinking is not

[3] John Dickinson, "Legal Rules in the Process of Decision," 19 *Univ. of Pennsylvania Law Review* 833 (1931), p. 839.

[4] Pound's statement of a similar view has already been cited. *Supra,* p. 80. Similar statements can be found in Morris R. Cohen, *Law and the Social Order* (New York, 1933), pp. 174, 178, 205; "Mr. Justice Holmes and the Nature of Law," 31 *Columbia Law Review* 352 (1931), p. 360; "A Critical Sketch of Legal Philosophy in America," *Law—a Century of Progress,* II (New York, 1937) pp. 308–9. See also Huntington Cairns, *The Theory of Legal Science* (Chapel Hill, 1941): ". . . the order which exists in human society at any given time is predominantly an achieved order, an invention at the center of which is man; it is not the order of the physical universe, which in physical theory is the product of the blind operation of nature . . ." p. 54. See also Lon L. Fuller, "American Legal Realism," 82 *Univ. of Pennsylvania Law Review* 429 (1934) pp. 429 n. and 456. Mr. Fuller takes the position that although one of the purposes of legal realism was to broaden the area of relevance in legal study, it really has operated in the direction of narrowing legal method, since the tendency has been to go completely outside the law to explain decisions. He holds that this is a false development of the first statement of legal realism in the writings of Bingham. His criticism of the positivism of legal realism is developed in *The Law in Quest of Itself* (Chicago, 1940) pp. 118–19, 131–32.

discovery; the judge who is called on to decide whether or not to award damages to a plaintiff is not, like the scientist, engaged in the discovery of new truth, or in adding to the sum total of human knowledge. The judge does not employ the case before him as a means of testing the validity of the rules which he employs in reasoning toward his decision.[5]

The analogy between the two types of law is also attacked on the ground that mere regularities of conduct, even nonjudicial conduct, do not furnish norms for decision. It has already been suggested that since such regularities are rarely perfect, they are of limited value in deciding particular cases. It can also be argued that social laws in the sense that the realists sought to state them lack the normative aspect necessary to the legal rule,[6] and it has been pointed out that the necessity for law arises out of the facts that behavior itself is not regular [7] and that a criterion is required by which desirable behavior can be selected.[8]

The limitation of the "scientific approach" leads therefore to a reassertion of the necessity and relevance of legal rules as guides to decision. The same result was reached by the critical tendency to reevaluate the relationships between logic and the law. There is again no tendency on the part of the critics to go back to the traditional conception of the judge as a logical calculating machine. Indeed, no one was more critical of the "phonographic" theory of the judicial function than were M. R. Cohen and John Dickinson. They continued to point out, nevertheless, that, properly used, formal thinking is a necessary and valuable part of the judicial process. It does not, perhaps, supply premises and it ought not outweigh more valuable as-

[5] *Ibid.,* p. 861.

[6] "An uncritical adherence to the behavioristic approach leads to another erroneous assumption, that norms of decision may be extracted directly from regularities of behavior, and that where you have a definite 'behavior pattern' you necessarily have a correspondingly definite norm of decision. Now this is demonstrably untrue . . . The mere fact that people habitually act in certain ways in certain situations is not itself a criterion on the basis of which law-suits may be decided. If a folk-way is relevant to decision, it must be because it has a 'normative' aspect." Lon L. Fuller, "American Legal Realism," *supra,* p. 457.

[7] "In modern heterogeneous and rapidly changing society the legal cannot be identified with the customary—indeed, it is the diversity of customs and their uncertainty under changing conditions that largely necessitate modern law-making." Morris R. Cohen, "A Critical Sketch of Legal Philosophy in America," p. 308.

[8] "There is, therefore, no way of drawing the distinction between legal and illegal behavior without reference to the system of ideas which authoritatively prescribe what we should and what we should not do." *Ibid.,* pp. 308–9. See also "Law and the Scientific Method," 6 *American Law School Review* 231 (1929), p. 237.

pects of law, but without it, the legal system would be chaos. As Cohen said:

> Law without concepts or rational ideas, law that is not logical, is like pre-scientific medicine—a hodge-podge of superstition, as has indeed been most of the world's common sense as distinguished from science.[9]

A similar attitude was expressed by Dickinson, who said:

> The need is for new distinctions based on the purpose of the law, but fixed distinctions, nevertheless; for new concepts of valid difference to secure a juster order and uniformity, rather than for the abandonment of legal definition altogether in favor of justice without rules . . . a mode of thinking other than the conceptual remains to be discovered which will fit the working processes of the human mind.[10]

Both Cohen and Dickinson were searching for a middle ground between absolute certainty, which both admitted was impossible, and the absolute discretion which might be found in some of the realist literature. To Cohen, the fault lay not in the inadequacy of logic, but in an inadequate logic,[11] and Dickinson expressed much the same

---

[9] "Law and Scientific Method," p. 237. See, further: "Like other useful instruments, logic is very dangerous, and it requires great wisdom to use it properly. A logical science of law can help us digest our material, but we must get our food before we can digest it. The law draws its sap from feelings of justice and social need. It has grown up and been improved by sensitively minded judges attending to the conflicting claims of the various interests before them, and leaving it to subsequent developments to demonstrate the full wisdom or unwisdom of the decision. The intellectualist would have the judge certain of everything before deciding, but this is impossible. Like other human efforts, the law must experiment, which always involves a leap into the dark future. But for that very reason the judge's *feelings* as to right and wrong must be logically and scientifically trained. The trained mind sees in a flash of intuition that which the untrained mind can succeed in seeing only after painfully treading many steps. They who scorn the idea of the judge as a logical automaton are apt to fall into the opposite error of exaggerating as irresistible the force of bias or prejudice. But the judge who realizes before listening to a case that all men are biased is more likely to make a conscientious effort at impartiality than one who believes that elevation to the bench makes him at once an organ of infallible logical truth." *Law and the Social Order* (New York, 1933), pp. 182–83.

[10] *Administrative Justice and the Supremacy of Law in the United States* (Cambridge, Mass., 1927), p. 140.

[11] "The limitation which underlies the old Aristotelian logic shows itself in the familiar difficulty as to the presence of discretion in the law . . . Individual discretion . . . appears to this view synonymous with the absence of law . . . This view, however, is based on an inadequate logic which fails to appreciate the necessarily provisional character of all legal classification and the consequent necessity of discretion to make definite that which would otherwise be really indefinite." "The Place of Logic in the Law," 29 *Harvard Law Review* 622 (1916), pp. 636–37. Here, Cohen is, of course, interested in criticizing the traditionalist overemphasis on logic. His remark, however, cuts both ways.

point of view when he asserted the desirability of the search for certainty even when it is admittedly unattainable.

> It may well be that no general rule is ever strictly possible because the same case never arises twice; but this does not imply that much will not be gained by bringing under an approximate general rule cases more or less alike . . . If we have not identities to work upon, we have at least resemblances . . .[12]

Implicit in the foregoing has been a theory of the judicial function which, by rejecting the discretionary and individualizing tendencies of some aspects of legal realism, asserts the value of the legal rule, as such, in the administration of justice. Both Cohen and Dickinson agreed with Pound that there are positive social values to be obtained by referring the particular case to the general rule. They were not in the end, therefore, too far separated from Holmes, who once defined his function as "to see that the game is played according to the rules whether I like them or not." [13]

II

The discussion of the questions raised by legal realism continued, but with decreasing intensity, through the 1930's, and the air of injured innocence with which the legal realists greeted the first onslaughts of Pound, Dickinson, and others [14] gave way to an attempt to restate legal realism in a fashion calculated to allay the fears of the more conservative group.[15]

It has already been said that the critics of legal realism tended at times to take the part for the whole and to attribute to the term "legal realist" more concreteness than it actually deserves. As was emphasized at the beginning of the discussion of legal realism, the common belief of the legal realists is extremely difficult to isolate.

---

[12] *Administrative Justice and the Supremacy of Law*, p. 119.

[13] "Ideals and Doubts," *Collected Legal Papers*, p. 307.

[14] It is at least possible that Llewellyn's reference to Pound's theories as "bedtime stories for the tired bar," ["A Realistic Jurisprudence—The Next Step," 30 *Columbia Law Review* 431 (1930), p. 435 n.] may have had something to do with the vigor of Dean Pound's reaction.

[15] Pound, of course, remains irreconcilable. See *Administrative Law* (Pittsburgh, 1942) and *Contemporary Juristic Theories* (Claremont, Calif., 1940). Jerome Frank's able defense of administrative agencies is found in *If Men Were Angels* (New York, 1942). Cohen also criticizes Pound's vehemence. "A Critical Sketch of Legal Philosophy in America," pp. 298–99.

Even on so central a point as the realist criticism of the legal rule, the degree of rejection varies from a total rejection to a partial rejection. Many of the realists, some of whom have been discussed, were not markedly behavioristic in their psychology. Therefore, the castigation of all realists as behaviorists was more total than was warranted by the evidence. On the other hand, in justification of the critics, it ought to be said that some realist could usually be produced who had committed one or all of the sins attributed by the critics to the group as a whole, and, further in their extenuation, it should be indicated that their tendency to state their opponents' arguments in the least favorable light is not unknown also among the realists themselves, despite the latter group's great fascination with scientific accuracy in legal study.

The attack upon the "scienticism" of legal realism resulted in an emphasis upon the fact that the "separation between Is and Ought" was at most only temporary. The legal realists insisted that although their approach did involve an increased attention to empirical data, they were conscious that the problem was not wholly empirical. As Llewellyn put it :

> The misconception lies in conceiving that everyone thinks facts are *all* that jurisprudence is concerned with, merely because he cries out for needed facts or in a particular preliminary study tries to report facts as objectively as possible; or that anyone conceives that all law has to do is to *follow* society because in a *particular* instance under discussion the following of society is urged to be the adjustment needed.[16]

Jerome Frank, whose provocative contributions to juristic literature made him the *bête noire* of the more conservative party, has gone so far as to describe the attempt to construct a legal science patterned on natural science as "fatuous," [17] and insists that careful reading of his works would have prevented his ever being associated with the idea.[18]

---

[16] "Through Title to Contract and a Bit Beyond," 15 *New York University Law Quarterly* 159 (1938), p. 162 n. Llewellyn insists that his statements about facts were misconstrued. It is in this article that he speaks of Pound's "queer blindness or willful perversity." Without taking the position that Pound's criticism of the realists is correct, it can be said that Llewellyn's enthusiasm laid him open to misconstruction.

[17] Preface to 6th printing, *Law and the Modern Mind*, p. xiii. In *Courts on Trial* (1949) he expands on this notion with particular reference to Harold Lasswell and Myres S. McDougall. See pp. 20 ff.

[18] As a matter of fact, Frank does appeal for a more scientific spirit in the sense of the willingness to experiment—a quality that he identifies with adultism. *Law and the Modern Mind*, p. 98. This is again a case in which an author might have been more careful to avoid misinterpretation.

He now re-emphasizes the idea that the unpredictability in the administration of justice is more importantly a trial court phenomenon than it is characteristic of appellate courts, and, in so far as he seeks to improve trial procedures, he places a greater value on predictability than his former writings would appear to indicate.

The tendency to lay less emphasis upon law as an objective uniformity of action is also evident in the willingness of the realists to concede the ultimately ethical quality of their problem. In point of fact, the realists' interest in the ethical question appears quite early in the movement, although ethical problems were not given the prominence that was accorded to other phases. Even so "realistic" a student as Felix Cohen admits the relevance of ethics to legal study:

> It is idle to hope that the interminable controversies of ethics may be forgotten in formulating a program for the positive, scientific study of law. For those who disagree upon the fundamental values of life will disagree as to what consequences of law are worth investigating . . . the rejection of all ethical absolutes will not help legal science to forget the war of ethical schools, since relativism gives to every individual the assurance of irresponsibility in the affirmation of his own personal ideals.[19]

Along with the revival of ethics, there is also indication that the extreme criticism of logic as useless to the process of decision is no longer, if it ever was, a characteristic of legal realism. Again, it is well to note, there is no return to the notion that the law ought to be a completely logical system, but there is acceptance of the idea that in its place logic is a useful device:

> But this discourse, in which law as logic expresses itself, is discourse about human experience which thus becomes part of the law when

[19] *Ethical Systems and Legal Ideals* (New York, 1933), p. 231. See also his insistence that even for purposes of study the ethical ideals of the judge are a fact to be considered. "Transcendental Nonsense," 35 *Columbia Law Review* 809 (1935), pp. 839–40. This article is quite realistic in tone, but see p. 833 for a discussion of the ethical problem. Compare: "I have no hesitation in declaring my belief that a realist examination of existing social and economic facts indicates defects in our social structure and that where a judgment will have the result of enlarging or lessening this defect, it is unrealistic to pretend that this is not so, and that it is no business of the judge to consider that fact. That commits us to a particular standard of better and worse. And where no such result is obvious or likely, I like to think of realists boldly facing the fact that their final problem is an ethical one and that good or bad is determined by moral ideals. Realists will find this moral ideal sometimes in a generalization from existing practices and sometimes in rules of conduct confessedly neglected in practice but admitted to be better than practice." Max Radin, "Legal Realism," 31 *Columbia Law Review* 824 (1931), p. 825.

lawyers talk about it. That human experience is not wholly or mainly logical in its process is now a commonplace. . . . Human experience, however, is also experience of the mind. It involves communication between persons . . . and within the world of this moving experience the law as logic is not so wholly a deportable alien as it is sometimes declared to be by anti-rationalist witch hunters.[20]

Perhaps the most elaborate attempt to restate legal realism and to take account of its demonstrated inadequacies and excesses is to be found in Edwin Garlan's *Legal Realism and Justice*.[21] Mr. Garlan's major interest, as his title implies, is in the realist approach to the problem of justice, and he sets up an able defense against the charge that legal realism sought to dispense altogether with the concept. Much that he has to say, therefore, does not bear directly upon the theory of judicial legislation. In his attempt to deal with the conflict between the realists and their critics over the area of uncertainty in the law, however, he takes the position that the area in which the legal system is not definite enough to provide certainty is of sufficient importance that to neglect it leads to oversimplification.[22]

It will be noted that Garlan does not say that there is no area in which rules do not govern decisions, but merely that the compulsive force of legal rules has been overstated. His statement is, therefore, more a criticism of traditionalist legal theory than of the post-Holmes development. He goes on to say, moreover, that even the existence of applicable rules does not preclude judicial discretion. Even in selecting a rule, or in determining whether such a rule exists, the judge must be guided by what he conceives to be desirable.

The position of the legal rule is, therefore, redefined. To assert that rules are not always the compulsive factors in decisions is not to say that they are valueless. The rules become instruments for

[20] Max Radin, *Law as Logic and Experience* (New Haven, 1940), p. 32.

[21] New York, 1941.

[22] "The extent to which law is uncertain; issues relatively indeterminate; possible issues and rules applicable to those issues in conflict or confused; particular judgments semi-autonomous, situationally localized, plural, and particular have been given less attention in our consideration of both law and justice than these matters deserve. Instead of accepting these features as accidental or irrelevant, they need emphasis as essential traits . . ." (P. 39.) This aspect of the law may be especially prominent in the United States because of the federal system and because administrative devices for securing uniformity readily have not been available. Each of the lower courts has enjoyed a considerable amount of independence. See R. H. Jackson, *The Struggle for Judicial Supremacy* (New York, 1941) and Felix Frankfurter and J. M. Landis, *The Business of the Supreme Court* (New York, 1927).

reaching decisions even though not the major premise for the decision.

> The process of legal judgment, as it is empirically observed, involves the use of rules and principles for a clarification of what the law is and what the issue presented for judgment may be treated as. This involves, in greater or less degree, a consideration of possible rules applicable to the case, of the conclusions of the case which would eventuate, and of the merits both of rules applicable and of their net effect on the particular case. The attempt to determine what the law is involves a simultaneous attempt to determine what is desirable.[23]

By the same token, an insistence that the legal system does not give absolute permanence and security does not imply a denial of the value of permanence and security in the administration of justice. "To insist that the value of any given decision must rest upon the evaluation of the consequences it effects is not to deny that faithfulness to uniform treatment is one of the values to be looked for and weighed." [24]

It will be seen that Garlan does not retreat on the point that in the legal process the judicial function is central. The constant motivation of the judge must be the administration of justice, but justice itself is an empirical matter.

> To the question of what justifies the values which compose justice, it suffices to give an empirical answer. Neither the idea of justice nor the formula of that idea do so; its concrete justification is not a matter of philosophy but of legal action. The concrete legal situation involves, as part of the situation, a context of competing values which are for the time being matters of justice.[25]

The solution of this problem in terms of the empirical demands to be adjusted constitutes the function of the judge.

In attempting to restate the common ground between the realists and their critics, Garlan appears to have achieved a formula that should prove satisfactory to both groups. In so doing, however, he dilutes legal realism to the degree that whatever distinction it ever had as a body of doctrine is nearly lost. It is interesting to note that although Garlan pays very little attention to sociological jurisprudence except as a forerunner of legal realism, he nevertheless frequently cites several of the leading figures of the sociological group—

[23] Garlan, *op. cit.*, p. 39.
[24] *Ibid.*, p. 81.
[25] *Ibid.*, p. 125.

especially Pound and Cardozo. There is at least an implication that he considers them to be somewhat the same as the legal realists. It is also apparent that the restatement puts us back on the familiar ground of sociological jurisprudence. Left unanswered is the question whether legal realism is not merely the name used by the sociological jurists of the later 1920's and '30's.

Chapter 8

CONCLUSION

The theories of the judicial function that have characterized recent American jurisprudence are integrally connected with the development of the modern state and the intellectual changes that have accompanied it. The modern jurist asserts that the judicial power is an apt instrument for accomplishing the adjustments forced upon the legal system by the dynamic character of our society. That he should turn to the judiciary for this purpose is deeply significant of the complexities of our constitutional and legal system as our national tradition has shaped it.

The emergence of the modern state predicated upon the concepts of social change and upon the conscious use of governmental power is, of course, a phenomenon common to industrial societies; in the United States, however, it has encountered constitutional and legal problems of exceptional complexity. The legal theory of the past seventy or eighty years is colored by those problems, and the form taken by much of our jurisprudence, particularly as it concerns the judicial function, can scarcely be understood without reference to them. It was largely because the emergence of the modern state in the United States presented issues of governmental power and because issues of governmental power are, or had become, judicial questions, that the need for a new theory of the judicial function became acute.

The problem to which the modern jurist addresses himself has been to devise a philosophy of judicial action that would induce the courts either to accomplish the necessary changes or, at the very least, to refrain from blocking the efforts of others to accomplish them. In point of fact, modern jurisprudence has attempted to accomplish both by means of what has come to be called the legislative theory of the judicial function, which, as we have seen, holds that courts should be sensitive to legislative considerations both in construing the powers of other agencies of government and in the development of those areas of the law traditionally in the keeping of the courts. The premise underlying both phases of the theory is that a dynamic society requires a dynamic legal system. The formulation of this theory of the judicial function has been deeply influenced by developments in the social sciences and in philosophy, from which the modern jurist draws concepts useful not only in the analysis of his problems but also in the guidance of the expanded judicial activity that he advocates.

Within the broad pattern set by its purposes and general position in American intellectual development, the appearance of the juristic theory of the past three-quarters of a century is therefore quite understandable, although the terms of the discussion were necessarily set by the particular problems which it encountered. However, much as its advocates may have tried to emulate other disciplines, there has been the essential consideration that modern jurisprudence has had always to combat a theory of the judicial function that was not only accepted but also official. The legal theory of the eighteenth century, institutionalized in the practice of judicial review, presented the judge with a closed system made up of universal and permanent principles. Within the assumptions of the system, his only functions could be discovery and deduction. The only way in which the system could be extended was by analogy, a further indication of the theoretical completeness of the principles upon which the whole was thought to depend.

The inner coherence of this complex of ideas is illustrated by the ease with which the idea of a written constitution could be fitted into it. So far as the judicial function was concerned, it made no particular difference whether the constitution was a legislative act of the sovereign power or was merely declaratory of eternally valid legal principles. In either case, the function of the judge was merely to apply the constitution, a function that fell within his proper sphere, not because he was empowered to enforce limitations on government, but because it was he who applied the law, of which the constitution was but another example. The duty might be one of peculiar delicacy and one into which special consideration might enter, but it was not one that required any alteration in the theory of the judicial function.

It is, perhaps, one of the most interesting aspects of modern American jurisprudence that although there is general dissatisfaction with the traditional conception of the judicial function, no commonly accepted theory has grown up to replace it. Any attempt to force contemporary theories into a general pattern cannot, with justice to the materials, go beyond the discussion of the most general tendencies. Certain of these may, however, be more suggestive of the major significance of the newer theories than are the points of variation between them. Of these general features, there appear to be at least two that are noteworthy: the reconsideration of the nature of law and its function in society, and the recanvassing of the available mechanisms of legal change.

The many-sided conflicts among the modern jurists should not conceal their common skepticism of the concept of law as a body of rules and their common interest in law as a technique of social control. It is a major premise of American legal theory that the important questions for juristic analysis are the social impact of law and its efficacy as a device for the achievement of prescribed ends. It is true that the description of the ends of the law did not as a rule proceed beyond rather obvious statements, but it is of importance to note the social orientation of these statements.

The acceptance of this position implies approval of certain others. When combined with the idea of a dynamic society, the conception of law as a social technique implies an acceptance of the impermanence of any particular set of legal relationships. This goes beyond the usual demonstration that the legal concepts that characterized late nineteenth-century United States were actually functions of time and place, to an assertion that any legal system defined in terms of its content will in time, by virtue of social development, either lose its contact with society or serve purposes different from those for which it was designed.

In modern juristic theory, therefore, the legal system ceases to be a social adjustment and becomes a process by which social adjustment is secured. However social adjustment is defined, the task of law is to define the relations between variable points, and, it is important to note, these points are always socially defined. Modern legal theory looks to the consequences of its activities rather than to the source of its authority or to any general principle to which it must refer its decisions.

The general social bent of the American jurists has also made them extremely receptive to the idea that law of necessity embodies a

statement of social policy and can therefore be appropriately judged
in terms of that policy. In these terms, law becomes an instrument
of social ends. Every court decision is positive in the sense that it
lends the support of the state to some interest that is seeking its protection. This concept goes far toward undermining the notion that
law is an impartial arbiter, rising in some undetermined fashion
above the interests of society, and it renders the law liable to evaluation in terms of its social policy in a way that was not formerly
possible.

As our survey of contemporary theories indicates, however, agreement on the point that law is a social technique does not prevent considerable variation among the modern group as to how law is best to
serve its function. The disagreements range from an inability to
agree either on the amount of stability desirable in society, through
widely varying interpretations of the actual amount of stability provided by a legal system, to the part played by legal rules in providing stability. Whatever criticism might be made of its accuracy, the
traditional theory was clear on these points: law was rules, and law
was stable. Whatever progressive theory of society might be held,
such social change could have no effect on the general principles that
made up the legal system. Although the moderns would agree in
rejecting that concept as stated, their agreement would imply no common doctrine to replace the traditional notion.

The situation is graphically illustrated by the spread of ideas on
the position of the legal rule, a spread which runs from "law is not
always rules," through "law is an accepted corpus of literature from
which rulings are drawn," to "law is purely a symbol that performs
psychologically satisfying functions." Pound and Dickinson, for
example, continue to support the idea of "law as rule," although both
are willing to admit a redefinition of the area in which rules are to
be considered fully operative. To Llewellyn, law is sometimes rules
and at other times is a statement of the uniformities of official behavior, and to Moore, law is a statement of the uniformity of behavior exhibited by human beings in defined situations. To the psychological group, law is an activity that satisfies certain symbolic
functions in response to psychological needs, and whether it performs
such functions well as opposed to other satisfactions that are possibly
better appears to depend on the psychologist. It is difficult to avoid

the conclusion that at some point in this development supposedly dedicated to empiricism, unannounced value judgments have entered the process.

The shift in the focus of juristic study and in the conception of law has, of course, important implications for the judicial function, although on this question as on many others there is a fairly wide range of choice among the various theories. The various judgments as to the degree to which the judge should feel free to alter the rules as the cases arise broadly parallel the positions taken on the binding force of legal rules—from "interstitial judicial legislation" to the concept of the judge as the "cheerful technician."

It would, of course, be possible to accept the modern criticisms of the nature and function of law without necessarily arriving at a legislative theory of the judicial function. In many cases one of the principal reasons for trying to bring the legislative function of the judiciary into the open was that overt recognition would perhaps operate to reduce it.

It would be logically possible to take the position that all laws ought to be legislative in origin and written in form. That such a notion is logically possible does not, however, make it feasible. Professor Rodell is possibly unique among the moderns in suggesting it. Generally, however, modern jurists not only take the position that judicial legislation is inevitable, but, on the whole, they seem to desire it. There are a number of reasons for this preference, but the principal argument appears to derive from the conception that legal progress is a matter of adjustments that can be made only by the expert. In general, these theorists take the position that legislatures, being bound to act in general terms and impelled to act only by strong pressures, are less capable than the judges for at least certain types of legislation.

It is necessary, nevertheless, that these arguments for judicial legislation be kept in proper perspective. There should be no implication here that the judges are being urged to usurp the legislative function. Rather it is proposed that they undertake to perform a necessary function, that would otherwise either go undone, or, given the necessities of the legislative process, would not be well done. Despite the tendency of its critics to overemphasize the legislative aspects of the theory, the newer jurisprudence is notably more receptive to changes in the legal structure through legislation than was the orthodox theory, at least if the experience of the United States is any criterion. The two ideas taken together throw into strong relief the underlying premise of all modern jurisprudence that our legal system, to be usable, must be adaptable. The concern with legal reform and change causes the acceptance of any instrument capable of effecting that change.

The issues that concern the modern jurist and his characteristic methods of attack having been surveyed, it remains to indicate briefly some of the results possibly to be attributed to the development and certain of the problems yet remaining. Although precision in such judgments is never possible, there is considerable reason to suppose that the energetic criticisms of the accepted theory of the judicial function made easier the shift in interpretation that features our constitutional law after 1937. It would perhaps be too much to say that the new legal theory is solely or even primarily responsible; there have been in our history equally significant changes in the orientation of constitutional decision without benefit of a redefinition of the judicial function. At the very least, however, the legal theories that have been studied provide much of the vocabulary of the change, and they can probably be credited at least in part with loosening the hold of precedents that might have made the shift of interpretation much more difficult. It is, moreover, noteworthy that so much of the newer trend in constitutional interpretation follows from the dissents of Holmes, Cardozo, and Stone, each of whom played an important role in the development of legal theory with which we have been concerned. The Supreme Court, for the present, at any rate,[1] has great respect for Mr. Justice Stone's position that the "power to govern" is at least shared with other agencies of government, including administrative agencies and state legislatures, and although such respect may not necessarily derive from sociological jurisprudence and legal realism, it is at least not inconsistent with those theories.

If we are to assume, however, that the influence of the newer jurisprudence is making itself felt in the course of decision, one regrettable shortcoming of the movement ought to be noted. This is

---

[1] That the trend of decision in the United States Supreme Court is actually being followed in the states is open to question. See Monrad G. Paulsen, "The Persistence of Due Process in the States," 34 *Minnesota Law Review* 91 (1950).

the basic failure to have achieved thus far any real clarification of the position of the courts in our total governmental structure. And perhaps no single fact illustrates the fundamental orientation of these theories toward the particular legal problems of the earlier twentieth century than does this failure to present a scheme for the solution of the problems that now face us. The rise of the theories of the judicial function that have been our concern roughly paralleled the development of what we have referred to as the "laissez faire" constitution, and much of the energy that the movement displayed was spent in combatting that development. The result, and this is particularly evident in the constitutional applications of these theories, was a program of legislative action. That primacy in defining the relationships between the government and the economy again falls to the legislative branch can be taken as established.[2] This change has, however, been accomplished by a redirection, not a redefinition, of judicial power. Although the instances in which congressional legislation has been invalidated in the recent past are few, there is no indication discernible that the power of nullification has been relinquished, nor do the recent bitter divisions of the Court over civil rights [3] or over the extent to which the Fourteenth Amendment includes the Bill of Rights [4] appear to presage any deep-seated consensus as to how that power is to be exercised. The recent history of the Fourteenth Amendment in the civil rights area suggests, however, that the invalidation of legislation under broad constitutional phraseology has not entirely disappeared, and thus far the efforts of various of the justices to show that they are not "legislating" in the constitutional field somehow fail to carry conviction.[5] That legislative activity should be most strongly suggested in the very field where the theory seems most firmly opposed to it does not render any easier the problem of evaluating the influence of either legal realism or sociological jurisprudence.

[2] *A. F. of L.* v. *American Sash and Door Co.*, 335 US 542 (1949) ; *Olsen* v. *Nebraska*, 313 US 236 (1941).

[3] *West Virginia* v. *Barnette*, 319 US 624 (1943) ; *Minersville* v. *Gobitis*, 310 US 586 (1940).

[4] *Adamson* v. *California*, 332 US 46 (1947). For discussions of the whole issue see Charles A. Fairman, "Does the Fourteenth Amendment Incorporate the Bill of Rights? The Original Understanding," 2 *Stanford Law Review* 5 (1949) ; Stanley Morrison, "The Judicial Interpretation," *ibid.*, p. 140.

[5] For a discussion of the problem see George D. Braden, "The Search for Objectivity," 57 *Yale Law Journal* 571 (1948).

Beyond the practical question of the actual influence on decision of the emergence of legislative theories of the judicial function, there remain some broader questions that the development itself does not answer. It cannot have escaped notice in the course of the survey of the various theories that, despite their attempts to broaden the scope of jurisprudence, with a few exceptions, the theorists approached the problem of the judicial function as if it were a legal problem exclusively. The question of judicial legislation is, of course, a major problem in legal theory, but it is also something more. The question on its face involves issues of the location and control of the legislative power. This is a basic question in any constitutional system, and especially is it so in the United States when the idea of "a government of laws" is still accorded great respect. The underlying issues raised by the development are, therefore, constitutional, not in the narrow sense of the congruity of judicial legislation with the text of 1787, but because the development of modern jurisprudence raises broader issues of governmental form and the political process.

Some of the problems for which the legislative theories of the judicial function have important implications are basic to all modern governmental theory, and for them no immediate answers or even standards by which to devise answers are available. They are raised, therefore, not in the expectation of supplying any solutions, but only in the belief that many of the modern jurists appear to have committed themselves to positions on these issues without, perhaps, fully exploring the implications of their theories. To a group generally receptive to the pragmatic argument, such considerations may be of secondary importance. To attribute any definite empirical results to judicial legislation, however, is, as we have seen, exceedingly difficult and likely to remain so in view of the extreme looseness with which the proponents of the theory defined the ends toward which the pragmatic results should tend. In the circumstances, therefore, it may still be permissible to turn to certain broader questions of governmental theory that appear to be raised by proposals for judicial legislation.

In considering these issues, it will not be necessary to do more than to indicate that, in so far as the judicial branch undertakes to legislate, there is a conflict with the formal theory of the separation of powers. This is obvious, but at the same time not of great importance, since the separation of powers is not an end in itself but only a means to another end which we shall discuss. Further, the separation of powers has never in the United States been a very active limitation on government and has had very little meaning in legal terms aside from that read into it by the judiciary in a comparatively few instances which are not always above question on their legal merits.

Of greater importance is the problem of the efficiency of the courts as legislative bodies. This problem has some very curious ramifications that arise out of certain ambiguities in the theories themselves. Despite the avowed intention to inform the legal process with more precise knowledge, none of the theorists whom we have studied has made any quantitative statements about either the amount of judicial legislation he favored or the extent of the changes he expected to accomplish thereby. In many cases, even among the realists, the language with which judicial legislation was advocated was rather more arresting than descriptive, since, apparently, no very extensive legislative activity was anticipated. In so far as this is true, of course, the problem of the efficiency of courts as legislative bodies does not arise in acute form, although, in such case, there is reason to wonder at all the controversy. Surely there was no necessity for a flood of books and articles to tell the judges that theory justified their doing what they were already doing. On the other hand, in so far as it was advocated that judges should legislate, there remain several questions that the theories themselves do not answer. Few of the writers, for example, deal directly with the problem of keeping the judiciary informed. In the course of the discussion it was indicated that, so far as practical devices are concerned, the Brandeis brief is almost unique. And, it must be remembered, the Brandeis brief is no guaranty of satisfactory results unless it is taken together with the appropriate presumption of constitutionality which, if honored, renders the brief unnecessary. In any event, the Brandeis brief, even as restricted, was most prominently a constitutional law device and, as has been shown, this was the area in which the modern theory tended generally to try to eliminate judicial legislation. It is regrettable that more attention has not been concentrated on the problem of keeping the judiciary abreast of the times in fields other than constitutional law.

Supposing, however, the development of some technique by means of which the judiciary might have a continuous and objective source of factual data upon which to draw, would we have the judiciary in any recognizable form? And if we are to consider changes of such magnitude, why attempt to get them by remodeling the judiciary? Unless the basic function of the judiciary to decide cases and controversies is changed, do we not encounter Bingham's argument that the judiciary would be deciding cases not before them? If this is to be the case, of course, what would be the advantage of having such matters taken care of by the judiciary? Is it not also relevant to suggest that if the basic function of deciding cases and controversies does not remain with the judiciary, the function will have to be performed elsewhere, where in all probability the whole controversy will arise again?

Pound and Cardozo argue, of course, that the tasks of keeping the law up to date is a highly specialized undertaking in which the expert knowledge of a trained judiciary is essential. Although not always so frankly stated, the assumption is implicit in nearly the whole development that we have surveyed. This assumption raises the age-old problem of the position of the expert in government, a problem that has been in the literature of political theory since Plato's criticisms of Athenian democracy. Although in the circumstances, then, it is quite possible that men may honestly differ on the issue, it is well to note that most of the modern American jurists have committed themselves on this point. Unfortunately they do not always give us the benefit of the train of reasoning by which they justify confiding so important a function to a group surrounded with all the constitutional protections customarily accorded our judiciaries. When this concession is taken together with the expositions of the duty of the "cheerful technicians" to manipulate society for "good ends" presumably defined by the "cheerful technicians" or the "social engineers," it is not difficult to see that we are making pronounced departures from our hitherto basic governmental ideas. It would plainly be foolish to attempt to label the whole development of modern jurisprudence in America as "undemocratic," even if one could be certain of the meaning of such a charge, although this would be to exercise more restraint than some of the jurists display towards one another. It might be appropriate to suggest, however, that on the whole the writers studied were prone to accept the most direct method of accomplishing the legal reforms they sought without fully considering the consequences of their choice of methods.

In so far as the movement we have studied tends to expand the judicial function because of the *expertise* of judges in the field of reform, it also raises questions relating to the traditional theory of popular, responsible government. In the field of judicial review, of course, the modern theory can easily present itself as enhancing popular control of government because a major goal was the minimizing of the judicial veto over legislation. In other areas, however, where more positive legislative action was urged on the judiciary and where forward-looking changes in the law were contemplated, it is difficult to avoid some difficulties with the theory of popular government.

Consideration of this problem leads to some rather curious conclusions. There is the possibility, of course, of asserting that the judges are representative of the deep and enduring desires of the American people as they are expressed in our constitutions. If this is true, however, there remain the problems arising from the determination of which values are permanent and which are less permanent, and who is to do the selecting. The sudden recourse to "permanent values" suggests a return to the constitutionalism of former days, and if the values to be represented by the judiciary are to be selected by the judiciary, where has there been a gain in constitutional theory?

It is difficult to escape the conclusion that the relationship between judicial legislation and responsible government has not been fully explored. We have already referred to Mr. Justice Frankfurter's characterization of the judicial power as "oligarchic." As he indicates, the judges do not indulge in press conferences, they are responsible to no one for their tenure of office, they deliberate in secret, and they announce the results of their deliberations in a special language that requires translation before the beneficiaries of their actions can understand it. That widening the legislative power of such an institution would produce better legislation is possible, although, as we have indicated, even that is by no means a self-evident proposition. But to say that widening the legislative power of a branch of government so constituted would be to strengthen popular control over government is, on its face at least, somewhat startling. It is difficult to avoid concluding that the final recourse is, indeed, the judge.

To indicate these unanswered questions is but to say that modern American jurisprudence reflects many of the difficulties that face modern American government in general. At base, the jurisprudence of the past seventy or eighty years has been concerned with practical questions. Its major problem was legal reform, particularly in the area of constitutional law. For whatever reasons, that reform has been on the whole accomplished, and, coincidentally, there has been a decline in interest in the problem of judicial legislation. As has been suggested, however, that reform was more nearly a redirection than a redefinition of judicial power. At base, the constitutional crisis of 1937 really settled none of the underlying issues of the judicial function, and neither, it can be concluded, did the juristic development that we have here considered.

Perhaps, ultimately, the most significant aspect of the whole movement is not any particular set of propositions that it produced but the very fact that it emerged. The nature of the American Constitution as it stood in the nineteenth century rendered it inevitable that the development of the modern state would require a recanvassing of many of our basic ideas about government, its form, and its proper function in American life. Perhaps nothing more clearly illustrates the anomalous position of the American courts than that the necessity to extend that re-examination has demonstrated to us the inadequacies of our traditional picture of the judicial function and our legal process. An accurate appraisal of the nature of the judicial power is an indispensable first step toward either its modification or intelligent public acceptance, either of which will stand as an advance in the achievement of responsible government in the United States.

INDEX

Adams, Brooks
  opposition to judicial review, 60–61
Adler, M. J., 34n, 98n
Administration of justice
  in Connecticut, 120–21
  studies of, 120
Administrative law, 52
Allen, C. K., 8n, 71n
American jurisprudence
  American writers on, 9, 19
  influence of evolution on, 22
  problems of, 160
  relevance to issues of American government, 6–7
Arnold, T. W.
  legal realism of, 130–32
Aumann, F. R., 9n, 16n
Austin, J.
  on judicial legislation, 19

Beard, C. A., 46n
Bent, S., 32n
Bentley, A. F., 75n
  and legal realism, 104–8
  social analysis of, 105–6
Berle, A. A., and Meuns, G. C., 55n
Beveridge, A. J., 61n
Biddle, F., 32n
Bill of Rights, 53
Bingham, J. W., Jr.
  and legal realism, 102–4
Blackstone
  views on judicial function, 9–10, 18
Boudin, L. B., 15n, 46n
Bowen, K. D., 32n
Braden, G. D., 69n, 93n, 155
Brandeis Brief, 90n
Bricker, J. W., 138n

Cairns, H., 140n
Cardozo, B. N., 19, 101n
  and ex post facto legislation, 88
  influence of, 83
  legal theory of, 83–88
Carey, H. C., 24n
Carr, R. K., 50n, 92n
Carter, J. C., 17n, 75n
Civil liberties, protection of, 92

Civil rights, 155
Clark, C. E., 93n, 120
  on function of trial courts, 121–22
Cohen, E.
  on ethics and legal study, 145
Cohen, M. R., 71n, 81n, 140n, 141n
  criticism of realists, 138, 141–43
Commager, H. S., 62n
Common law, 85
Constitution of the United States; see
  also Fourteen Amendment
  "meaning" of, 5n
  since 1937, 31
  trends in interpretation of, 154–60
Constitutional law and sociological jurisprudence, 89–94
Cook, W. W., 117n, 125n
Cooley, C. H., 22
Cooley, T. M., 12
Coolidge, C., 13n
Corbin, A. L., 71n, 85n
Corwin, E. S., 22n, 46n, 51n, 53n, 54n
Courts
  as legislative bodies, 157–58
  powers of, 3–4, 8
Coxe, B., 46n
Currie, B., 116n
Curtis, C. P., 46n
Cushman, R. K., 92n

Darwin and social forms, 23
Democracy and judicial review, 59
Dewey, J., 77n, 78n
  and legal realism, 108–12
  on rationality, 28–29
Dickinson, J., 71n
  criticism of realists, 138–39, 140–43
Dorsey, R., 32n
Douglas, W. O., 85n, 124n
Due process, 5, 54–55, 91–92

Edgerton, H. W., 50n, 62n
Ehrlich, Eugen, 19n
Evans, L. B., 50n

Fairman, C. A., 155n
Federal legislation, judicial review of,
  49–52

161

Federalist, The
  Hamilton quoted in, 10
  nature of, 11
  No. 51, 53n
Fete, K. B., and Rubenstein, L. B., 61n
Flexner, B., Oppenheimer, R., Lenroot,
  K., 120n
Fourteenth Amendment, 51, 54–56, 92
  and civil rights, 155
  expansion of, 65
Frank, J., 16n, 19, 22, 97n, 98n, 122
  legal realism, of, 132–34, 144–45
Frankfurter F., 32n, 47n, 62n, 93n
  and Landis, 67n, 146n
  legal theory of, 66, 68
  oligarchy in American government, 8
Fuller, L., 140n, 141n

Gabriel, R. H., 22n 25n
Garlan, E.
  on legal realism, 146–47
Geny, F., 19n
Gmelin, H., 19n
Goodhart, A. L., 8n
Goodnow, F. G., 63–64
Gray, J. C.
  legal theory of, 99–102
Green, L., 122n
Gross, B. M., 104n

Haines, C. G., 46n, 50n, 62n
Hale, R. L., 62n
Hall, J., 105n
Hamilton, A.
  on judicial review, 10–11
Hamilton, W. H., 66n
Hand, L., 41n, 92
Handlin, Oscar and Mary, 54n
Hartz, L., 54n
Hockett, H. C., 16n
Hofstadter, R., 22n, 27n, 29n
Holland, Thomas E., 39n
Holmes, O. W., 19, 31
  concept of law, 34–39
  function of judge, 39–43
  influence on American law, 32–45
  on Fourteenth Amendment, 51–52
  on Spencer's *Social Statics,* 71n
Hook, S., 98n
Hope, T. S., 119n
Hopkinson, J., 16n, 17n
Hough, C. M., 52n
Howe, M. D., 34n
Hughes, C. E., 5n

Income tax, 58

Interstate commerce, federal regulation
  of, 56–57

Jackson, R. H., 13n, 20n, 46n, 52n, 146n
  on judicial review, 53
James, W.
  significance for jurisprudence, 27–28
Johns Hopkins Institute of Law, 119
Johnson, William, 15n
Judges, functions of, 39–43, 83, 90,
  122–25, 159
Judicial function
  and marginal cases, 123–24
  and modern state, 149
  Aristotle on, 18
  Bentham on, 18–19
  disagreement on, 152–60
  English writers on, 9–11
  expansion of, 159
  Holmes concept of, 34–45
  legislative theories of, 149–51, 156–60
  mechanistic theory, 18
  modifications in theory of, 21–22
  psychology and, 22
  theory of, 123
  traditional concept of, 3, 7–9, 18, 21
  unorthodox theories of, 9
Judicial legislation
  and judicial review, 46–69
  and responsible government, 159–60
  as distinguished from judicial review,
    4–6, 18–20
  importance of, in U. S., 19–20
  theories of, 3, 19
  views on, 153–54
Judicial supervision of administrative
  agencies, 52–53
Judiciary ; *see also* Courts
  American idea of, 7–9
Jurisprudence, sociological, 79–96

Kallen, H. M., 28n
Kent, J., 12, 16n
Kiss, G., 19n
Konefsky, S. J., 66n, 91n, 92n

Lafollette, R. M., 62
Laissez faire, 48
Lasswell, H., and McDougall, M. S.,
  144n
Law
  and pragmatism, 94
  and social policy, 151–52
  and social sciences, 97
  and society, 94
  disagreement on function of, 152–60

Legal realism, 81
 and free judicial decision, 122–26
 and "science of law," 114–22
 and sociological jurisprudence, 104–8
 criticisms of, 136–48
 development of, 97
 diversity of, 97
 in American jurisprudence, 113
 nature of, 97, 99
 of Arnold, 130–32
 of Bingham, 102–4
 of Frank, 132–34
 of Gray, 99–102
 of Robinson, 126–30
 of Rodell, 134–36
 problems of, 113–14
Legal realists, 9
Legal reform and science of law, 125
Legal theorists, American, 4
Legal theory
 American, 6, 70, 94
  on judicial review, 62–63
 and courts, 31
 and judicial review, 6
 of judicial function, 21
 of modern state, 93
 modern, 151–52
Legislation, constitutionality of, 5
Legislative judgments, Holmes on, 40
Legislative power, problems of location, 3
Lenroot, K., and Landberg, E. O., 120n
Lerner, Max, 32n, 43n
Lindsey, B., and O'Higgins, H. J., 120n
Llewllyn, K. N., 19n, 97n, 98n, 102n, 127n
 on legal realism, 144
 on study of law, 116–18, 122–23
Lockmiller, D. A., 9n
Lusky, L., 93n

McIlwain, C. H., 47n
McKinnon, H. R., 32n, 33n, 34n
McLaughlin, A. C., 49n
Markey, J. F., 129n
Marshall, John
 and judicial review, 60
 on judicial supremacy, 12
Mathews, J. M., 62n
Meigs, W. R., 46n
Miller, S. F.
 on power of government, 7
Moore, W. U., 45n
 on legal methodology, 119–20
Morrison, S., 155n

Natural law, 23, 29
Nominalism, 102–4

Odegard, P., 75n
Ogburn and Goldenweiser, A. A., 72
Ogg, F. A., and Ray, P. O., 61n
Oligarchy, judicial, 31
Oliphant, H., 117n

Palmer, B. W., 33n, 34n
Paterson, W., 11n
Paton, G. W., 71n
Patterson, G. W., 124n
Paulsen, M. G., 154n
Persons, S., 22n, 27n
Police power of states, 55–57
Pollock, F., 33
Pound, R., 9n, 16n, 19n, 98n, 105n, 120n, 128n, 143n
 criticism of realists, 138, 143, 148
 influence of, 82
 legal theory of, 71–83
 on American realists, 137
Pragmatism
 and legal theory, 108–12
 influence on social thought, 26–27
Pringle, H. F., 62n
Pritchett, C. H., 14n, 121n
Property, constitutional protection of, 53–56

Radin, M., 123, 125n, 145n
Realism; see Legal realism
Recall
 of judges, 62
 of judicial decisions, 14, 62
Report of the Attorney General's Committee, 52n
Roberts, O. J.
 on judicial function, 13
Robinson, E. S.
 legal realism of, 126, 130
Rodell, F., 66n
 legal realism of, 134–36
Roosevelt, F. D.
 Court Plan of 1937, 7, 62
Roosevelt, T.
 recall of judicial decisions and, 14
Root, E.
 on judicial function, 14
Ross, E. A., 72n, 82n
Rule of administration of Thayer, 65

Schneider, H. W., 27n
Schroeder, T., 134n
Shulman, H. N., 120
Small, A. W., 75n
Smalley, H. S., 62n

Smith, J. A., 47n
  opposition to judicial review,
    59–60
Social activism, 22
Social analysis, methods of, 22–23
Social sciences and social analysis, 24
Social theory and change, 29
Sociological jurisprudence
  criticism of, 95–96
  of Cardoza, 83–88
  of Pound, 71–82
  of Stone, 89–93
Spencer, H.
  on evolution, 22–23
Stare decisis, 48, 117
State
  and social change, 149
  in modern society, 6
  legal theory of modern, 69, 93
Statutes, invalidation of, 4–5
Stone, H. F.
  and civil liberties, 92
  legal theory of, 89–93
  on American jurisprudence, 102
  on function of judge, 89–90
  on judicial veto, 7
Stone, J., 94n, 116n, 136n
Story, J., 12, 16n
Strong, F. R., 51n, 54n

Sumner, W. G.
  social philosophy of, 23–26
Supreme Court and social policy, 57
Sussman, G., 120n
Sutherland, G., 5n, 43n
Swisher, C. B., 57n

Taft, W. H., 14n, 47n
Thayer, J. B., 9n, 67n
  legal theory of, 64–66
  rule of administration, 65
Townsend, H. G., 27n
Trickett, W., 46n
Twiss, B., 139n

United States Supreme Court and
    Roosevelt, 7

Veblen, T.
  influence on social thought, 25–27
Veto, judicial, 62–63

Warren, C. E., 46n
Wayland, F.
  economic analysis of, 24
White, M. G., 98n, 108n
Willoughby, W. F., 120n
Wilson, J.
  on judicial power, 11